Georgeanna Muirson Bacon, Eliza Woolsey Howland

Letters of a Family During the War for the Union. 1861-1865

Volume 2

Georgeanna Muirson Bacon, Eliza Woolsey Howland

Letters of a Family During the War for the Union. 1861-1865
Volume 2

ISBN/EAN: 9783337021382

Printed in Europe, USA, Canada, Australia, Japan

Cover: Foto ©Suzi / pixelio.de

More available books at **www.hansebooks.com**

LETTERS OF A FAMILY

DURING THE

WAR FOR THE UNION

1861-1865

VOL. II

CONTENTS

CHAPTER VIII.

SECOND YEAR OF THE WAR—Continued.

CHAPTER IX.

CHAPTER X.

CHAPTER XI.

THIRD YEAR OF THE WAR.

CHAPTER XII.

CHAPTER XIII.

FOURTH YEAR OF THE WAR.

CHAPTER XIV.

CHAPTER XV.

THE WAR ENDED.

CHAPTER XVI.

SECOND YEAR OF THE WAR

(CONTINUED)

CHAPTER VIII.

E's Journal.

We have just been transferred to this big boat, while the Wilson Small goes for repairs. This boat will accommodate four or five hundred men in bunks, now being put up by the carpenter and filled with mattresses stuffed by the "Lost Children" who are garrisoning Yorktown. . . .

May 18. My entry was broken short by the arrival of 160 men for the Knickerbocker, and we were once more very busy. They were all fed,—numbered, and recorded by name, (Charley's work), and put to bed. Next morning arrived 115 more, for whom the Elizabeth with Miss Wormeley, Miss Gilson, and two men of the staff had been sent up Queen's Creek— tired, miserable fellows, who had been lying in the wet and jolted over horrible roads. There was another tugboat full, too, and Mrs. Griffin and I took charge of both till the men were moved into the Knickerbocker.

The Hospital Transport Spaulding.

We are now steaming up towards White House, all on deck enjoying the sail except Mr. Knapp and Charley, who are unpacking quilts for the bunks now ready.

G. to Mother.

May 19.

We are lying in the Spaulding just below the burnt railroad bridge on the Pamunkey. It is startling to find so far from the sea a river whose name we hardly knew two weeks ago, where our anchor drops in three fathoms of water, and our ship turns freely either way with the tide. Our smoke stacks are almost swept by the hanging branches as we move, and great schooners are drawn up under the banks, tied to the trees. The Spaulding herself lies in the shade of an elm tree, which is a landmark for miles up and down. The army is encamped close at hand, resting this Sunday, and eating its six pies to a man, so getting ready for a move, which is planning in McClellan's tent.

E. writes.

White House on the Pamunkey.

Half a mile above us is the White House naming the place, a modern cottage if ever "white" now drabbed over, standing where the early home of Mrs. Washington stood. We went ashore this morning, and with General Franklin and his aides strolled about the grounds

—an unpretending little place, with old trees shading the cottage, a green lawn sloping to the river, and an old-time garden full of roses. The house has been emptied, but there are some pieces of quaint furniture, brass fire-dogs, etc.; and just inside the door this notice is posted : " Northern soldiers, who profess to reverence the name of Washington, forbear to desecrate the home of his early married life, the property of his wife, and now the home of his descendants. (Signed)

A GRANDDAUGHTER OF MRS. WASHINGTON.

Some one has written underneath in pencil, " Lady, a northern officer has protected this property within sight of the enemy and at the request of your overseer." It is Government property now, and the flag waves from the top, and sentinels pace the piazza.

After wandering about the grounds General Franklin sent for General FitzJohn Porter, who, with General Morell and their staffs and Will Winthrop, whom we met by chance, came back to the Spaulding with us and were treated to clean handkerchiefs, cologne, tacks, pins, etc., from our private stores. General Seth Williams also made a long, friendly call on deck, during which we dropped half a mile down the river and anchored.

Mr. Knapp has gone down to bring up the rest of the Commission fleet, and White House will be our headquarters for the present.

The army of the Potomac was all this time advancing, and McClellan was at New Bridge, within eight miles of Richmond, his base of supplies being White House on the Pamunkey, a feeder of the York River; and there the hospital fleet assembled and the Sanitary Commission established its head-quarters on the line of the railroad running to Richmond.

Our forces held the road, and trains of wounded, and men dying of fever from the swamps of the Chickahominy, arrived at any and all hours.

A. H. W.

New York, May 19, 1862.

My Dear Children: I am writing in a book-store down town. . . . We had a famous letter on Saturday from you, Georgy, and another, half Eliza's half Charley's. I did not discover at first at what word one broke off and the other began. Your adventures are like those of the fox and the goose and the bag of corn. I hope you will all come together after awhile, perhaps have done so already, as both these letters were directed in Charley's handwriting. Charley himself ordered your Tribune transferred to our house, and it is coming regularly. I have all the numbers from May 1, and I understood Mother that she had in one of the trunks all the numbers up to that date. . . . Baskets of flowers, vegetables, mushrooms, butter, etc., came down on Saturday from Fishkill. . . .

I have bought all the shirts I could find at the employment societies. . . . Do you need grey or red *flannel* shirts. You may as well say out and out what your observation decides is needed, and don't be mealy-mouthed as to asking, or in mentioning quantities. We can as well send hundreds as dozens, except that it takes a little more time to collect them. Money is no barrier, of course. If all we can do is to *send* things for you to make useful, do let us send enough! and do you use up fast enough. . . . Thomas Denny & Co., Mr. Aspinwall, Robert, and others have just made their money over to Jane, " for you and your sisters to spend in any way for the soldiers," and they all refuse to say what we shall buy or precisely how much shall be used here or sent there.

You remember I said Carry had gone down in search of Captain Parker, of the 16th. She picked out the handsomest man in the barracks, with pale complexion and long blonde beard, but he was in bed, undressed and fast asleep.

The lists had not been made out, and no one knew if that were he. She had no flowers— nothing but a soft old cambric handkerchief which she cologned and laid on his pillow, but she had to come away without finding out who he was. . . . You must send any wounded officer to our house, using your discretion of course about it—those officers who have been used to refinement, and who need care. We should be very glad to entertain them and take care of them as they pass through the city, above all any officer of Joe's regiment. Captain Curtis must certainly come to us when he is well enough to move. . . .

Jane has gone to the City Hospital this morning with her usual illustrated papers and pots of jelly. The mortality in the North house, where the fever patients are, is very saddening. They hardly seem sick at all, but they die. She takes down things one day to a man, and next day he is dead. Five or six is the daily number. . . . Good-bye, dear girls and boy.

From H. L. H.

ON BOARD HOSPITAL SHIP "WHILLDIN,"
CHESAPEAKE BAY, May 21, 1862.

Dear Georgy: We are again on the Bay on our way to join the army. I was very sorry that we moved up to Queen's Creek for the wounded of Williamsburgh before Eliza and yourself examined the Commodore. For a few days we were very busy. Some 1,500 wounded men passed under our charge.

I was home for a day or two and saw Hatty. Mother enjoyed her visit very much. I send this to you, though I do not know where you are, simply to announce that I hope soon to see you. As we both have the same object in view, may we arrive at the *same spot again*, no matter where that may be.

E. to J. H.

FLOATING HOSPITAL, SPAULDING,
OFF WHITE HOUSE, May 22.

We are to go on shore presently to see what we can do for the large field hospital there. Two of our doctors, Ware and Draper of New York, spent the day yesterday trying to organize it and make the men tolerably comfortable. They furnished from the Commission nearly a thousand mattresses, secured them fresh water in hogsheads (which they were entirely without) and saw that all who needed medicine got it. System and food seem to be the great wants, and to-day we ladies will attend to the latter, take them supplies and show the hospital cooks how to prepare them. There are 1,200 or more sick men there, and until the Commission took hold they were in a most wretched plight, lying on the damp ground without beds, without food

or water, and with little or no care. . . . I
hope *you* take all necessary precautions in this
wretched climate. *Don't give up your quinine.* . . .

Later.—Directly after I wrote you this morning Georgy and I went to the shore to breakfast
the men we had dinnered and teaed yesterday,
and there we had a little house nearby, which
Dr. Ware had found, nicely cleaned out for a
hospital or resting-place for the sick when the
other overflows. The floor of one of the rooms
up stairs is six inches deep in beans. That
makes a good bed for them. . . . Meantime
Mrs. Griffin and the others got this boat in
order for sick, and this afternoon fifty odd have
been brought on board. To-morrow it will fill
up and leave for New York.

G. to Mother.
Steamer Spaulding.

The Spaulding is bunked in every hole and
corner. The last hundred patients were put on
board to relieve the over-crowded shore hospital late last night ; stopped at the gang plank,
each one, while Charley numbered all their little
treasures and wrote the man's name. Though
these night scenes on the hospital ships are part
of our daily living, a fresh eye would find them
dramatic. We are awaked in the dead of night
by a sharp steam whistle, and soon after feel
ourselves clawed by the little tugs on either side

of our big ship, and at once the process of taking on hundreds of men, many of them crazy
with fever, begins. There's the bringing of the
stretchers up the side ladder between the two
boats, the stopping at the head of it, where the
names and home addresses of all who can speak
are written down, and their knapsacks and little
treasures numbered and stacked. Then the
placing of the stretchers on the deck, the row of
anxious faces above and below decks, the lan-
tern held over the hold, the word given to
"lower," the slow-moving ropes and pulleys,
the arrival at the bottom, the lifting out of the
sick man, and the lifting into his bed ; and then
the sudden change from cold, hunger, and
friendlessness to comfort and satisfaction, winding up with his invariable verdict, if he can
speak, "This is just like home."

The Spaulding being all ready was now
started northward, and the "staff" moved
back to the Small once more, from which
they were busy day and night receiving the
sick and wounded, fitting up hospital ships,
and starting them to northern ports.

A. H. W. to G. and E.

May.

My Dear Children : . . . Doesn't Charley
want something? Mother is racking her brain

to think what it can be, as he no doubt *does* want
something, going off in the hurry he did. She
is afraid, too, that he is exposed to illness—
running risks from the climate, from contact
with soldiers' clothing, from the atmosphere of
the hospital ship, etc., etc.

Yesterday, Jane, Carry, Mrs. Buck, and Col.
Bliss and a few others, started from Park
Barracks for Bedloe's Island on a committee of
investigation. They chartered a little steam
tug at ten dollars an hour, and went from the
Battery, not staying very long, and quite enjoying the trip. They found the hospitals extremely
comfortable. Some sick in the brick barracks,
and some in three large hospital tents—close on
the shore, with the sea breeze driving through
them, and the waves rippling up close by. The
men they saw were as pleased with their accommodations as could be, and everything looked
ten times better ventilated and more hopeful
than at the City Hospital, for instance. They
have about a hundred men on Bedloe's Island—
mostly from the Ocean Queen—and not many
now are alarmingly ill. The ladies took down
four large baskets of oranges, jelly, towels, etc.
—some of the abundant supplies that have been
pouring in at the Park Barracks—and we are
to get together next week some books for a
library. Jane says she has seen what does her
heart good at the City Hospital—some tidy,

sensible, once-upon-a-time-fashionable ladies,
nursing men every day in the fever wards—
Mrs. Charles Strong, Miss Irving, and four or
five others ; they went down and offered their
services, which were accepted—such was the
great number of sick, and the necessity of an
immediate increase of nurses ; and they go down
every morning at seven and go away at seven,
taking their meals down there. Hired nurses,
men, watch at night. Here was an excellent
chance to put some of the port wine uncle E.
sent us, into use. Jane came right up for a jug
and put it in Mrs. Strong's charge, and it has
been of inestimable use already to some of the
patients. These ladies must have served a week
or ten days now, and will continue daily. They
do everything for the men, under the direction of
the doctors, administering food and medicine.
It is really most praiseworthy and delightful,
and, as in the case of your young doctors whom
you like so much, gives you a better idea of
human nature — *their* human nature, at all
events. I cannot say so much for the young
doctors of the New York Hospital as you do
for yours. They made a strike the other day
for increase of salary, writing the Trustees
quite an impudent letter, reminding them what
advantages the State now offered to volunteer
surgeons at Yorktown, etc., and requesting an
immediate answer. They did have a very imme-

diate one. The gentlemen assembled next morning and sent the young doctors word that they could have just so many hours to pack up and quit,—an answer that astonished and mortified them. You see it was very mean, for it was just when the largest number of sick that the house could contain were being brought in. The Trustees intended to increase the corps of surgeons, but *that* these residents would not listen to, "they were fully competent to do all." . . . Jane went down this morning with Mrs. Professor Hitchcock, Mrs. Smith, and Mrs. Buck, to take their turn at 194, but found that the last week's committee and their friends to the number of twenty, were so firmly established still, that they refused all hints about "relinquishing the keys," being "tired of the service," etc., etc.; "Oh, no; we are as fresh and interested as possible:" and indeed they were, though they were at the rooms until one last night, when Colonel Howe chartered an omnibus and sent them home. They had received all those who came yesterday afternoon by cars from Baltimore, and had worked faithfully, and hated to give up to the new set.

A. H. W. to E.

Dear E.: The returning Spaulding takes to you 12 Boston rockers, 6 boxes of brandy (if it gets there), 1 package of mosquito bar (getting

very scarce), a bundle and a basket, and chewing tobacco, for Charley to distribute! . . .
Tell him the 22d marched in splendid order;
their own uniforms and long yellow leather
leggings. The cheers and fireworks and interest all along the line were as great as the 7th ever
elicited. Carry and Charles Johnson sat on a
stoop on Broadway, till ten o'clock night before
last, to see them pass. We hear that they are
ordered to Harpers Ferry.

J. S. W. to a friend in Europe

May 23, 1862.

We all talk politics now. I asked a wide-
awake cousin to-day, "What do you think about
England now?" "England? England?" was
the answer, "I had entirely forgotten that there
was such a country!" . . . Our English friends
sent us Mr. Gladstone's speech. Mr. Gladstone
is a fair representative Englishman, and a man
whom everyone must respect; but hear him!
the same mysterious incapacity to understand us.
Hear his excuse for England's lack of sympathy.
He says an expression of sympathy with us would
have alienated six or ten millions who *might have
become* an independent nation! But why alienate,
for their sakes, eighteen or nineteen millions,
already an independent people? Because the
friendship of the rebel section (granted in-
dependence), was better for trade. How the

shop shines through! Then he uses the false
analogy of the rebels of '76, etc., etc., and that
is the best they can do. But at the same time I
honor the fortitude, and pity the sorrows of
Lancashire, and don't despair of even "sympathy" when Bright and Stuart Mill live and lift
up their voices; though it seems sometimes as if
Great Britain had wantonly thrown away the
friendship of this country, between the South,
which hates her because she has not yet broken
the blockade, and the North, which distrusts her
intentions. Probably there is no other question
on which both sections are so completely
agreed. . . . I think I must have done my little
duty by the affairs of the nation, and descend
from these topics to the comparatively ridicu-
lous items of personal narrative. We are
connected with one or two organizations for
receiving the disabled volunteers on their way
home, . . . helpless, wasted, gaunt, fever-smitten,
worn-out men. It is the old story; camp sickness immensely in excess of wounds. A great
many have died at the city hospitals, and a great
many are still here, slowly going, or slowly
recovering. We do what we can. There is
nothing they need or fancy, they cannot instantly
have, but it is heart-breaking work; I feel as if
I had been wrung out and dried: and how nobly
the men behave! I *must* testify to their patience
and sweet humor through everything, dying in

torment with a smile in their eyes and grateful thanks on their tongues ; praying for their country and *their nurses* in their last delirium. I could tell you twenty stories, but I'll only tell one. Private Jones, hurt mortally in the charge on the rebel rifle-pits at Lee's Mills, and forced to have the bad regimental surgeon's work done over again here, showed great fortitude, the tender-hearted surgeon told us, during the dressing of his wounds. We repeated the surgeon's praises to him and asked him if he really found it easier than he feared. " O, no !" the dear boy said, " it was *very* bad, but I saw the tears in the doctor's eyes, and do you think I was going to let *him* see how much he hurt me ?" My head and heart have been so full of these things that they *will* come out through the inkstand. The " boys " have a great deal to say about the " mean whites," and several of them have told me emphatically that they consider them much less worthy of freedom than the negroes. Sergeant Eaton tells me " their faces are dirty, their clothes are dirty, and their conversation exactly matches their dress." . . . Mrs. Howland and Georgy, who are in the transport service on York river, say no praise can do justice to the untiring and tender carefulness of the volunteer doctors. They speak very highly of Mr. Olmsted, who directs it all, finding, as they say, continual comfort in his administrative genius.

They explored the forsaken works at Yorktown, and saw the wreck and the indiscriminate, wanton destruction of the flight. They saw many tin plates left with bits of pork upon them, and nasty tin cups with dregs of coffee, but almost every plate and cup they saw, was slashed with an axe. Here and there all through the camps were stakes driven with the warning, "dangerous," graves of torpedoes and other infernal apparatus. Charley saw one in a water-jug. He is volunteer purser, and he and the ladies go from one transport to another, as they are wanted. . . . The siege-approaches, or whatever they call them, are killing work for the men. I asked a wan, crippled creature at the Park Barracks last week if he had been in battle. "Oh, yes," he answered, "in many battles, but I fought them all with a shovel."

Georgeanna Howland born.

Mary's fifth little girl was born at Astoria, May 24th, '62. Various names were proposed for the "bright little thing with dark steel colored eyes "—Bella ("horrida bella" Jane said) among them, but she was generally known as "Pamunkey," Abby writes,— that being a household word at the time. When she was old enough however, she was, in honor of her Aunt G., who was doing hospital work, taken in from Astoria to the

chapel of old St. Luke's Hospital on Fifth
Avenue and 54th–55th Sts., and baptized by
her father's old friend Rev. Dr. Muhlenberg,
"Georgeanna,"—Sarah Woolsey being god-
mother. The record is in the books of the
hospital chapel, no doubt.

One of the favorite relics to send home
from the front used to be shot and shell
picked up on battle fields. Carry seemed to
feel less grateful than we expected for those
forwarded to 8 Brevoort Place, from the
immediate front of the Sanitary Commission.

C. C. W. to C. W. W.

FRIDAY MORNING.

Dear Charley: We live in mortal fear of the
projectiles going off, the grape shot exploding,
and the cannon balls doing something else
equally unpleasant. There is no reason why
we should not set up an armory, we have such
a variety of arms. But really the grape has
never been used and I see nothing to prevent
its suddenly igniting; at all events, I don't
mean to hammer on the nail at the top, which I
firmly believe to be a fuse. The day it came
Mr. W. was calling and, though I was deeply
interested of course in what he was saying, I
could not help hearing the conversation that
went on in the entry between mother and the

city expressman, whom mother took to be a
soldier from the Daniel Webster and treated
accordingly, gave him half a dollar (12½ cents
being the price) and, not exactly invited him
in to dinner, but offered him some there! . . .
We have a quantity of things to send to the
girls on the return hospital transport. Uncle
Edward sent here yesterday 100 shirts, some to
go to Eliza, and 1,000 pocket handkerchiefs.
. . . Mother and I went to the Park Barracks
yesterday in Jane's place. There is a system of
passes now, and no lady can get in without one,
except myself, who go and come freely and no
questions asked,—I don't know why, unless there
is a natural dignity and committee expression in
my face that no one is discerning enough, except the admitting policeman, to see. . . . Write
when you can and tell us all you do. We still
direct Cheeseman's Creek.

From Mother.

8 BREVOORT PLACE, FRIDAY MORNING.

My dear Girls and Charley: All your notes
and letters are of thrilling interest to us now,
and though we think it very kind of you to take
a minute even for us, in the midst of all that is
going on around you, we are craving enough to
cry for more, more. I was a little disappointed
not to see you, Charley, by the Daniel Webster,
but I am not surprised at your staying behind.

. . . I meant to have given more time to my pen
for you, but spent all day yesterday at the Park
Barracks, nailing blue cambric over wooden
clothes-horses for screens around the men's
beds, a very tiresome job, and I came home used
up, and went to bed at once. This morning I
feel all right again. My quiet three months in
Washington and a drive out, instead of a dragging walk every day, has spoiled me for the
distracting noise and cares of New York, or else
I have grown old and feeble! I want very
much to slip into Jane's place at the hospitals if
she will let me, for she is breaking herself down.
It is not half so pleasant here in these places as
it was in Washington or Alexandria, as you
could go in there amongst the soldiers and talk
with them, and give them, yourselves, the clean
handkerchiefs, all cologned! and the books and
papers, etc., but here you are not allowed to
do this; can only be admitted to the committee
room by ticket. . . . This system is carried to
a hateful excess. . . . The greatest quantity of
goods and food and drink and every thing you
can imagine is constantly being sent in—people
send them here (to No. 8), too. Our front entry
is literally filled up now with immense bundles
and packages of shirts, drawers, stockings, shoes,
everything. One item is one dozen boxes of
cologne from your Uncle E. . . . Abby has *bought
out* several industrial societies in shirts and

drawers. Charley, I saw one poor soldier walking off yesterday with what I instantly recognized as one of your old shirts I had given to Mrs. Buck. She said he was so proud of his plaited bosom! They prefer old fine ones to new cotton without bosoms or stiff wristbands. And they all ask for neckties to wear home, so I am going out this morning to buy a great lot of them. . . . Carry is writing to you, dear Charley, and Abby is scratching away to some of you. Pico and Mac are yelping and ravenous for breakfast. . . . Do come up for a run one of these days, but not to take turns in night-watches on board with the sick, in a crowded cabin. I want you to have a little rest and some fresh air. . . . Did Charley find the gimlets and corkscrew? I stuffed such little things in where I could find room, for his stateroom. I should judge he had not much room to hang a coat from the looks of his den on the transport when I saw it. With ever so much love to you all, and the earnest wish that you would *send for me*,—I want to go down exceedingly—

YOUR LOVING MOTHER.

E. W. H. to J. H.

FLOATING HOSPITAL,
OFF WHITE HOUSE, May 27.

Still not a word from you for a fortnight now. I am beginning to be very hungry,—not

anxious, only *hungry*, for letters. I only hear
in indirect ways that our division was near the
Chickahominy a day or two ago and was
ordered to march into Richmond the next morning; and again yesterday that the whole army
was to move in light marching order, leaving
wagons and tents behind the Chickahominy.
I dream about it all, and wonder, but *know* nothing. . . . We moved to the Knickerbocker from
the Small and found a great state of confusion
consequent upon having the Elm City emptied
into it. . . . The event of this evening is the
return of the old Daniel Webster, which we all
look upon as a sort of home. . . . Dr. Grymes
always invites us over "home" when he arrives
in it, and we had a very nice dinner with him
to-day. He rose as we came in and said, "I
give you welcome where you have a right."
Mrs. Trotter returned in the Webster and Mrs.
Baylies, Mrs. Bradford and Miss Mary Hamilton came down from New York this time. The
two latter are to stay, and be replaced on the
return trip by some of our force who want to
go home. The Webster brought us more bundles and stores from home and lots of letters
and papers.

Captain Curtis of the 16th, who had been
a patient on board our Headquarters boat
the "Small," since his wound at West Point,

went up in one of the transports to an Alexandria hospital. He found there our friend Chaplain Hopkins, still hard at work among the sick and wounded. The following letter from the chaplain is inserted to show the success of our effort to have hospital chaplains appointed by the government. Mr. Hopkins received his commission and was under military orders from this time.

ALEXANDRIA, June 3d, 1862.

My dear Mrs. Howland: As you may have noticed, the bill for hospital chaplains has become a law. . . .

Hospital Chaplains bill a law.

After several ineffectual attempts to see the President, I at last gained access to him yesterday, to ask the appointment of a hospital chaplain in my place, and found his excellency in a most genial frame of mind. He was fairly exuberant; told funny stories! volunteered the remark that he "was afraid that fellow Jackson had got away after all," etc., etc. He told me that he had that very day appointed a man to help me—Bowman, he believed. "A very good man, isn't he?" Mr. B. had been condoling with him on the loss of his son Willy. My application he seemed to be most favorably impressed with, endorsed what I had to say on the back of it with his own hand, rang for Mr.

Nicolay, and—I say it with pain, but not without hope—*had it filed away.*

The moment Richmond is taken I shall apply to be removed there, and shall hope to join you and Miss Woolsey in many an excursion into the to-be historic environs. How you ladies can preserve calmness and elasticity of spirit I do not understand, but I know that you do.

On May 30 and June 1, '62, the terrible battle of Fair Oaks was fought.

The Commission had had a new Hospital tent pitched on shore at White House, near the railroad landing, for a kitchen and store-house, and we women took charge of it, feeding nearly all of the three or four thousand men who were brought down from the battle-field. The Commission established a bakery, and 100 fresh loaves were stacked on our tent table daily. *Shore Kitchen estab-lished.*

G. to Mother.

June 3.

The trains of wounded and sick arrive at all hours of the night, the last one just before daylight. As soon as the whistle is heard Dr. Ware is on hand and we are ready in the tent, blazing trench-fires and kettles all of a row, bright lights and piles of fresh bread and pots of coffee ; tent door opened wide, the road leading to it from the cars dotted all along the side with little fires or lighted candles. Then comes the first procession of slightly wounded, who stop at the tent door on their way to the Hospital boat, and get cups of hot coffee and as much condensed milk as they want—these followed by the slow-moving line of bearers and stretchers, halted by our man, Wagner, detached from the Duryea Zouaves, and the poor fellows on the stretchers have brandy, or wine, or iced lemonade given them. It makes but a minute's delay to pour something down their throats and put oranges in their hands, and saves them from exhaustion before food can be served them, in the confusion that reigns in the regular Government boats! When the worst cases have been put on board, the rest are sent to the twenty Sibley tents pitched for the Commission along the railroad, and our detail of five men start, each with his own pail of hot coffee or hot milk, crackers, soft bread, lemonade, and ice water, and feed them from tent to tent. For these men no provision has been made by the Government, and they are left on our hands, sometimes three days at a time. They would fare badly but for the sleepless devotion of Dr. Ware, who works among them night after night, often until two or three o'clock in the morning.

Without exception, the Government boats so far have been inadequately provisioned, wretchedly officered, and in a general state of confusion,—Dr. Agnew calls it "damnable."

One Government boat, which had been lying here waiting for wounded for a fortnight, would have left this morning, crowded with suffering men, without food (except hard-tack), but for the Commission ; without a cup, or a basin, or a lemon, or a particle of lint, or bandages, or old linen, without clear water for bathing, and without an ounce of beef,—though their official report had been to the Commission that they were "all ready." One man had been without nourishment all day until an hour before his shoulder was taken off. Then the surgeon hurried over and asked us to take him beef tea and egg-nogg, and I crossed the coal barges and fed him myself, and two others ; this after the doctor had himself told me that they needed no help. This is just where the Commission comes in— kettles of soup and tea with soft bread and stimulants are sent from the tent kitchen, and with them go cups and spoons and attendants to distribute the food. It is just the same with lint and bandages, and splints, all of which the Commission supplies freely.

We fed from our kitchen 600 men for two days on two of these Government "all ready" boats.

Some of the hurried notes in the small blank books we carried about with us (G's tied to her belt) are characteristic, and somewhat mixed at the distance of 36 years.

"78 pillow-cases, and 4 mattresses. Whiskey for 10, brandy for 4. W. T., 49th Ga., Co. D. C.G., both legs ; handkerchiefs, arrowroot, bay-rum. V. W., shoulder off, 17 Cedar St. E. D., lowest berth ; Waters, top berth."

And in the midst of it this note :

"To Mrs. I., 3 Milligan Place.

My dear Mother : You must not be anxious about me as I am not wounded, only sick. I was not in the battle because I was not strong enough to hold my gun. The battle began Sunday while I was in bed. We had to jump up and take our arms. I asked the lieutenant to let me fall out ; he said I might, and stay there. The rebels came right up to the pits. Our men began to retreat very fast, and one came and told me to get up or I would be taken prisoner. So the doctor sent me down in the woods. Three nights I had nothing to cover me, slept just under the dew. The doctor put me on the cars and I was brought to White House. I am lying now in better condition and being better taken care of."—Beef essence, tea, oranges " —— ! Etc., etc. etc.

We used to say :

> "In the great history of the land
> A lady *with a flask* shall stand."

A. H. W. to G. and E.

NEW YORK, MONDAY.

Georgy's letter of the 23d, written on the Spaulding from White House, came in this morning at breakfast, which is more prompt than usual. It tells of the proposed opening of hospital tents ashore, and *two thousand* sick ready to put into them at once. Why the Commission should have had to work long and perseveringly to accomplish this, I don't know. . . . The accumulating number of sick is frightful, especially when we remember that hundreds probably die unknown on the roads, literally from starvation and exhaustion. . . . *God's* curse, and not his blessing, is evidently on the whole country now, and will be while such pro-slavery policy as we have had is persisted in, and such burning sins as the Fugitive Slave Law gives rise to are perpetrated on the very Capitol steps at Washington.

Here is Banks, the embodiment of " success," which is his motto, his command pursued and scattering; the Baltimore & Ohio road and the termini of those other important communications, all abandoned. Mobs in Baltimore, panic everywhere, and we just where we were more than a year ago ; the *7th Regiment ordered off this afternoon* for the defense of Washington. . . . Why, the war proper hasn't so much as *begun* yet. . . .

Later :

Carry took Jane's turn at Park Barracks yesterday afternoon. They have gone lately on alternate days, and as Carry is very chatty with the men and very communicative when she comes home, we hear a great deal of funny talk and pleasant incident. She helped get tea for them last night at 194. Smoked beef and boiled eggs, tea and toast and butter, all on little white plates, and each man served on a separate little tray at his bedside, if he was weak and in bed.

A. H. W.

NEW YORK, June 2d, 1862.

My dear Girls : Charley's letter of Thursday came in this morning. He explained to us his system of numbering and sorting the men's luggage, etc., which interested us very much, and shows us what his duties are in some of their details. We are glad the nutmegs and lemon-squeezers happened to fit in a gap. What else can we send ? I hope Moritz, with the rockers and brandy, will all arrive safely. Do you want more air-beds ? . . . Dorus Woolsey has been in for a final goodbye this morning.

He will get a furlough as soon as possible, for
his business affairs hardly allow of his being
absent so soon. The 7th, 22d and 37th are
doing police duty at Baltimore. I mean they
are the military guard of the city. . . . Rev. J.
Cotton Smith went too as chaplain. The night
before, he tried to make a speech to them in the
regimental armory, but was cheered so that he
had to stop. "Go on, go on!" they all cried,
and he managed to make himself heard, and
said "On the whole I won't go on now; all I
want to add is that I am *going on to-morrow*!" at
which there was tremendous cheering again.

Night was made hideous with Herald extras,
screamed through the streets between eleven
and twelve. We waited till this morning, and
got the news in the morning papers of that horrible battle, and what is worse—that *in*decisive
battle. It has shattered the strength of Mc-
Clellan's army—what poor creatures were left
in it, after all the sickness and fatigue of the
march—and has accomplished *nothing*. . . . Charley says that 3,900 men of Casey's division were
lost on the march. God help them and their
families, who can only know that they died like
dogs on a roadside with fatigue and hunger.
This makes four full regiments out of a division which only had ten to start with. No wonder it was overborne and broke line and scattered! Never accuse such men of cowardice.

. . . We are much worked up this morning with this news of our disaster, and with the information that North Carolina slave-laws are re-enforced and Colyer's black schools disbanded by government direction. What Government that commits such an act, can expect anything *but reverses* to its arms !

Worst of all, as far as *our* petty little hopes and interests are concerned, here is the order promulgated this morning, by which General H. B. takes supreme military command of all sick and wounded arriving here on transports. They are to be unloaded at Fort Hamilton and Bedloe's Island, and the ladies' game at Park Barracks and at 194 is blocked. B. is a regular of the regulars as to primness and military order, and personally has no more heart than a mustard seed. . . . Jane has gone down this morning full of wrath, to kidnap Abbott, of the 16th, if possible, and send him to his friends in Maine. She wants to get a ticket transferring him to 194 Broadway, when, if necessary, he can be " lost on the way," and whipped into a carriage and down to the Fall River boat ! . . . All these volunteer efforts at comforting and clothing the men must come to an end. Fort Hamilton is too far out of the reach of ladies with oranges and clean pocket handkerchiefs, unless they hire a tug at ten dollars an hour, and go through all the formalities of military passes.

A little later E. writes to J. H.:—

I enclose some comments about Casey's division, and we all agree here that justice was not done to the men. It is surely hard enough to lose as terribly as they did without being reproached for cowardice. Abby says in a late letter—"Anna Jeffries came on from Boston yesterday in the train which brought many of the Daniel Webster load, scattering them all along at or near their homes. One gentleman was asking another whether Casey was of Rhode Island or Connecticut, when a wounded soldier cried out from some seat nearby, overhearing Casey's name—a cry of anguish and anger—'They didn't run! they didn't run!' He tried to stagger to his feet, being wounded in both ankles, and then added—'I can't stand, but I tell you they only broke, they didn't run.'"

H. L. H. to G.

PHILADELPHIA, June, 1862.

Dear Georgy: Once more our paths have separated. . . . Upon my return with the wounded from the battle of Fair Oaks, I received an appointment to a large hospital (1,500 beds) now building in West Philadelphia. I will live at home, but will be *there* a part of each day.

[margin note: H. L. H. appointed to a Philadelphia Hospital for Wounded.]

The Pennsylvania delegation to which, as you know, I was attached when at the White House and elsewhere, has been dissolved.

H. R. W. to G. and E.

New York, June.

Dear Girls: I write more for the sake of sending a letter by Dr. Draper, than because there is anything to tell you about. . . . I think Abby looks miserable and needs rest. I don't believe even you, "the working sisters," as Dr. Ferris calls you, do as much as Abby does, for there is certainly something that pays in giving nice little things to soldiers and having them so grateful to you and seeing them get well under your care,—there is an excitement in it all which cannot be got out of homely un-bleached cotton, yards and yards and hundreds of square yards of shirts. . . .

Think of my having a chance of becoming a nurse up at the Mott Hospital in Fifty-first street. Mrs. Ferris offered me a place of that kind, out of consideration for my merits and the one hundred dollars Uncle E. had given them the week before, but I foolishly gave in to the family row. They had me laid out and buried twenty times over of malignant typhoid, diphtheria, and other ills which flesh is heir to.

. . . Carry is engaged in finding a summer retreat for the family. . . . The combinations absolutely necessary are: sea and mountain air, a place near the city with speedy communication, and no New Yorkers.

I send Charley's wine, Dr. Draper having offered to take anything for us.

We must give you a little breathing place. Victories elsewhere. Your Aunt Abby's dark views for the country, with her eyes persistently kept on the Army of the Potomac, were not justified to anyone willing to take a wide sweep of the horizon. McClellan was not our only general, happily. All round the edges of the map of the rebel states, inroads were being made, and the army and navy at large were giving us hope and courage. Admiral Foote had reconnoitered the Mississippi for a long distance. Garfield (later President) had successes in Kentucky. Hatteras, N. C. was occupied, and a provisional loyal governor congratulated that state "on its salvation." General *Grant* had taken Fort Henry, on the Tennessee River, and Fort Donelson with 15,000 prisoners. Roanoke Island was captured off North Carolina by the army and navy. Springfield, Mo. was taken. Mitchell (professor of Astronomy in Dudley Observatory) was in charge of the troops who took and occupied Bowling Green, Ky. Pope in Missouri had captured three Generals, 6,000 prisoners, and 100 siege-guns. Nashville, Tenn. was evacuated and held by the U. S. troops. Columbus, Ky. saw another sight, — the national flag raised where the rebel colors had been hauled down. And on April 11th Fort Pulaski, off Georgia, had surrendered to the National guns fired from Tybee Island, and the 7th Connecticut (F. B. included) had taken possession of it.

On April 26, Farragut had captured New Orleans, and the Mobile Register about this time announced to its readers, " The enemy is raging along our lines on coast and frontier." Better than all these was the action of both houses of Congress, abolishing slavery in the District of Columbia.

These were some of the victories since '62 began. So that although there was sorrow enough, and discouragement, we were on the whole, running our race with a bright look ahead.

E. W. H. to J. H.

OUR SHORE TENT, June 5th.

. . . I am very glad of the chance of sending you a note by Quartermaster Davies, who has just looked in at our tent door and been fed with coffee and bread and oranges, and seated on a box-end and generally well treated. . . . I have captured a darkey from the country who brought fresh butter for sale this morning, and promised peas and strawberries for to-morrow ! We have had pine-apples and bananas from

New York and fresh eggs from Fishkill! which
Moritz brought down, and which I wish you
could share with us. He reports everything
looking lovely at home and descants largely on
the sunshine and sweet air and the pleasure of
sitting on the piazza. . . .

I write with chattering all about me, for Mrs.
Griffin and G. and Drs. Ware and Haight are
sitting on boxes and barrels talking and laughing and enjoying the respite we are having.
We are both well: also Charley, who is doing
good service, is very cheerful, and thrives on it.

The quartermaster waits. The only thing I
think of to send you is some fresh bread,—I also
put in a package of concentrated beef tea for
two or three 16th men who I hear are very sick,
and some farina, arrowroot and handkerchiefs
for the same. . . .

Only 100 wounded came down this morning,
and have gone on the State of Maine, which is
in beautiful order for them. We fed about 600
yesterday, three meals each.

G. to Mother.

June 6, WILSON SMALL.

We have on our boats nine "contraband" Ex-
women from the Lee estate, real Virginia dar- slaves at
keys but excellent workers, who all "wish on House.
their souls and bodies that the rebels could be
put in a house together and burned up." "Mary

Susan," the blackest of them, yielded at once to the allurements of freedom and fashion, and begged Mr. Knapp to take a little commission for her when he went to Washington. "I wants you for to get me, sah, if you please, a lawn dress, and a hoop skirt, sah." The slave women do the hospital washing in their cabins on the Lee estate, and I have been up to-day to hurry them with the Knickerbocker's eleven hundred pieces. The negro quarters are decent little houses with a wide road between them and the bank, which slopes to the river. Any number of little darkey babies are rushing about and tipping into the wash-tubs. In one cabin we found two absurdly small ones, taken care of by an antique bronze calling itself grandmother. Babies had the measles which would not "come out" on one of them, so she had laid him tenderly in the open clay oven, and with hot sage tea and an unusually large brick put to his morsels of feet, was proceeding to develop the disease. Two of the colored women and their husbands work for us at the tent kitchen. The other night they collected all their friends behind the tent and commenced in a monotonous recitative, a condensed story of the creation of the world, one giving out a line and the others joining in, from Genesis to the Revelation, followed with a confession of sin, and exhortation to do better ; till—suddenly—their deep humility seemed to strike them as uncalled for, and they rose at once to the assurance of the saints, and each one instructed her neighbor at the top of her voice to

> " Go tell all de holy angels
> I done, done all I kin."

Just as they came to a pause, the train from the front with wounded arrived—midnight, and the work of feeding and caring for the sick began again. Dr. Ware was busy seeing that the men were properly lifted from the platform cars and put into our Sibley tents. Haight was "processing" his detail with blankets, and our Zouave and five men were going the rounds with hot tea and fresh bread, while we were getting beef tea and punch ready for the sickest through the night. By two o'clock we could cross the plank to our own staterooms on the Wilson Small.

E. to J. H.

FLOATING HOSPITAL, WHITE HOUSE.

Sunday, June.

We are having a delightful quiet Sunday—such a contrast to the last few days. A hundred and fifty men, to be sure, came down last night, but unless we have two or three hundred we think nothing of it nowadays. We are going for a walk, and Dr. Jenkins of the Commission is to have service for us under the trees. We have almost lost sight of Sunday lately in the press of work.

There are large bunches of laurel and magnolia in our parlor-cabin and dining room, and the air is full of their fragrance..

Miss Dix spent last night with us, but is off now.

C. W. W.'s letter to the N. Y. Post.

Carry writes Charley June 6: We were surprised and pleased to see your letter in the Post last night, and sent out and bought up all the copies in the neighborhood, and have mailed them to James Gibson (Ireland) and elsewhere.

C. W. W. to New York Evening Post.

SANITARY COMMISSION, FLOATING HOSPITAL,
PAMUNKEY RIVER,
OFF WHITE HOUSE, Va., May 31, 1862.

The work of the Sanitary Commission, as connected with the army of the Potomac, is just at this time, as you doubtless know, a most important and indispensable one. More than two thousand sick and wounded men have been shipped by the Commission to New York, Washington and Boston during the past month, and it is safe to say that the lives of hundreds have been saved who would otherwise have died in camp and on the march.

The vessels used by the Commission are chartered by the government, and are first-class ocean steamers and Sound boats. They are supplied with all the necessary hospital apparatus at the expense of the Commission, and are furnished, so far as possible under the circumstances, with every convenience for the transportation of the sick, who are too often victims of neglect in regimental sanitary regulations. If your readers care to know something about the detail of management on board a hospital ship, let me give them briefly the program of a single day's routine—a routine in the case of the majority on board, let them remember, of inevitable and monotonous suffering or sleepless pain.

Four bells,—but the day does not begin then, it is only a continuation of yesterday and the day before. On a hospital ship night and day are alike to all hands, and " on duty " for a nurse means only his "watch," whether it comes at noon or midnight. Dr. Some-one is medical and military chief, and every well man on board, except the ship's officers and crew, is subject to his authority. His command consists of four or five surgeons and physicians, a commissario-quartermaster, a purser perhaps, a varying number of volunteer nurses, eight or ten contrabands, and from one hundred to four hundred or five hundred sick men, according to the capacity of his vessel. On the ocean steamers the greater

number of bunks are between decks, and roughly
built of secession lumber, in tiers of three ranged
on either side the length of the ship, and a double
row down the centre. On this deck also are a
dispensary, with an apothecary to preside, and a
room or space reserved for the exclusive use of
the lady nurses.

The sick are divided into several wards, each
with a ward-master, generally a medical student,
and the watch is arranged by the medical chief—
the twenty-four hours being divided into three
watches, of six hours each, and two dog-watches,
of three each. Let us divide all the doctors and
nurses on board into two squads, or reliefs,
called A and B. Squad A relieves squad B at
seven in the evening ; B goes to bed and quickly
to sleep until one o'clock, when it relieves A ;
A turning in until 7 A. M., when it relieves
B again, and so on. The dog-watches in the
afternoon reverse the order, so that neither
squad may have the same hours of watch two
successive nights. The satisfactory arrange-
ment of these watches to all parties concerned is
no small matter.

The bulletin at the main stairway displays a
record of the ward arrangements for the day,
the hours of the house diet, the most explicit
directions in case of fire, and more than the
usual number of warnings with respect to the
use of lights in the cabins.

By far the most formidable part of the work is getting the sick men on board and then landing them. The steamer lies out in the stream, and the sick men are in their camp hospitals on shore, it may be several miles inland, or perhaps left exhausted on the roadside, in the advance. A day or two ago thirty-six men arrived on the shores of the Pamunkey who had fallen off from the army, in this way, unable to proceed from fatigue and exhaustion. They said they had walked fourteen miles since midnight, and had had no food for three days. When they applied at the Government tent hospital at White House for food and shelter they were told that there was no room for them, and that they had better look along the shore for a hospital ship. In this condition they fell into the hands of the Sanitary Commission, were transferred to the Spaulding, and were speedily fed, clothed, washed and convalescent. Up to the 29th instant General Casey's division had lost in this way three thousand nine hundred men since leaving Yorktown.

The difficulty is to get the sick men from the land to the floating hospital—from the hands of the government to the Sanitary Commission. Convalescents can walk and in some measure help themselves. The sick must be lifted, (and not always with the tenderest care,) first into an ambulance, then jolted to the shore (even ambulances jolt in Virginia, those vehicles that offer

every facility for accidental death), then put on
a tug to be taken out to the steamer.

On the Sound boats the process of embarka-
tion is comparatively easy, as the decks are low.
In the case of an ocean steamer a tackle is rigged
from above, fastened to a fixed frame into which
the stretcher and all are placed while on the deck
of the tug.   The tackle is then hoisted, with the
sick man and his effects, to the upper deck.   Before being lowered to the receiving doctor below,
who assigns him to a berth, all his baggage, including his gun and blankets—new blankets
being furnished him—is taken from him and
firmly tied together.   His rank, name, regiment,
company and postoffice address are noted down,
and a number assigned to him and a correspond-
ing number pasted on his baggage.   In this way
his baggage is cared for, and much confusion,
which without some such system would prevail,
is avoided.*

Necessarily, now and then, a blanket or pair
of shoes loosely packed, or a likeness carelessly
put in the haversack, is lost or unclaimed.   Occasionally a soldier, much to his chagrin, may
be obliged to carry home some one else's gun,
new, perhaps, from the factory, instead of his
own trusty rifle that has shot, to his certain
knowledge, at least half a dozen rebels.   Jones,

---

* This was Charley's work.

of the Third Maine Cavalry, who is stout, may be obliged to put up with a coat belonging to Jenkins, of the Tenth Indiana Infantry, who is slim, etc.; but, in the main, the men have their baggage returned to them intact at the end of the journey.

A detail of men sometimes accompanies the sick, who are employed as nurses. When every bed is filled and order begins to come out of the seeming chaos, a meal is served to those who need it, the gangway is lowered, the whistle blows, and the ship, with its strange cargo, is in motion for New York or Washington. The doctor makes his rounds, giving particular directions about the sickest, and the watch begins. Down the York river, round the cape, and so, with the flag of the Sanitary Commission waving at the mast-head, out to sea. Convalescents, who are well enough, smoke their pipes on deck, and in picturesque groups talk over the wonderful scenes they are leaving, or discuss the superior merits of their several regiments.

Up stairs, we are a lot of soldiers off duty, on a pleasure trip down a peaceful little Virginia river. Down stairs, how different! Occasionally a death occurs on the passage (though the proportion is very small), and a vacant bed in the long line marks the soldier's last resting place while living. His knapsack and gun are taken by some friendly hand to be returned to

his family, and thus the soldier ends his fight—
sadly, yet in a noble cause ; his heroic aspira-
tion crowned so soon with their utmost result.

A dark side there must necessarily be, but a
bright side is by no means lacking. Chloride
of lime and the lady nurses contribute largely
to the brighter half. Whitewash and women on
a hospital ship are both excellent disinfectants.
Men are nurses of the sick only by study and
experience, women by intuition. A man can
dress an ugly gun-shot wound or prescribe for a
typhoid case better, perhaps, than a woman, but
a woman's hand must knead and smooth the
bed that supports the wounded limb, or much
medical science may go for nought. Masculine
gruel, too, nine cases out of ten, is a briny
failure ; but gruel, salt tempered by feminine
fingers, is nectar to parched lips.

Creature comforts abound in the presence of
lady nurses, and from their culinary retreat
between decks come forth at all hours of the
day a sizzling sound as of cooking arrow-root ;
armsful of clean white clothing for the newly
washed, and delicacies for the sick without number, sometimes in the shape of milk punch, or
lemonade squeezed from real lemons, sometimes a pile of snowy handkerchiefs that leave an
odorous wake through the wards. Again, a
cooling decoction of currants for the fever case
nearest the hatchway, or a late *Harper's Weekly*

for the wounded man next him, (who to his surprise and delight recognises his last skirmish,
though feebly reduced to the consistency of
printer's ink, with his identical self in the fore-
ground), or oranges, cups of chocolate and many
a novelty, but never a crumb of hard tack, (unless
in the pulpy disguise of panada,) or ever so faint
a suggestion of too familiar salt pork. . . .

Suffice it to say that the services of the ladies
who are here as nurses of the sick are invaluable to the Commission and duly appreciated by
the battle-tried and camp-worn soldiers. A simple word of sympathy or encouragement from
a genuine woman is sometimes more potent to
cure, than brandy or quinine from the hands of
the most skilful physician. The kind looks and
deeds of our nurses, and their kindlier words
go straight to the hearts of the sick men and
bring them nearer home by many a weary mile.
We have other bright features, too.

Of articles contraband of war there are several
specimens on board. They are always jolly and
grinning, and ready for the hardest kind of
labor, and breathing a "mudsill" atmosphere has
not made "sour niggers" of them. Strange as
it may seem, too, at uncertain intervals, they
even make use of an ejaculation peculiar to that
genus of article in a sportive and jocular yelp:
"Yah! yah!" says Aaron to Jim (not Moses)
"dis yer's a heap better than Massa Coleman's";

whereupon James performs an affirmative comedy of " Yah, yahs," and looks all teeth. Moreover, these men seem to take kindly to the wages (!) that are paid them from time to time, and especially on these festive occasions are they exceeding lavish in their display of ivory, and blithesome to a degree passing strange.

A little while ago I witnessed the novel spectacle of an "article" earning his living. Six weeks ago he was an "indefinite" article—a chattel—a non-entity ; now sole proprietor of his own muscle and able to convert the sweat of his brow into legitimately-gotten shining metal. He was rolling a barrel of northern pork aft, and I saw him halt three several times on his march to the kitchen, in order to execute a *pas seul* from his favorite plantation jig. It was a march of triumph to him, for he knew that every revolution of his barrel rolled out for him at least the fraction of an expected dollar, the just recompense of his free labor, and his ungainly "juba" was only the natural overflow of his exuberant glee upon attaining at length his long-denied manhood. There is a "down East" smack and flavor in this their first taste of freedom that seems to be peculiarly grateful to the contrabands, and which I doubt if prolonged years of tasting will expunge.   c. w. w.

J. S. W. to G.

Charley's letter to the Post was quite a success and I advise him to continue his communications. The Vanderbilt, Government Hospital Ship, got in last night at six or seven, and will be emptied to-day, I suppose. There has been a great and general muss on the whole subject (of course) between General B—— and Satterlee and their underlings, parties of the first part,— and all the State agents and volunteer doctors, parties of the second part, the old fight between regulars and volunteers—conflict of authority and efforts to sustain small personal dignities at the expense of everything else. In the meantime however, the patients, contrary to the usual course, have *not* suffered very much, as the public have had pretty free access to them and their wants have been supplied. Now, all transports are obliged to anchor in the stream and report to the regular quartermaster. . . . The Vanderbilt is the first arrival under the new régime and we shall see how it works. As much flourish of authority as they like, if it only shows fruit in the comfort of the patients, a subject on which I have misgivings. Fort Hamilton is the new depot; that and Bedloe's Island. We went to the Island on Friday and found things improving. A few weeks ago Dr. Agnew (I think) or one other of the Commission went down and found the doctor drunk, the stewards on leave given by themselves, and the fever patients dying of neglect. He, whoever he was, cruised about the Island, found ten pounds of beef, cut it up and made broth himself, and spent the night feeding the sick men. They have got a new surgeon now, but I think the steward steals. One reform at a time. We are determined, we "females," to make the place much too hot for him if we can *prove* anything. But how many weak-minded sisters there are! I never realized before how few people in the world are *really clever* and how very few are capable of "taking the responsibility." I have also discovered that there is nothing like philanthropy to bring out the quarreling propensities. Two young gentlemen called yesterday and asked for Charley, expressing great surprise that he hadn't got back, as they saw him driving his horse a day or two ago. They might have mistaken the man, but they appeared confident on the subject of the horse. So, Charley, Mr. Coles may be guilty of some black-hearted treachery. My mind always misgave me that Wilson's men went out o'nights with Nelly Bly. *What* is the news from Joe and the 16th? We search the papers in vain to find his whereabouts. Yesterday in the Herald, in a chance letter, was this, " General Franklin, in crossing a brook to-day, got mired in the soft earth banks and was thrown, but instantly emerged unhurt, dripping, puffing and laughing." That is the only public news I have seen of the Division for ten days. *Where* are they?

CHAPTER IX.

E. W. H. to J. H.

The Commission has sent out to establish a camp hospital at Savage's Station on the railroad about twelve miles from here, a depot for supplies, and a little encampment of twenty tents or more as a resting-place for sick and wounded stragglers, and a kitchen to feed the sick from as they pass by. Mr. Rogers and Mr. Holman are the agents of the Commission there, and Mrs. Fogg. It is a nice thing, and will greatly decrease the sufferings of the poor fellows. . . .

We have no news from you to-day. 250 more wounded came down last night, mostly rebels, and are being cared for on the "Louisiana." Georgy has just been giving them clean handkerchiefs, and our dear Mrs. Griffin has come in, blooming, from her rounds, saying she has had "a delightful morning." The rebels are very badly wounded, and so have better care than our own men; for the worst cases, whether Union or rebel, have the best treatment. They

The Chickahominy Swamp.

ought to be impressed by the kindness they
receive, and many of them are. I offered wine
and water to one fine, manly-looking fellow
who was carried on a stretcher past our tent,
and he answered gently, "No, sister; thank
you; I don't want any." Another little Geor-
gian was "so sorry to give Georgy so much
trouble" when she took him a pillow. . . . If
only I could see you now and then! Tell me
when you write what you mean by the *swamp*.

The "swamp," by which, and in which,
the army of the Potomac was operating, was
the deadly Chickahominy to which so many
thousands were sacrificed.

Edward
Mitchell.

While we were lying at White House in
the Wilson Small, one day, Mr. Olmsted
came to G. with the statement that " young
Mr. Mitchell of New York, who had come
down to help in the Commission's Quartermaster's department, was ill on the supply
boat Elizabeth." G. went across the plank
to him at once, and found a most attractive
six or seven feet of future brother-in-law
cramped into an uncomfortable little hole of
a cabin. This was E. M.'s first introduction
to the family; he was looked after a little,
and sent home in a returning hospital ship

to recruit. Mr. Olmsted had his father's private instructions to keep him out of the army.

A. H. W. a little later, writes:

Mr. Mitchell called yesterday afternoon to say good-bye and to offer to take anything to Georgy. Dr. Agnew had sent for him in a great hurry to go back as quartermaster on the Elm City. He had promised to go back on three or four days' notice, and had hoped to spend those at the seaside, where his physician had told him he ought to go. We had nothing for Georgy,— the Elm City lying at Jersey City, it would not have been convenient anyhow—but Carry took to his house in 9th street a letter to Georgy, and a large bundle of candy for himself.—(C's first present to her future husband).

J. S. W. to G. and E.

Sunday, June 8th.

Dear Girls: Being at home from church on account of the rain, I may as well do the next wickedest thing, write a letter. I have given up trying to get ahead of Abby, but am able to cut in now and then when she is out of town. With great exertion we got her off with Mother for a few days in Norwich. . . . We sent up after them Georgy's pencil note telling of your being at the railway terminus feeding the wounded in transit. I envy you from the bottom of my heart, but it is also my opinion, kept pretty much in that sacred receptacle, that you are killing or will kill yourselves. It is not only the positive fatigue, but the awful drain on your sympathies, and the excitement, etc.—you will be wrung out and dried—yellow and gray, if you ever get home at all. I have no doubt Abby will be horrified to hear that you are at the White House Station ; and all your softening of your labors for family use does not take us in in the least. However, as I said, I envy you, and I respond to the little song you are no doubt singing out of Maud,

> " What matter if I go mad,
> I shall have had my day."

. . . Dr Agnew says that he is " not using too strong terms when he says the government's neglect of its wounded is damnable." . . . The St. Mark is to go down, probably, on Wednesday. We will send the few things you mention by her, and hope to hear in the meantime of something more that you want. Dr. Bellows goes in her. It seems to me that some people with money are not half waked up to the need of giving it in this cause. I alone, could name a dozen who don't seem to know or care anything about hospital matters. *Poor* people give a great deal—dozens of plain men and women come with clothes, provisions, etc., to the different barracks, but many of the better able ones neither come nor send. By and by their day of opportunities and grace will be over.

Hatty writes :

June 10.

We shall send you the things you ask for by the steamer St. Mark to-morrow, and hope you may get them, though I have my doubts as to Charley's wines making a sea journey safely with government employees on board ready to drink them up. William Hodge has just walked up the street with me, says Lenox has come back for an appointment in one of the government Hospitals in Philadelphia.

E's Journal.

WILSON SMALL, June 13.

Little to do. As we were sitting in our parlor-cabin Wednesday, trying to keep cool, Joe ran up the stairs into the midst of us. Everything was quiet at the front and in the regiment, and General Franklin told him "he would rather have him come than not." He and Captain Woolsey Hopkins rode the twenty-five miles down together, over roads more frightful than they ever were near Washington. We took them into the Commission for the

Ordered off from White House.

night in spite of the new rules excluding outsiders. As there was little to do, we ran up the
river in the evening, in the "Wissahickon,"
past the broken bridge and Colonel Ingalls'
encampment and the lily pads, far up into the
moonlight. . . .

Later. . . . It was Friday night our stampede
happened. We were all quietly at work in our
tent on shore (having fed a hundred or more
sick men), preparing for the night, when a
wounded soldier came by with the news that
the train which was just in had been fired into
by rebel cavalry near Tunstall's Station, about
three and a half miles from White House. One
man was killed, and six or eight wounded, but
the train pushed on and gave the alarm. We
felt no fear whatever for ourselves, but I was
very anxious to hear of J.'s safe arrival in camp
the day before. A peremptory order from
Quartermaster-General Ingalls came to Mr.
Olmsted : "Put your women behind the iron
walls of the Spaulding, and drop down below
the gunboats."

Edward Mitchell went up to headquarters to
see if there was no mistake, and came back with
the message : "Drop down below the gunboats
at once, and look out to keep clear of vessels
floating down, on fire." So we reluctantly hurried on board the Small with all the staff,

(except Drs. Ware and Haight, who stayed with
the sick on shore) and skedaddled ignominiously.
Once moored alongside the Spaulding, Mr.
Olmsted came back in a rowboat for news, and
found all the camp followers, teamsters, sutlers,
railroad and barge men organizing in companies, and arms and ammunition serving to them.
Edward Mitchell, who had volunteered for this
duty, had a company.

The sickest men from the tents were all taken
on board the Small, a detail of twenty-five
doctors and men from the Spaulding acting as
bearers.

It was now after midnight, but we made up
about forty beds, got beef tea and punch ready,
and about thirty, including the wounded from
the train, were made comfortable. They were
to have been transferred to the Spaulding, but a
new order prevented this, and Saturday morning
we once more took our old place at the White
House wharf. Simultaneous with the attack on
the train was one on the forage landing, a little
above here on the Pamunkey, where two hundred government wagons were burnt, forage
destroyed, and several of the teamsters killed.
A schooner was also burnt, and we supposed
the light of it to be that of a burning bridge.
The scare has blown over.

A. H. W.

8 BREVOORT PLACE, June 17th.

My dear Charley: We had just been reading in the Times about the scare at White House
when Georgy's letter arrived. We have read it
aloud over the breakfast table, and are now
going to enclose it to Mary and Carry at Astoria,
that they, too, may have the private version of
the affair. It was a bold and very clever dash
of the rebels; just what might have been
expected, however. They are up to all sorts of
thievish, daring things. . . . It would not have
been out of place for you all to have been much
more frightened than you profess to have been.
Georgy's letter, in fact, we presume, was prepared for *home consumption.* She always tries to
"draw it mild" for our benefit; is always having
a lazy, lovely good time, perfectly well, and in
the best of spirits, and as to the scenes of suffering about her, not caring a bit; has to pinch
herself, I dare say, to see that she isn't stone—
thinks she "hasn't any heart," etc., etc. Tell
her, of course she hasn't, or won't have soon—
it's *ossifying*, that, or something kindred, is what
all surgeons die of—suppressed emotion. Tell
her we insist on her coming home for a few
weeks; now that you are with Eliza, she has not
that excuse for staying.—Eliza, of course, we
cannot induce to leave, it would be useless to

try. Tell Georgy her known imprudence in overdoing herself, her known obstinacy about precautionary and remedial measures, impel me to insist on her taking a northern trip and a little rest just now. . . . Mrs. Gibbons goes back to her Winchester hospital next Monday. I am going up to see her, hear some of her tales and offer what supplies we have on hand. She and her party were obliged to fly for their lives when the rebels drove Banks out, lost on the way their three trunks, containing all their clothing, and Mrs. G. was without a bonnet. They have been very busy sewing up a new outfit, and I hope won't be interfered with again, though Jackson threatens another raid up the valley with 70,000 men as soon as the harvests are ripe. . . . I have saved our only piece of news till the last—the engagement of Pussy Wheeler; make Georgy guess who to. . . . It is Dr. Ceccarini, the Italian oculist, an accomplished man and skillful surgeon. . . . Mother says, " Tell Charley how glad I am always to get his letters, and tell him that when he cautions Georgy on the subject of health, to be sure to be prudent himself." You are in a most useful and important place, and we would all rather have you there than in any part of our army.

Mother to C. W. W.

NEW YORK, June, '62.

My dear Charley: Here are lots of scraps
for you. Our basket is just going off to the
steamer. I hope you will enjoy the gingerbread. We are all anxiety for further accounts
since the battles of the last few days. The
paper this morning states two deaths on the
Knickerbocker of poor wounded men. What
trying scenes again for you ! I agree with you
in all you say of Georgy's health, but know
that persuasion is useless. You ask about coming home. We do not *need* your aid in getting
out of town, however pleasant it would be to
have you. There is no prospect of our going
at present ; we have no place in view at all. . . .
Have the rebels cut the telegraph lines, that we
get no news from the army ? Where are you
all to rendezvous now that the White House is
given up ? Some of the movements seem so
mysterious to us—such as this, and the falling
back of McClellan's army to Savage's Station,
and some other strange doings. I hope it will
all come out right. Do take care of yourself
and the girls. I am so much better satisfied to
have you where you are, than with the 22nd.
Your Cousins William and Anna have been on
to Baltimore to see Lloyd ; they are greatly distressed at the idea of his being sworn in, even
for three months ! . . .

Farewell dear boy.   Mother's love and blessing to you.

Northern hospitals in many places were
all this time filling up with wounded from
the front, and women were volunteering as
nurses in them also.   The following letters
show what was being done at the New
Haven General Hospital, years before its
Training School for Nurses was organized.

S. C. W. to G. M. W.

NEW HAVEN HOSPITAL, June.

I have been so very busy that my conscience
does not reproach me at all for not writing. . . .
A fortnight ago our wounded came—240 of
them, all dreadfully neglected and needing
attention of every kind.   I cannot just this moment recollect the name of the ship which
brought them, but there was only one surgeon
on board to care for them, no nurses and hardly
any provisions ; the wounds of many had not
been dressed for nearly a week when they got
here, and seven or eight died on the passage.
For the first few days most of them were placed
in tents on the hospital grounds, but since then
the new Barrack Hospital has been finished, and
all except about twenty very bad cases are quartered there and doing very well.   They would

not let any young ladies enter for the first three or four days, the sights and sounds were too bad for them. Such was the enlightened decision of the excellent incapable in charge, but Friday I worked my way in, and since then have been there nearly every day, taking charge of the linen room and giving out clothes, etc. to the men. At first everything was in dreadful confusion, but gradually our department is getting into order, and in the course of three or four days will be thoroughly systematized. A good old lady and myself are to take turns in presiding over the clothing supplies, and as she is rather inefficient and feeble, I hope to take a very big half of the time. The small corner they give us as a store-room was yesterday all shelved and cupboarded under my direction, and will be capable of holding three times the supply it did before. . . . I go up at nine and stay till seven, and all day long the nurses are coming after sheets, and shirts, and bandages, and rags, and towels, and soap, and the men stopping at the door to ask for trousers or coats, and in time I hope to get the true tailor's measure in my eyes. Such fine, manly, patient fellows as they are. Many of them, almost all, from Michigan and Pennsylvania and New York ; not one Connecticut man among them. From the linen room one can organize little rushes into the wards to see special cases, etc.,

so it is not to be despised even though not as
satisfactory as the actual nursing would be.
Just outside of our long wooden barrack is a
small wooden kitchen, and there Harriet Terry
and Rebecca Bacon preside over the diet for the
special cases who cannot eat the hospital rations,
and if one looks in there about twelve, such a
smell of good things greets the nose as it does
one good to experience ; and arranged on the
table are such nice little messes all labelled and
numbered—such brown crisp toast and savory
chops, and smoking beef-tea, and little messes
of this and that ; and later the great trays come
in and carry them off down the long entry, and
so, many poor fellows are made comfortable.
One building, which holds eight wards, and
comprises four tents full of sick, is all well
managed, orderly and thriving, with good paid
and excellent unpaid nursing ; but in the main
hospital where the housekeeper has control, it
is all mismanagement, confusion and waste ;
really sickening to see.   The men are doing
pretty well though, and all of them are so happy
and grateful for the care taken of them.   A
very nice man from the 105th Pennsylvania, for
whom I was writing a letter yesterday, told me
to tell his mother not to feel anxious about him,
for he was cared for just as if he was at home,
and had everything he desired.

S. C. W. to G. M. W.

LINEN ROOM, NEW HAVEN HOSPITAL,
June 26th, '62.

My dearest G.: A lull in business gives me
a chance to write a few lines to you and tell you
how glad I was last night to find your letter
waiting for me when I got home from my day
here. . . . What wonder that you have not written when *I* have never found time to write until
after ten o'clock at night. . . . One of my pets
here among the men is sure that you and Eliza
are the ladies who were in a large tent on shore
at White House, and brought him some bowls
of bread and milk and swigs of strong drink of
some kind. He was so interested to make sure
of the point that I promised to bring up your
picture for him to see and compare with his
recollections. . . . The Surgeon-General has
written to Dr. Jewett to say that he hears such
favorable accounts of the state of affairs here
that he is going to send 300 of his worst cases
for us to care for. Inspector-General Hammond
is coming on Saturday to see with his own eyes,
and we are to be swept and garnished for his
benefit. Mrs. Hunt ("H. H.") helps me here
often ; mends clothes by the hour and comes
for three days during the week to write letters
for the men. . . . My fortnight's experience
here convinces me that I could soon acquire the
art of keeping, not an "Hotel," but a small

country variety store. There is the same run of customers, the taking of stock, the arranging of the goods, the sweeping-up and closing of the shutters at night. My stock comprises almost everything—shirts and collars, cravats and suspenders, coats and trousers, vests and shoes, handkerchiefs, sheets, pillows and pillow-cases, rags, bandages, soap, thread, needles, tape, buttons, combs, brushes, hats, fans, cotton wadding, water beds (2), stockings, oranges, lemons, bay rum, camphor, stationery, towels, dust-pans, brushes and mosquito netting, and this morning a woman bolted in, saying, "Is it in this room that the *corpse* is?—they tell me that it is in this end of the passage, and I thought I should like to see him!" I didn't happen to have one, however, and she seemed quite aggrieved. . . . Jenny is somewhat better, and the baby lovely as can be. . . . She is a dear little puss, and one of the great obstacles to my entire devotion to my country.

From Edward Mitchell.

WHITE HOUSE, June 20, 1862.

My dear Father: Heavy firing in the advance this A. M. Since writing to Fred. I have had no time to write another word. Sitting up late that night, I was waked up, with Drs. Jenkins and Haight, to go ashore for 24 hours at 3 A. M. In consequence of being routed out at this unusual hour, yesterday was spent, so far as leisure hours were concerned, in deep sleep. . . . I now write to thank you for your kind expressions of regard for my health, and of love for me ; and for your desire to see me with you once more. . . .

My health—it is excellent. . . . And so far it has been possible to find an assistant, who though stupid to an extent and lazy, is willing to go twice a day to wait an hour or more for commissary stores;—it would be perfectly disgusting to me. . . . I doubt much if Mr. Olmsted will be willing to let me go home for some months at least. The staff is now well organized, and the departure of one would throw very much labor on another who would not understand it at all. This is especially so in my case. The drawing of rations requires much care, and to know what stores the Commission has, and where they are, one must be continually among them. . . . *You* were right about the rebel cavalry, not I. It was very bold. Gen. Stuart commanded. In case *we* had been called out, I had intended to use only the bayonet and to creep round if possible on the flank of the enemy and charge at my own time—have lain in ambush, in other words. I think Sawtelle would have been willing to allow me my own way, for as he was a regular, he of course placed not much reliance, if any, on such a Falstaff army. . . .

Olmsted has a deal of tact ; as much as a woman. Also much shrewdness and a very quiet manner. In some characteristics he reminds me a little of you, or rather what you would have been if you had been called more actively into public life. . . .

A battle is *predicted* to take place in three days, by Capt. Sawtelle ; time will show.

The Webster and Spaulding go to New York. Dr. —— goes in charge of the latter. In my capacity of aide I delivered his sailing orders to him. He may be a very nice man and an excellent physician, but he has an unquenchable and unalterable desire to spread himself and his authority. I received instructions to *bully* him into staying on board in case he should attempt to come back to the White House ! Some funny things occur here !

I regret immensely that I will be unable to be present at Neil's commencement. I would rather loose $50 than not to be there. . . .

E. to J. H.

WILSON SMALL, June —.

This morning I have your Sunday note with the charming little poem. Who wrote it ? Be sure and tell me. It *is* a poem, and though entirely undeserved, I value it very much indeed.

[Poem by a Lieutenant of the 16th N. Y., dedicated to
E. W. H.]

To Mrs. Joseph Howland.

———

From old Saint Paul till now,
  Of honorable women not a few
  Have quit their golden ease, in love to do
  The saintly works that Christ-like hearts pursue.

Such an one art thou, God's fair apostle,
  Bearing His love in war's horrific train ;
  Thy blessed feet follow its ghastly pain
  And misery and death, without disdain.

To one borne from the sullen battle's roar,
  Dearer the greeting of thy gentle eyes,
  When he aweary, torn and bleeding lies,
  Than all the glory that the victors prize.

When peace shall come, and homes shall smile again,
  Ten thousand soldier hearts, in Northern climes,
  Shall tell their little children, with their rhymes,
  Of the sweet saint who blessed the old war times.

E. to J. H.

June 20.

I am much entertained by the regiment's
vote of thanks to *me* for the hats with which I
had nothing whatever to do. [J. H. had himself
ordered straw hats for the 16th, to help guard
against the intense heat of the Chickahominy
swamp, and gave them in E's name.] . . . Quartermaster Davies has gone off with an order for
the delivery of the musical instruments, and you

will probably receive them to-morrow. Let me
know if they are good ones. I have a "Psalm
of the Union" for you, which I will send by the
Quartermaster—a composition of old Mrs. Hill's,
Mother's opposite neighbor. It is sent to you
with her compliments. "She always expresses
her emotions in harmony."

We ran down at daybreak yesterday to Yorktown to see the floating hospital, the "St. Mark,"
just arrived from New York with Drs. Agnew,
Draper, Carmalt, and others on board. . . .

Later—The Small came back during the evening, and brought Dr. Agnew and Dr. Carmalt
(Annie Woolsey's brother-in-law), and a number
of the St. Mark's force, to go out to the front
to-day. We all spent most of the evening in
the tent, with the front curtains down and the
back ones open to let in the blaze of the camp
fire, over which on the pot-hooks hung the kettles
of tea and coffee and soup which were preparing
for 200 or 300 sick who were expected down on
the trains. Nearly 500 came before morning
and were provided for. The Commodore is fitting up and will leave for New York to-morrow.
. . . Another party, the third of Congressional
picnickers, came down to-day, but were refused
transportation to the front by General McClellan's orders. I rejoice in it. . . . Won't you tell
Dr. C. to pin the *name and address* of all his sick
men somewhere about their clothing, if he has

to leave them, and however *little sick* they may
be. So many men come down and die here
without name or token, and then—so many
families are left in sorrow and suspense.

G. to Mother.

June 22.

The Commodore, government boat, lies at
the dock nearly full. Sixty Sisters of Charity
had arrived yesterday and to-day, and were to
be established at the White House and work at the
General Hospital—on shore. They came down
unexpectedly by some one's orders and *would*
have done good work, but now they sat on their
large trunks on the Knickerbocker's deck, forbidden to stay by the Padre, who was in a high
state of ecclesiastical disgust at not finding full
provision for them on shore, including a chapel !
I labored with the old gentleman upon the
unreasonableness of expecting to find confes-
sionals, etc., on a battlefield, but to no purpose.
There sat the Sisters clean and peaceful, with
their sixty umbrellas and sixty baskets, fastened
to their places by the Padre's eye, and not one
of them has been allowed to come over and help
us to put the Commodore in order. So our
staff went to work among the 500 patients. We
asked for basins ; there were none on board this
government vessel. We secured all we needed
from the Commission's stores, however, and be-

fore the boat started that night, the sickest men
were fed and washed, and beef tea and punch
enough made to last the worst cases till they
reached Fortress Monroe. We wrote all the
names and home addresses of all the sickest who
might be speechless on arrival and pinned the
papers inside their pockets. The Sisters now
gladly took hold of the work and returned to
their convents, as nurses on this hospital steamer.

E's Journal.

WILSON SMALL, June 23.

A very anxious day. An orderly from
Brigade Headquarters brought word from Captain Hopkins that Joe was ill and unable to
write. I at once put up a basket of stores for
him—bedsack, pillows, sheets, arrowroot, etc.,
etc., to go by the orderly, and Charley telegraphed Generals Slocum and Franklin to
know the truth, while Mr. Olmsted arranged
with Captain Sawtelle for a pass to take me
to the front to-morrow morning. My mind was
relieved, however, by the telegraphic answers
and better accounts, and I have given up the
idea of going out.

. . . June 25th. General Van Vliet says that
if I want to go to the front at any time and will
send him word, he will have his wagon meet me
and take me over to J's camp. This morning
Dr. Bigelow came back to our boat from the
front.

. . . June 26th. Running away down the
Pamunkey again as fast as we can go, escap-
ing from Stonewall Jackson !

All night the wood choppers were at work
cutting down the woods at the White House to
give the gunboats a chance to command the
land beyond, and just now as we passed, the
banks were shorn and the pretty little place laid
bare. The pickets had been driven in, and
Jackson was supposed to be close at hand.
Eighty wounded were brought down last night
and put on board the Knickerbocker. Twelve
more and a few sick came down this morning.
The Whilldin follows us, nearly full of sick and
wounded.

The rumor to-day is that all communication
with the front is stopped, to conceal an advance
of our army.

June 28th. We went as far as West Point,
followed by a train of schooners and barges
running away like ourselves. There we lay
through the evening and night, watching for the
flames of burning stores at White House which
did not burn, and for booming of guns which
did not boom—without news or orders, until
after dinner, when we turned and ran up the
river again in search of both. Near Cumber-
land we met the Arrowsmith with Surgeon
Vollum on board, who hailed us and told us all
we yet know of yesterday's action at the front.

Colonel Vollum then pushed on to Washington for medical supplies and we kept on up here to White House again.

We little knew at the time that "yester- Battle of day's action at the front," to which E. Gaines' Mill. alludes so quietly, was the desperate battle J. H. wound- ed. of Gaines' Mill, June 27, 1862, the first of the terrible seven days' battle before Richmond. It was in this action that J. H. was wounded at the head of his regiment. His command- ing officer (General J. J. Bartlett) said, in his official report of the battle: "The enemy were slowly but surely forcing back the right of the entire line of battle. At this juncture I ordered forward the 16th New York Volunteers, Colonel Howland com- manding. From the position of the regi- ment it was necessary to change front for- ward on first company under the most terrific fire of musketry, with the shells and round shot of two batteries raking over the level plain, making it seemingly impossible for a line to withstand the fire a single instant. But with the calmness and precision of veteran soldiers the movement was executed. . . . To Colonel Joseph Howland I am indebted for maintaining the extreme right of my line, for nobly leading his regiment to the charge and retaking two guns from the enemy. Whatever of noble moral, physical and manly courage has ever been given by God to man, has fallen to his lot. Cheering his men to victory, he early received a painful wound, but with a heroism worthy of the cause he has sacrified so much to maintain, he kept his saddle until the close of the battle."

Lieutenant-Colonel Marsh of the 16th was mortally wounded in this engagement at Gaines' Mill, and apart from the Colonel and Lieutenant-Colonel, the loss of the regiment in killed and wounded was 260 men, rank and file, fully one-quarter of its effective force on that day.

It was "for gallantry at the battle of Gaines' Mill, Virginia," that the rank of Brigadier-General by brevet was later conferred on J. H. by the President of the United States.

Story of old Scott, Joe's war horse   When the battle at Gaines' Mill was all over and Joe began to realize his own fatigue and wounded condition, he dismounted and lay down under a tree not far from the field, and presently fell asleep. He did not know how long he had slept, but it was dusk when he was waked by something soft touching his cheek, and rousing himself he found it was his war horse, old "Scott," rubbing his nose against his face. He had got loose from where he was tied and had looked for his master until he found him. Joe was not ashamed to say that he cried like a child as he put his arm round the dear old fellow's neck.

He brought him home and rode him after the war until he grew to be old and no longer sure-footed. Then his shoes were taken off and he was turned out to grass to have an easy time and nothing to do the rest of his life. After a little, however, he moped and refused to eat and was evidently dissatisfied with life. So Thomson came to Joe and said, "Do you know, Mr. Howland, I believe old Scott would be happier if he had *something to do.*" And accordingly, although he had never been in harness in his life, he was put before the lawn-mower, and to do active light farm-work. The effect was excellent; he grew happy and contented again, and proved to be one of the best working-horses on the farm for several years.

It was Scott's last shoes as a saddle-horse, when he was turned out to grass, that we mounted and hung in the office at our Fish-kill home.

The news of J.'s being wounded reached us at White House through a telegram kindly sent the morning after the battle by Dr. McClellan, Staff Surgeon at Army Headquarters, as follows: "The Colonel has a slight flesh wound. He is in my tent, and will be taken good care of until he can be sent down."

At almost the same moment communication with the front was cut. We telegraphed for more details, in vain. The rebels were upon us. Stoneman sent in word that they were in sight. We stayed as long as they would let us and then went off into the dark, taking what comfort we could in the one word, "slight."

G. M. W. to Mother.

WILSON SMALL, June 28.

Sanitary Commission falls back. White House abandoned.

The telegraph wires had been cut just as we received the news of Joe's wound, and a mounted messenger announced the enemy at Tunstall's. Stoneman's cavalry were worrying them till we were all safely off, when he would fall back, and the rebels would walk into our deserted places. So we steamed away, watching the moving of the last transports, and the Canonicus (Headquarters' boat for the army officers at White House), with Colonel Ingalls, Captain Sawtelle, and General Casey and staff. The most interesting thing was the spontaneous movement of the slaves, who, when it was known that the Yankees were running away, came flocking from all the country about, bringing their little movables, frying pans, old hats, and bundles, to the river side. There was no appearance of anxiety or excitement among them. Fortunately there was plenty of deck room for them on the forage boats, one of which, as we passed, seemed filled with women only, in their gayest dresses and brightest turbans, like a whole load of tulips for a horticultural show. The black smoke began to rise from the burning stores on shore (fired to keep them from the enemy), and now and then the roar of the battle came to us, but the slave women were quietly nursing their children, and singing hymns. The day of their deliverance had come, and they accepted this most wonderful change with absolute placidity. All night we sat on the deck of the Small, watching the constantly increasing cloud of smoke and the fire-flashes over the trees towards the White House, as we moved slowly down the river.

The Wilson Small, with the whole fleet of hospital ships, made its way to Fort Monroe, and lay waiting for news from the front, cut off from all communication with the army and our own special part of it, Joe.

McClellan retreats to the James.

During this time the seven days' fighting before Richmond took place. The line by the York River was abandoned, and the army made its fearful and humiliating retreat across the Peninsula, through the deadly Chickahominy swamps, fighting and retreating upon the James, as a change of base. On July 2nd the gunboats headed by the Galena pushed cautiously up the James from Fortress Monroe, followed by our headquarters boat, the Wilson Small, to Harrison's Landing. Our retreating army had reached that point almost at the same moment, and to our joy we saw the flags flying as we neared the shore.

Arrived at Harrison's Landing, the Sanitary Commission at once began establishing its depot of supplies and made ready to receive the wounded. Almost immediately Joe was helped on board the Small. He had been brought across the Peninsula, wounded, and ill with Chickahominy fever, in a headquarters' ambulance—a very painful experience in itself—but he was safe now, and *with us*.

Mother to C. W. W.

June 29 or 30.

Your last letter this moment come! We know not what to think. Dear E., what a heroine she shows herself. This slight wound may be the means of saving Joe from greater danger, as he *must* now *lie by*. Dear boy, how sad we feel about him. Our best love to him when you can. How very anxious we are to hear more. Thank you and G. for letters. We feel thankful it is no *worse* with Joe. Let this feeling keep up all your hearts. Our dear love to Eliza; I am rejoiced she is so brave. I wish I were there to help take care of Joe. Let us hear at once all you know.

Mother to E. W. H.

July 3, '62.

My dear Eliza : What times you are living through! in the very midst, too, of everything as you are!—and how dark, very dark, it all looks to us this morning as we read the last "reliable" accounts from the army before Richmond! Think of six days' continuous fighting. When I looked over the list of horrors, my first thought and exclamation was, "just think what Joe has been spared!" I really look upon his "slight wound" as the greatest blessing which could have happened to us all, and I am thankful for it. It may have been the means of sav-

ing his life. Abby is writing you, but I put in
my own words of tender love and sympathy. . . .
I rejoice that Charley is at hand with you.

A. H. W. to E.

July 3.

Georgy's letter sent ashore at West Point
came this morning; Charley's came yesterday.
Both are postmarked Old Point. We learn of
Joe's wound, and trust it may be no more than
you describe it, and that his previous illness
will not be against his recovery from this fresh
drawback. We shall be extremely anxious to
learn all particulars. No doubt if any one is
well taken care of, he will be, as he is so near
his General and other army friends. But what
are the thousands and thousands of our poor
wounded to do, cut off from railroad transportation, left in a swamp, without supplies? We
see by the morning papers that hundreds from
the fight on the *left* were carried to the banks
of the James River, where were neither supplies
or surgeons or transports. Some were huddled
on a government tug, but who can tell the distress and disorganization that attends such a
reverse as ours. Not a word of intelligence
have we had since the last date, Saturday evening, on our right, and nothing from the left for
days and days. The city has been full of wild
and gloomy rumors, which may well fill us with

doubts and anxiety. . . . I hope you have all had enough of McClellan at last.

Captain Curtis stopped here a few moments yesterday, on his way back to the 16th. He went by the 5 P. M. train. " Not well enough to go, as a man, but well enough as an officer," he said. Joe will be glad to feel that *he* is at his post once more, in his own absence. I hope you won't let Joe worry about his regiment, though I do pity the poor men now. . . .

We are thankful, as you are, Eliza, that Joe is safe from the desperate fighting we have had for six days and the worse that is to come. Everything looks like a terrible reverse. It leaks out that our loss in two days was ten thousand, including, I suppose, Porter's fight on the right. The call for three hundred thousand volunteers shows, as I have seen all along, that so far from ending the war on the 4th of July, we should only have to begin it all over again. Well! we must be thankful that as a family we have been so mercifully spared so far. The papers are not allowed to publish a word, and as *good* news is never held back, we are left to the wildest and gloomiest rumors. How many families must be in painful suspense. There were twenty calls here yesterday : Rockwells, Aspinwalls, Johnsons, etc., all happening in, all much concerned, and all sending much love. General Porter lost eighteen pieces of artillery we see, in that hor-

rid fight and retreat at Mechanicsville and
Gaines' Mill. Thank God that Joe came out of
it so well. Jane has seen at the New England
Relief several of the 7th Connecticut, wounded
at James Island lately; Corporal Hooks and
Private Cook and others, who all spoke in the
warmest terms of the bravery and kindness of
Surgeon Bacon, who was in the very front, taking care of the men, lifting them out of danger,
etc. Corporal H. had had his arm amputated,
but so well was it done, that he says he never
has had a sensation of pain in it from the first
moment. The surgeons say that all the surgery
on these 7th Connecticut men was splendidly
done.

Corporal H. sent home eleven dollars to his
mother out of thirteen. He laughed a loud
laugh when Jane said to him, "Your arm was
too much to give to those rebels, wasn't it?"
"Law! they might have the other and welcome,
if they'd only let me go back!" He had promised to write to Dr. Bacon, but asked Jane if she
wouldn't do it for him; "he hadn't got used to
having only one hand, and couldn't hold the
paper steady."

We shall not keep a very merry Fourth anywhere in the North to-morrow.

One of the hospital duties of all the nurses
at the front was writing letters home for the

sick and wounded men, and sometimes the sad work of telling the story of their last few hours of life. That such letters helped to comfort sorrowful hearts, the following answer to one shows. The soldier was mortally wounded in the seven days' fight, and in E's care on the hospital ship.

To Mrs. Joseph Howland.
July 2nd, 1862.

Madam: Your letter of the 26th ultimo, conveying the mournful intelligence of the death of R. P., was received on Monday, the 30th ult. . . .

Until I received your letter, I had indulged the hope he would survive the injury; and had —not ten minutes before it was delivered to me— been informed by a lady, whose son is in the same division, that he was wounded, and that the other members of the company were preparing to send him home. This information, with a knowledge that he was of a robust constitution, and perfectly healthy, induced the belief he would recover. . . .

Madam, that letter of yours, although it was a messenger of death, when it was received by those who were being tortured by alternating thoughts of hope and fear, was like the visit of an angel; for it relieved their minds of a torturing anxiety.

I am requested by R's father to let you know that he is utterly unable to express his gratitude; that the only way he feels able to compensate you is by offering his heartfelt thanks.

Madam, the occupation which it appears you have chosen, that of alleviating the condition of those who are in affliction, is for its labor paid in a still secret way, which is not fully appreciated by any, except they be like you; for I doubt not, that on receipt of this, (when you will have known that you have been instrumental in conferring a lasting favor,) a lady of your nature will feel she is somewhat repaid.

A. H. W. to E.

8 BREVOORT PLACE, SATURDAY, July 5th, '62.

My dear Eliza: Georgy's and Charley's letters from Harrison's have just arrived, the last date being a postscript Thursday, July 3, which brings us into close correspondence again you see. These letters have relieved the painful anxiety that began to possess us, about Joe's condition and whereabouts. We thought perhaps that if his wound were really slight, he had been tempted to rejoin the regiment, and had shared in that horrible battle of White Oak Swamp. . . . Mother says that if it is Charley's *desire* to stay a little while longer, she consents; he is evidently so useful, that she should not have the heart to insist on his coming back. As for Georgy, if you leave her behind, we shall never forgive you. She *must* come. Mother cannot stand the anxiety much longer, nor can Georgy bear the constant strain. By-and-by, perhaps, if necessary, she could go back ; *now* she must come home with you. We should be better pleased to have Charley and all once more together, at the end of this battle-year, and before we all begin on other years of separation and distress. Have C. come too. Poor, poor Colonel Marsh ! mortally wounded at Gaines' Mill. What a mercy it would have been had he been killed on the spot. . . . We shall never know all that this week of desperate fighting has cost us ; our dead and wounded being left behind, or crawling painfully along in the trail of the retreating army. Here and there an officer picked up in a passing ambulance, as Joe rescued the four you speak of. Our great, beautiful "Army of the Potomac," dwindled down to an exhausted handful. . . . *Fifty* thousand in all destroyed by fever and wounds, in McClellan's brief campaign ! No wonder if the President has hesitated to send more troops to be used up in swamps, when so little was being done to show for it. . . . Any fool might have known that Beauregard and the bulk of his army had come to Richmond ; but then our generals are not even fools, but something less if possible. . . . It may be God's will to destroy this nation by inches. It is certainly the devil's will to put dissension into the hearts of our leaders, and blundering darkness into their minds. God overrules all evil, even this, I suppose, to his own glory. I have no question that this and all other defeats are intended to drive us, as a nation, to a higher moral ground in the conduct and purpose of this war. As things stand, the South is fighting to maintain slavery, and the North is trying to fight so as not to put it down. When this policy ceases, perhaps we shall begin to have victory, if we haven't already sinned away our day of grace.

I don't know who kept Fourth of July yesterday; there was not much for public rejoicing, though many families had private mercies and deliverances, like ours, to be thankful for. Hatty and Carry went with the Bucks to Bedloe's Island, with a tug load of ice cream and cake, and flowers, and flags, and a chest of tea, forty quarts of milk, and butter, and handkerchiefs, papers and books, to set out a long table and give a treat to two hundred in hospital there. To their distress they found that H—— B—— (malisons on him) had ordered away the day before, back to their regiments (via Fort Monroe I suppose), all who were strong enough to move about. They cannot possibly carry their knapsacks or guns, and must go into hospital again from relapse.

The forty convalescents left on the Island had a glorious feast, the doctor giving his full consent that even the twelve sick ones, in bed, should have as much *ice cream* as they wanted. Mr. Lasar, the singer, and one or two others, went about twice in the course of the day, from tent to tent, singing patriotic songs and hymns, winding up with "Lord, dismiss us," by particular request of the men; and then the men escorted the whole party, after tea, back to the tug, with three cheers and overwhelming thanks. Each man had at least a quart of ice cream, Carry thinks, and each a glass of Catawba wine, and a good slice of cake, and no doubt there will be many made sick, and the ladies will be blamed as the cause.

If you have a hold on Hammond, do get him to look into the hospital rations in the hospitals here: Bedloe's and David's Islands. There seems to be no "special diet" provided—nothing but coffee (no tea), dry bread and stew, rank with onions and white with grease. I have written to the ladies at New Rochelle, begging them to take David's Island in hand, and open a "ladies' kitchen," a "gruel kitchen," as Sarah says theirs in New Haven is called. But they say the surgeon looks with disfavor on the visits of ladies, and they feel "satisfied that the men are *well* taken care of." . . . They will find out by-and-by that surgeons and hospital stewards are not all angels in uniform. . . .

People kept coming yesterday, having seen Joe's name in the newspaper lists, and to-day we have notes of inquiry from all directions. . . .

Edward Walker's account of the fight at Gaines' Mill agrees with the Tribune reporter's —black masses of men coming upon our guns with *orderly joy* determined to take them, and falling under our fire in solid blocks, others pressing forward to fill the gaps.

J. H. and E. go home.

The Daniel Webster was now filling up again with wounded and sick taken on at Harrison's Landing,—J. H. among them,— and, with Eliza as hospital nurse-in-charge, it sailed July 5th for New York. Charley and G. stayed on a little longer, till the army fell back towards Washington.

A. H. W. to G. at Harrison's Landing.

8 BREVOORT PLACE, July 7, 1862.

My dear Georgy: Eliza and Joe came safely through yesterday (Sunday) morning. Jane and I were just going to the front door on our way to church when their hotel coach drove up. They had a pleasant voyage, only Joe says (in joke) *he* was neglected—Eliza and Miss Lowell directing their attention to other men ! . . . Joe hobbled up on his broom-stick for a crutch, and we swarmed round, having so many questions to

ask that we didn't know where to begin, and so
were silent. Some broth and sangaree were
quickly served and relished. I should say that
Charley's telegram from Washington came Saturday afternoon, and gave us notice enough to
send out and get what extra supplies we needed.
. . . Mother and Uncle E. drove right in from
Astoria, and Joe has had the story to go over a
great many times.

A. H. W. to G.

8 BREVOORT PLACE, NEW YORK, July 10th, 1862.

Eliza, Joe and Jane have gone off this morning to Fishkill. . . . Joe's place here was in the
long lounging-chair by the front parlor window, while we received ordinary folks whom he
wouldn't see, in the dining-room. He has worn
a full white suit of Charley's, which Hatty happened to lay her hands on, and went off in it
this morning, home, via Newburgh. . . . He did
not mean to go till this afternoon, but got a
letter yesterday from Mr. Masters (who has
been one of the callers here) written in great
haste, and full of excitement. It was to Eliza,
saying that the people of Fishkill were so full
of enthusiasm for her husband, that they were
bent on having a demonstration on his arrival,
which he knew would be contrary to Eliza's
taste, and injurious to Joe's health. He therefore advised that they should change the hour

and way of their proposed coming, and if they would telegraph him to Newburgh—*under an assumed name* (isn't it funny?)—he would be there to receive the message and would let Thomson and Moritz know! . . . We think it a shame to disappoint the people so much, but Joe *would* get up at five this morning and leave the house at six, with his sword, etc. done up in a brown paper parcel. He thinks if there is such enthusiasm, he ought to be able to turn it to account for *recruiting*. It is really pleasant to know that the country people have such a spirit —for the cause. It is a good sign. . . .

The farmer, Mr. Thomson, wrote me a letter of thanks for mine to him, describing Joe's wound, etc. He said there had been "such reports in Fishkill as never was. Some had it his nose had been shot off, and some, his *jaw*, and the story was 'Mrs. Howland was pris'ner,' " etc. Great discussions took place in the church porch on Sunday, whether his moustache would grow over such a very bad scar, and Mr. Masters was so besieged for details that he ended by reading from the pulpit part of a letter of Carry's to Mrs. Charles Wolcott.

The neighbors have all been in, or sent in to offer their services to us and our wounded hero, having watched him get out of the coach that Sunday morning. Carry was so intent on watching the Hills from her window, and so

desirous that they should all be ranged at their
front windows, looking, as they *were*, that I believe she missed seeing Joe get out herself! . . .

Did anyone tell you of your friend Mr.
Mitchell's call the other night? He brought
your note and was very pleasant. We had no
candy for him, but he drank iced lemonade.
His father won't let him enlist, so you may see
him back again. Jane recognized him as some
one she had seen at Philharmonic rehearsals fifty
times or more.

Mrs. Trotter writes G. about this time:
"John met Edward Wright (of the army) to-
day. He spoke in the highest terms of Mr.
Howland. He says he is the idol of the
regiment, and there is not a man who would
not do anything for him. I trust his reward
will be as great as the sacrifice."

E. W. H. to G.

NEW YORK, July 7th, '62.

Dear G.: I am just going out to get the
things you need, and so cannot report in advance as to their loveliness. Will make a pencil list at the end if I can. I shall send two
"Agnews"—one for Miss Wormeley. It is very
nice to be here, but I am overwhelmed with the
luxury of everything, and lie in bed measuring

the height of the ceiling "in a maze like." . . . Strange to say they (Mother particularly) seem quite contented to have you stay, that is they think you did right, though they are very much disappointed at not seeing you. . . . We had a very good voyage, perfectly smooth and fine, and delicious nights. The men were mostly very slightly sick or wounded, and the principal occupation was dressing them up in clean clothes, including gorgeous linen bosomed shirts, of which there were lots. There were only half a dozen very sick — one of whom died; — one consumptive of the 5th Maine sent to me for "just a little piece of meat to suck," and was profoundly grateful to "Lady Howland," who, he told one of the nurses, had been in his regiment "thousands of times." Lieutenant Hill was dressed up in Joe's second suit and has them on now at the Brevoort House, where Mrs. VanBuren was hovering over him yesterday when I sallied round with some grapes and some old linen for his arm. I have some lovely flowers for him to-day, which I wish you of the Wilson Small could share. I think of you all, all the time, and pine for you. Give my love to the staff, particularly Miss Wormeley, Mrs. Trotter, and dear Mrs. Griffin, who has probably joined you by this time. Write me all the details, and all you want. I hate to be clean while you go dirty. The pile of filthy things I am sending to the wash would, however, console you. To-day is hotter than any we had on the Pamunkey. Love to Charley.

E. promises on the first page of this letter to send on "two Agnews": an explanation is in order. The red flannel shirts of the Garibaldian troops used to be called Garibaldis when adopted as part of a lady's outfit, after the Italian battles. When Dr. C. R. Agnew came down to the front in a delightful black and white flannel shirt, the eye of the shabby-looking G. was fastened upon it, and she made bold, cut off from all supplies as she was, to say to the departing Doctor, "*Please* give me your shirt for my own wear." He did, and from that time we wore "Agnews."

E. to G. M. W.

FISHKILL, July 13.

Except for seeing how much good the rest and the home scenes are doing Joe, I would much rather be at Harrison's Point. He is improving nicely. His wound is not healed yet, but the inflammation has all gone and it looks better every day, . . . and but for a good deal of debility and shakiness of leg and hand, he would be quite himself. . . . Did they tell you of the demonstration the village people had

prepared, and how we had to change our time
of coming and telegraph secretly to Mr. Masters
at Newburgh in order to escape it? They had
actually arranged to take the horses out of the
carriage and drag Joe home themselves. Fancy
the struggle we should have had, to maintain an
expression of mingled gratification and humility
all through the three miles!

Joe received the other day the company reports
of the 16th's part in Friday's battle, and their
simple story is exceedingly touching — all of
them speaking particularly of the coolness and
cheerfulness of the men. Lieutenant Corbin,
who wrote the little poem, makes out the report
of Company C, which in its quaintness and
simplicity reminds one of the old days of knight
errantry. "Four of my men," he says, "fell
dead *fighting bravely and pleasantly.*" Company
C, you know, is the color company, and of them
he says, "The colors, which my company had
the honor to guard, *were safely kept*, though they
bear many an evidence of the hot fire in which
they stood." The reports are nearly all equally
simple, and one captain says, speaking of the
order to cross and reinforce Porter, "This
seemed highly pleasing to the boys, and with
elastic step we took up our march for Gaines'
Mill." Joe says they came out of the fight, too,
with equal bravery and cheerfulness, and he got
a smile from every man he looked at that day.

They all seem to want him back again, and his great anxiety is to be with them.

C. W. W. to J. H.

WILSON SMALL, HARRISON'S LANDING,
SATURDAY, July 12th.

Dear Joe: I saw, to-day, your adjutant, surgeon, and quartermaster; the former is much better, he says, and is going home in a day or two. He reports the 16th in good condition and in excellent spirits. This is unmistakably the case with the whole army. Exhausted and disappointed they naturally are (or were), but they have never lost heart, and the morale of our army is as good as ever. Having but little to do on the boat I have been on shore about the camps for a day or two, and have got a good idea of the strength of our position. It seems to me impregnable even without the earthworks we have thrown up at the weakest points. With these, we are very strong and can surely hold our own. Taking Richmond, however, is quite a different thing.

Send us the " Fishkill Standard " containing the account of the " ovation," and do not stand too long poised on one leg when you harangue the assembled multitude from the Tioronda balcony.

Georgy is going home soon, and perhaps myself. Love to E.

Yours affectionately,   C. W. W.

Sarah Woolsey to E. W. H.

NEW HAVEN, TUESDAY NIGHT.

I am just home from a very hot day at the New Haven Hospital, and so glad to find Jane's note with the news of your arrival that I must write a line before going to bed to tell you of it. And thus our week of suspense ends, and while so many thousands are straining eyes and hearts towards the bloody Peninsula, we may draw a long breath and refresh our thoughts with a picture of our dear Joe safe and resting his "honorable scars" amid friends and comfort and home and peace. . . . Do you know that one of our hospital cases here, on seeing your *carte de visite* the other day, recognized you as the "lady who gave him some very nice wine as he lay on a stretcher at White House, and bowls full of bread and milk afterward"—upon which he quite took on over it. He is one of the

"Ten thousand soldier hearts in Northern climes."

. . . Dr. Frank Bacon is here, having come up on a twenty-day furlough to recruit himself. I have not seen him but hear that he looks wretchedly—utterly broken down by overwork.

F. B. on the Corps of Surgeons of Volunteers.

The James Island fight occurred early in June, '62, and in the official report of the general commanding, F. B.'s regiment is singled out for mention: "The 7th Connecticut moved up in a beautiful and sustained line." "The 7th Connecticut had been on very severe fatigue duty for three days and three nights." "The 7th Connecticut advanced in the open field under continued shower of grape and canister." "The medical officers were unwearied on the battlefield and in the hospital."

After this service F. B. went home on sick leave. Later he resigned from the 7th Connecticut, passed the examination for the Corps of Surgeons of Volunteers, and was assigned to duty in charge of the Harper's Ferry Hospital.

Here he found a large accumulation of army supplies and a hospital in what he considered an exposed position. On reporting this to Washington and recommending its breaking up, he received prompt orders to carry out his own views, and had the satisfaction of getting the patients and supplies safely off on the last train, before a rebel dash captured the place. He writes to J. S. W. that if he had continued the hospital at Harper's Ferry he should have wanted a select party of ministering angels, and asks whether we write M.A. after our names now, "after the manner of a mature female in the Har-

per's Ferry laundry, who sent up a requisition with 'D. R.' after her signature, and on
a demand for explanation said 'daughter ot
the regiment, sir, which I have been adopted
by the 109th.'"

F. B. was then assigned to duty in Washington on General Casey's staff, to examine
outlying camp hospitals and break them up
when expedient, and to overhaul new regiments and their doctors as they came in.
Here, a little later, having got permission to
join the troops at the front, he had the miserable experience of marching in from the second battle of Bull Run with the Army of the
Potomac, defeated again on their old first
field.

CHAPTER X.

While waiting for the army to make some Army and Hospital Fleet at Harrison's Point. move, G. ran up to Washington with Mr. Olmsted and Charley, on the Small, to secure more hospital supplies, and took news to Mrs. Franklin of her husband the General, at Harrison's Point.

A. H. W. to E.

8 BREVOORT PLACE,
July, '62, FRIDAY MORNING.

Dear E.: Enclosed are a lot of letters for you, Georgy's own among them. . . . She describes their doings at Washington, voyage, etc., and says the best thing Mr. Olmsted did was to get Meigs to give him fifty hospital tents, each holding twelve patients. Also to get him to promise to send the old tents stored since last winter, enough to shelter fifty thousand men. Our poor, wretched army, she says, "lies tentless and blanketless at Harrison's Point, smitten by sun by day, and moon by night, and it only makes her cry to hear them cheer." . . .

General Franklin to G., sent on board the Small at Harrison's.

CAMP NEAR HARRISON'S BAR,
July 10, 1862.

My dear Miss Woolsey: I am exceedingly obliged to you for the trouble you took in bringing me the two bundles, and for your kindness in presenting me the tea and the sherry. The round bundle I am happy to say contained straw hats and white sugar, and the other, musquito bars. My wife knows my tastes too well to send me cakes. The tea and sherry were particularly acceptable, and General Smith and myself have tested the qualities of both articles with very high approbation.

I am glad that you saw my wife and that you thought she was braver than her sister army ladies. I see from her letters that she is cheerful and looks on the bright side of things. If I have time or opportunity I shall be very glad to call to see you.

I hope that you hear good accounts of Colonel Howland. Please give him and his wife my kind regards when you write.

Truly your friend,
W. B. FRANKLIN.

A. H. W. to G.

July 11th.

Dear Georgy: Your letter arrived this morning—letters I may say, enclosing multitudes for

Eliza. We have forwarded them to her at Fishkill. . . .

Dr. Carmalt was here last night. Does not
go back on St. Mark. Mrs. Dr. Jenkins was
here this morning to see Eliza, who had seen
her husband. She is pretty and pleasant. . . .

General McClellan's "caution," Georgy, has
ruined the country. It is too expensive a policy.
We are bankrupt already.—Stewart, and Lord &
Taylor began yesterday to give change to their
customers in postage stamps;—handed Carry
a tiny envelope stamped U. S. 50 cts., in change
for something, which she in turn handed out in
payment for a piece of ribbon at Aitkin & Mil-
ler's; all right, no words exchanged. So we go!
Aspinwalls and Uncle E. blue as indigo. Don't
know what to do about our property and their
own too. I would give every dollar of *mine* if it
would end this accursed war and slavery to boot.

In July, 1862, Cousin William Aspinwall
sent to the War Department his check for
$25,296.60, his share of the profit on a con-
tract for arms purchased by Howland &
Aspinwall and sold to the Government.

The Secretary of War ordered that "the
thanks of the Department be rendered to
Mr. Aspinwall for the proof which he has
furnished of the spirit which animates the

people of the United States and the assurance given that its citizens prefer public welfare to private gains."

This was true of a large proportion of the people, if there *were* contract swindlers and speculators, to our grief.

G's Journal.

July 12.

Medical Department improved.

Lying off Harrison's Point in sight of the hospital on shore to which we went the other evening. The fifty tents we brought from Washington are going up and are partly filled—men on cots, and not very ill. The place is to be used as a rest for a few days for men who can then join their regiments. The Medical Department is greatly improved, and the Sanitary Commission, who were chiefly instrumental in putting in the new Surgeon-General (Hammond), who in his turn has put in all the good new men, finds its work here at an end, and might as well retire gracefully. Four thousand sick have been sent north from Harrison's. Soup, and food generally, are being cooked all the time, without the aid of the Sanitary Commission, and they would leave now but for the flag of truce sent in by Lee to arrange for the bringing away of our wounded left behind in the retreat. The transports are under orders.

Commodore Wilkes is here in charge of the Flag of the Rebel Gun Boat gun-boat fleet, and Captain Rodgers sent his small boat for us the other day, and took us all over his vessel and then over the Monitor and the Maratanza. The Galena was full of cannon ball holes. The Maratanza gave me a piece of the balloon found on the rebel gun-boat Teaser. It was made of the old silk dresses of the ladies of Richmond, forty or more different patterns. They gave me, too, the signal flag of the little imp. We went over her to see the damage the shell did her, bursting into the boiler and disemboweling her.

The army is quiet and resting, and the surgeons of the regiments have been coming in constantly to the Sanitary Commission supply boat with requisitions for the hospitals. We are giving out barrels of vegetables. The Small will run up the river and be ready to fill a gap in bringing off our wounded prisoners, and it will be a comfort to do something before going home ignominiously. The last two weeks of waiting has been wearing to us all, and Miss Wormeley is a fascinating wreck.

Your father—Elsie—having been asked for Edward Mitchell and the Sanitary Commission. some account of his later connection with the Sanitary Commission, sends us this modest résumé of what was a laborious and important service for two years and a half.

"You remember that Mr. Olmsted assigned
me to duty rather as a personal aid on his
staff of assistants, and, when I parted from you
on the James River, he took me with him
to Washington some time in July, 1862. Soon
after I was sent to the front with a wagon-train
of Sanitary Commission supplies, for one of the
Corps of Pope's Army, then engaged in the
"Second Bull's Run." Returning to Washington, I was sent with a train of fresh supplies for
the Army of the Potomac, as far as Antietam, in
September. In November or December, 1862,
I was ordered to sail with the Banks Expedition, destination unknown. On reaching New
Orleans and reporting to Dr. Blake, who was in
charge of the Sanitary Commission there, I was
put in charge of the store-house, receiving and
issuing supplies until the Spring. In March or
April, 1863, I was started out with a wagon-
train to accompany an expedition through the
Teehe country and to Baton Rouge. At Baton
Rouge I established a depot, supplying the hospitals there and the hospital boats coming down
the Mississippi, until after Port Hudson was
taken. In the winter of 1863 I was dispatched
to Matagorda Island to receive and distribute
potatoes and barrels of pickles and sauer kraut
to the troops under command of General Napo-
leon Jackson Tecumseh Dana, who, when some
one complained to him of his Commissary in

general terms, asked, "What charge do you make against him?" and being answered somewhat vaguely that he was "generally unpopular," replied, "I would not give a d—m for a popular Commissary."

In the Spring of 1864 I was ordered to proceed to Alexandria with two assistants, and a large assortment of various stores, and establish a depot there for the use of the "Red River Expedition," which was composed of General A. J. Smith's troops, who came down the Mississippi and united with General Banks' army.

After returning to New Orleans I resigned from the United States Sanitary Commission, but went with General Smith up the Mississippi, and, either at Cincinnati or Nashville, meeting Dr. Newberry of the Western Branch of the United States Sanitary Commission, I, at his request, spent some time at Murfreesboro, Chattanooga and Knoxville in the service of the Commission. In the autumn of 1864 I returned to New York and the Columbia College Law School, but for many years after, I was constantly stopped on the streets by men, quite unknown to me, who begged me to "take a drink," insisting that something distributed by me had saved their lives.

Floating
Hospital
service
finished.

Somewhere about July 14, '62, Charley and G. must have gone home from Harrison's Landing, probably in a returning hospital ship. The record is lacking—Sarah Woolsey's letter of July 22 being the first mention of it. She had been serving all this time at the New Haven Hospital.

S. C. W. to G.

NEW HAVEN.

AT THE BARRACK HOSPITAL, July 22.

. . . When the family leave you a little gap of time, write me one line to make me feel that you are *really* so near again. I cannot help hoping that if you go back, there may be a vacancy near you which I can fill. The work here is very satisfactory in its way, but is likely to come to an end before long if the decision about "Hospitals within military limits" is carried out. . . .

This is Sunday, and I have been here since half past nine—it being about 5 P. M. now . . . It has not been very Sunday-like, as I've mended clothes, and given out sheets, and made a pudding, but somehow it seems proper. Mary would laugh if she knew one thing that I've been doing—distributing copies of "A Rainy Day in Camp" to sick soldiers, who liked it vastly. I had it printed in one of our papers for the purpose. To-morrow I am going to

change employments—take Miss Young's place
in the kitchen, and let her have a day's rest,
while Mrs. Hunt supplies mine here. Meantime
as a beginning I must go and heat some beef tea
for a poor fellow who hates to eat, and has to
be coaxed into his solids by an after promise of
pudding and jelly. . . .

P. S —Have come back from service and ad-
ministered the beef tea, though it was an awful
job. The man gave continual howls, first because the tea was warm, then because I tried to
help him hold a tumbler, then because I fanned
him too hard, and I thought each time I had
hurt him and grew so nervous that I could have
cried. Beside, there is a boy in that tent—an
awful boy with no arms, who swears so fright-
fully (all the time he isn't screeching for currant
pie, or fried meat, or some other indigestible),
that he turns you blue as you listen.

The whole staff of the Wilson Small seems
now to have scattered and "fallen back" on
Washington. The letter of July 21 is from
Miss Katherine P. Wormeley. She and Mrs.
William P. Griffin had been delightful
friends to us. We were the four "staff"
women on the Wilson Small through the
whole Peninsular campaign. Miss W. came
home on our old hospital ship the Daniel

Webster, in charge of her last load of wounded from the Peninsula, Mrs. Griffin remaining at Hampton Roads in a receiving hospital for some weeks longer.

Miss Wormeley to G.

NEWPORT, R. I., July 21st, '62.

Dear Georgy: How did you take to civilization? I got along perfectly till I was caught going off the boat without paying my fare. Captain T's mother was on board, which was a capital thing, and induced him to behave himself. I found intimate friends on board who were dear to me because they escorted me to supper. Georgy! if you ever take passage on the Metropolis, go down to supper for my sake and imagine how it affected me. My friends rather apologized for their desire to go down ; for my part all I could do was to conceal my disappointment at not being able to eat everything. It seemed to me there was everything good that I had ever heard of, ending with peaches and ice cream.

I put the wounded captain into an express wagon (the nearest thing to an ambulance) and got home myself at 4 o'clock, to be finely cackled over by Mother. The next day the town called on me, beginning, like a Fourth of July procession, with the mayor and clergy. The next day I stayed in bed till after visiting hours. By-the-

by, isn't a bed delicious? I can't believe it is
the same mattress, the same blanket and sheets
that I had before I went away. Of course you
know that Dr. Wheaton with 1,700 men are
here (six miles from here). Excursion boats
run from here and from Providence to the
camp. It is the fashionable drive, and the dear
creatures are all female sutlers with baskets of
pies and cakes and pickles and sweetmeats.
Colonel Vollum is here. I have sent him
word that if I can do anything sensible with
authority I will, meanwhile I do not intend
going near the camp. . . . I am truly sorry that
Colonel Howland's furlough is shortened.
Fanny Russell told me about it, and we spent
all the time we were together in adoring " Mrs.
H." I have said one hundred times " I will tell
that to Georgy," but behold I have forgotten
everything. Yesterday was a happy day to me,
the dear little chapel was so peaceful and full of
love and praise. I thought of Mr. —— as I sat
there. . . . No large mind doubts God or the
excellence of life with Him merely through
looking at the mean lives of others.

Good-bye, love to Mrs. Howland and C. W. W.
I am yours faithfully,
K. P. Wormeley.

J. H. kept up constant communication
with the 16th and his commanding generals,

always in the hope of going back, in spite of all discouragements.

Gen. Henry W. Slocum writes to him:

HARRISON'S LANDING, July 19, '62.

My dear Colonel: Yours of the 16th has just come to hand. I am sincerely glad that you are doing so well and I shall be rejoiced to see you back. I think the major is doing well, but there is nothing like having the head present. Still I hope you will not think of returning till you are *fully* recovered. If you come back feeling weak, you will be obliged to leave again. This climate is very debilitating, and nearly all the officers, even the strongest, are affected by it. . . . My advice to you is to remain at home until some move is made here.

. . . As to your conduct and that of your regiment on the 27th, I hear but one opinion—all speak in terms of praise, the strongest terms.

. . . General Franklin told me to say to you that you must not come back till you are well. He (Franklin) is about half sick. I am in the same condition—too sick to be worth much and too well to go home. . . . Remember me to Mrs. Howland and tell Miss Georgy that her favor has been received and that I will "follow them with a sharp stick" as requested.

Yours truly,

H. W. SLOCUM.

By July 22 Joe could not be kept away
from the army, and only half well, he
started back, probably in a hospital return
boat, to the regiment at Harrison's Landing.
It was, however, only to break down again.
The Historical Sketch of the 16th, prepared
for their reunion at Potsdam in 1886, says:
" Colonel Howland visited the regiment for
the first time since the battle of Gaines' Mill,
His suffering was plainly seen, and the men
showed their love for him by going to his
tent and relieved each other's guard, so that
everyone might take him by the hand."

E. writes him from Astoria, July 23 :—

Dear Joe : It is the dull twilight of a dull
November-like day and I am afraid you have
had a cold, dreary passage. Once at Harrison's
Landing, however, cold weather will be better
and healthier for you than hot. I suppose you
must have arrived to-day. . . . Georgy and I
drove out yesterday with Robert, found Mary
well and the children asleep. To-day we have
had the full benefit of them within doors and
have fought with the little rebel Bertha and
played with the strange child Una, and studied
the fascinations of the little new baby, most of
the time. Georgy is an unusually sweet, bright
little baby, and Una is a real beauty. Bertha's

J. H. returns to his regiment. but breaks down again.

affectionate greeting was : "I throw you in the bushes, and pull your head off for me dinner."

. . . The Elizabeth at Harrison's Landing is the Sanitary Commission store boat and has plenty of hospital clothing and supplies, and the Medical Director's boat has plenty of farinaceous food, farina, arrowroot, etc. . . .

E. and G. meantime were planning to join the hospital service again, and keep near Joe, under the Sanitary Commission auspices.

Frederick Law Olmsted to E. W. H.

U. S. SANITARY COMMISSION,
NEW YORK AGENCY, 498 BROADWAY.

NEW YORK, 25th July, 1862.

Dear Mrs. Howland: I have just received your note of the 22d.

It is expected that the "Euterpe" will leave here on Saturday for Old Point, there to "await orders." Dr. Jenkins writes me that Dr. Cuyler changed his mind and his orders about the use of the hospital vessels two or three times a day, and he could form no plans. . . .

I hope some decided and tangible line of work may be determined on. At present everything remains as when we left James River. . . .

The Commission would, of course, be glad to have you and your sister take passage upon the returning hospital ship if you wish ; and you can do so without placing yourself under any obligation to remain upon her. You could, upon arrival at Fortress Monroe, determine, by consultation with Dr. Jenkins, whether you could find duty at Berkely. Most respectfully yours.

Early in August J. H. broke down once more with malarial fever and was sent home by the army surgeons, this time not to return to the regiment, and our going to the front was given up.

E. W. H. to Mother.

Fishkill, Aug. 15.

Dear Mother: In answer to my letter Dr. Draper came up yesterday noon and stayed till this afternoon. . . . The visit was part professional and part for pleasure and was satisfactory in both ways. He finds Joe improving, though more slowly than he had hoped, but he says he must not think of returning to camp. That if fever got hold of him again he would stand very little chance of recovery. It would permanently break down his constitution, if it was not immediately fatal. . . . It is very disappointing. He hoped to gain fast enough to go back the end of this month, and is greatly depressed about it, for he has made up his mind that under the circumstances it is great injustice to the regiment and to Major Seaver to continue to hold his commission, getting the credit as it were, while the Major has all the care and responsibility. He wishes to do only what is most for the interests of the service.

J. H. resigns from the service. J. H. resigned from the service by the advice of Dr. W. H. Draper of New York, whose medical certificate stated that he was suffering from extreme nervous exhaustion and debility, and was unfit for duty. The resignation was received by his superior officers with expressions of great regret, and letters full of affection poured in upon him.

General Bartlett, commanding the brigade, writes:

HEADQUARTERS 2D BRIGADE.
Sept. 4th, 1862, "CAMP FRANKLIN," VA.

Dear Howland : I received your papers just as we were embarking at Newport News, and you cannot imagine how badly I felt at the thought that perhaps we should never be associated together in the field again, and perhaps never again see each other. We all agreed that you ought not to come back, all seemed actuated by the same feeling of love for you and all expressed their sorrow that you would no longer be with us. . . .

The old 16th are still "A. No. 1."

General Bartlett writes again:

HEADQUARTERS 2D BRIGADE,
NEAR BAKERSVILLE, MD.
Oct. 1st, 1862.

My dear Howland: I enclose to you the acceptance of your resignation and honorable discharge from the service.

I had much rather it had been your appointment as brigadier, for I don't believe the service can afford to lose many such officers, and yet I would rather see you recover your health and strength than to be made a major-general, myself.

On the 14th of August—McClellan's attempt to reach Richmond via the Chickahominy swamps having proved a disastrous failure—the transfer of the army to Washington began. *Our poor Army retreats from the Peninsula.*

Lieutenant Robert Wilson of J. H.'s regiment wrote home at the time a letter which might easily have come from *any* regiment in the Army of the Potomac. "Six days' march," he says, "to Newport News, choking with dust, parched with thirst, melting by day and freezing by night, poorly fed and with nothing but the sky to cover us. You can judge of our exhausted condition when I tell you that six miles before we reached the camp at Newport News the 16th Regiment, N. Y. Vols., numbered only 184 men in the ranks, though men straggled in, so that there were 400 in the morning, *and the 16th is no straggling regiment.* Next day embarked on transports and arrived at Alexandria, sorrowful and humiliated when looking back over a year and finding ourselves on the same ground as then. The débris of the Grand Army had come back to its starting place with its ranks decimated, its men dispirited, its morale failing, while the thousands who sleep their last sleep on the Peninsula demand the cause of their sacrifice."

Second Bull Run Battle.   The retreat from the Peninsula was almost immediately, (August 29, '62,) followed by the "Second Bull Run" disaster, which again filled the Washington and Alexandria hospitals to overflowing and taxed the hospital workers to the utmost. Chaplain Hopkins, still on hard service in Alexandria, writes:

OFFICE OF GENERAL HOSPITAL,
12 O'CLOCK SUNDAY NIGHT.
ALEXANDRIA, August 31st, 1862.

My dear Mrs. Howland: These days are more terrible than any thing the nation has yet seen, and their horrors are at our very doors. Yesterday we sent 375 men to the north, and 433 to-day, and yet to-night we have opened a hall where, strewn on the floor, without even blankets, lie scores of wounded men unattended, with rebel lead festering in their bodies, but thankful for even that accommodation. Many of them came all the way from the battlefield in horrid army-wagons after lying in the rain and mud upon the field through the night ; — patient, unmurmuring men. The best of New York and Boston blood oozes from their undressed wounds. I have just come from doing all that I could for them and am resting for the next train, which we momentarily expect at the foot of Cameron Street. . . . You have seen all this at Harrison's Landing, but in my wildest dreams, when I first reported to you in Washington, I never thought of such scenes. Through all the wards confused heaps of torn and dirty clothes and piles of bloody bandages, tired attendants doing their best to make comfortable the poor fellows torn and mangled with shot and shell in every imaginable way. Things now, from what I hear in the hall, are coming into order, several surgeons having just reported themselves to Doctor Summers, besides large numbers of citizen attendants from the departments in Washington and from this city, too.

By the time this reaches you the papers will have informed you that last night the main part

of our army on the left wing was compelled to
fall back on Centreville. This morning the
whole army was concentrated there, utterly dis-
organized, with the exception of Sumner's Corps
and some other fresh troops just arrived. They
formed in front with their splendid artillery, and
the rest of the army began to gather itself up
for fresh encounters. The fight began again at
three o'clock this afternoon, and men who left
there at four o'clock say that it was going
against us. God grant that the tide may have
since turned.

Don't apprehend our capture here, for the forts
have been fully manned and supplied with ammunition ; besides, we are going to whip them
on the present battlefield to-morrow. I hear the
whistle of the expected train with wounded and
must stop this hasty letter.

The tide did turn. Chaplain Hopkins'
prayer was answered. The "fight which
began at 3" the afternoon he wrote, ended
with the repulse of the rebels by McDowell,
and our troops rested that night at Centreville. There was a drop of comfort for H.
H.'s poor men in the knowledge, later, that
their courage and suffering had not been all
in vain, though the poor army was again,
after all its frightful losses, just where it
stood in March, six months before.

Chaplain H. H. to G.

ALEXANDRIA HOSPITAL, Sept., 1862.

My dear Miss Woolsey: In great haste I
write to say that to dispense anything which
will do the bodies of these poor sufferers good
will be a most welcome task. . . . Outside of
the house, at the Mansion Hospital, we fed
1,100, 1,900, 2,100, and 1,600 patients passing
North on successive days, so that those inside
suffer some lack of care and of good food. Last
night 75 came in from beyond the lines by flag
of truce. I thought I had seen weary and worn-
out human beings before, but these bloody,
dirty, mangled men, who had lain on the battlefield, some of them two and three days, with
wounds untouched since the first rude dressing,
and had ridden from near Centreville in ambulances, were a new revelation. We cut their
clothes from them, torn and stiff with their own
blood and Virginia clay, and moved them inch
by inch onto the rough straw beds ; the poor haggard men seemed the personification of utmost
misery. But some of them were *happy*. One
nobleman who attracted me by the manliness of
his very look in the midst of his sufferings, when
I spoke to him of the strong consolations of a
trust in the Saviour, threw his arms about my
neck and told me, weeping, that for him they
were more than sufficient. Some of these fellows I love like brothers and stand beside their

graves for other reasons than that it is an official duty. . . .

"Mor-
tally
Wound-
ed." It was for such heroic sufferers as the "nobleman" described by Chaplain Hopkins that Mary wrote these verses:

"MORTALLY WOUNDED."

I lay me down to sleep,
  With little thought or care
Whether my waking find
  Me here—or THERE !

A bowing, burdened head,
  Only too glad to rest,
Unquestioning, upon
  A Loving breast.

My good right hand forgets
  Her cunning now ;
To march the weary march
  I know not how.

I am not eager, bold,
  Nor strong,—all that is past !
I am willing *not to do*,
  At last, at last !

My half-day's work is done,
  And this is all my part :
I give a patient God
  My patient heart ;

And grasp His banner still,
  Though all its blue be dim ;
These stripes, no less than stars,
  Lead after Him.

Weak, weary and uncrowned,
I yet *to bear* am strong ;
Content not even to cry,
"How long! How long!"

Mr. Lincoln's call for 300,000 more troops Call for 300,000 answered.
was being answered. All over the country
camps were being formed and boys drilled
in all the pleasant villages of the land.
Mother and all of us went to rest awhile,
after Charley and G. came home, in Litchfield, and watched the drilling and recruiting.

A. H. W. to H. G.
LITCHFIELD, Sept. 3, 1862.

My dear Hatty (Gilman): I should like you
to see the beautiful camp of the 19th C. V. here
before it is all broken up. We are to have a
flag presentation from Mr. Wm. Curtis Noyes,
and a religious farewell service was appointed
to be held to-day in the Congregational Church.
Good Dr. Vail will pray, I dare say, as he did
on Sunday : "God bless our 19th Regiment,
the colonel and his staff, the captains, and all the
rank and file." . . .

The calm air, the physical comfort and peace
we have here, make mental peace easier I suppose. We cannot be too thankful, we say to
each other, that we are not in New York, heated

and tired and despondent. It is infinitely sad, all this desperate fighting and struggling ; this piecemeal destruction of our precious troops, only to keep the wolves at bay. But how well the country is going to bear it ! I suppose these poor, innocent, confident new lives will be in the thickest of the fight at once. They will have their wish ! be put to the immediate use for which they enlisted. . . . I grow stony and tearless over such a *mass* of human grief. I am lost in wonder, too, at the generalship, the daring and endurance of the Southern army. We are to fight it out now, even if it becomes extermination for us and them. . . .

A camp for sick and wounded had been established at Portsmouth Grove, near Newport, R. I., and as a matter of course it appealed to Miss Wormeley, its near neighbor. She was allowed only a short rest before earnest request came to her to take charge of the nursing there. We were all hankering for our active life in the thick of the fight. Mr. Olmsted used to say :

"My heart's in the Pamunkey."

G. to E. W. H.

LITCHFIELD, CONN., Aug. 26, '62.

Miss Wormeley had a nice note from Mr. Olmsted which she sent me to read and which I returned to her—all about "the staff" on the Wilson Small—complimentary, but saying that he wonders at himself for having been at the head, and never could attempt to say how he felt towards all those who were associated with him. She wrote to ask his opinion about accepting the directorship at Portsmouth Grove Hospital. . . . I can't find her note. It told me that the Surgeon-General, Hammond, had been to see her and had asked her to take the lady directorship. She hesitated and he sent the surgeon-in-charge to see her, who wouldn't take "no" for an answer; said he liked women, and agreed at once to write for Dr. Robert Ware. He did write, but the Dr. could not be found.* . . .

[margin note: Portsmouth Grove Hospital proposed to G. M. W.]

She asks what I think about it. I advised her to take it, and if she could not live in the hospital, to go out several times a week, and keep her paw on it, and insist upon order and system in the housekeeping department and kitchen arrangements. I hope she will, it is too good a chance to miss, and it is certainly a great compliment from the Surgeon-General.

---

* Dr. Ware volunteered for service further South, and died there of fever contracted on duty.

The interchange of letters between Miss Wormeley and G. ended in an agreement that they should join hands again for hospital work at Portsmouth Grove, and as G. made bold to propose your Aunt Jane and Sarah Woolsey as co-laborers, all three of them were given the chance they coveted. Miss Wormeley's plan for organizing will give you an idea of your aunts' duties thirty-six years ago.

Miss Wormeley to G.

NEWPORT, Sept. 5th, '62.

Plan of work for Portsmouth Grove Hospital

My dear Georgy: I found the new surgeon inclined to one woman for each ward (twenty-eight wards or barracks, of sixty men in each). I hunted him out of that idea however. Everything in the domestic management of the hospital being left to me, I shall *gently* avail myself of the courtesy. Now then for your advice. My ideas are these. Please give your decided opinion on them. To give five wards, sixty beds to each ward, to the superintendence of five friends—you, your sister, cousin, H. Whetten, and a lady here whom I esteem and consider efficient. Under these I should put one, two, or three women nurses, as occasion may require. These five ladies would be responsible for everything connected with their wards, *in general.*

You know what general supervision means,—cleanliness, beds, linen, due washing thereof, etc., etc., in all of which the women under you should do the actual work whilst you see that they do it. . . . I want to have *the men* intelligently looked after, as only a lady can. I should therefore wish that the ladies should go round with the surgeons *invariably*—to make short notes of each patient's treatment, medicine, and diet. Medicines I should want her to make sure were properly and timely given. The special diet lists ordered by the surgeon I should wish to be handed in to me as soon as practicable. I shall put a special diet kitchen at each end of the Barrack St. with a female cook in each, whom I shall attend to myself. . . .

This is in general a sketch of my ideas. What do you say? Will you come? . . . I want to point out to you that no ladies have ever *been allowed* to come into a *U. S. General Hospital* in this way—much less warmly requested, and thanked, and confided in, as *we are*,—for of course it has nothing personal to myself in it ; it is General Hammond's first cordial reception and experiment of ladies in hospital, and is in consequence, as he told me, of the grateful sense he had of what we did at White House. . . .

Now as to our own living there. A house is building for us, to be finished by the 12th of this month. It has bedrooms for all the female nurses, a dining-room for ditto, an office for me. We shall have to carpet our own rooms, and adorn them as we see fit ; the Government supplies the common necessities of a bed, etc., for the nurses in general. . . .

I should want to have you with me at the start. Can you arrange to come ? . . .

Write me at once, please. What a vile place you are in ; the mails take a week to go.

A. H. W. to H. Gilman.

LITCHFIELD, Sept. 22.

Charley prom- ised a Lieuten- ancy.

Charley is trying for a Lieutenancy in one of the new regiments, and Governor Morgan has promised, as all governors do, to "see about it." This is going to be a great drain on Mother's spirits and strength, if the application succeeds, and will bring us all continued personal interest and anxiety.

Georgy was telegraphed ten days ago to come immediately to Newport to a great military barrack hospital.

On September 17th the fierce battle of Antietam was fought by the Army of the Potomac,—a drawn battle, little better than a defeat for us ; and though the rebels retired there was no following up on our part, and no result worth the enormous loss of life.

And now the moment had come for the war-measure Mr. Lincoln had held in reserve. The Government had been fighting to uphold the Government, and announcing all along that if the abolition of slavery proved needful to that end, then slavery should cease.

On September 22, 1862, Mr. Lincoln issued a preliminary proclamation declaring that in all States found in rebellion on January 1, 1863, slaves should "thenceforth and forever be free." Congress, however, delayed to take the action urged upon them by the President, until the time limit expired.

Abolition of slavery promised.

J. S. W. to a friend abroad.
8 BREVOORT PLACE, N. Y.
October, 1862.

The fighting at Cedar Mountain and Gainesville and on futile fields of Manassas, the mysterious ups and downs of commanders, the great invasion scare, the mean dissensions and the sad delays, have kept us constantly agitated, the more so that we were in the tauntingly still and sweet country, where the newspaper train was sure to fail in great emergencies. There *was* a time,—I confess it because it is past, when your correspondent turned rather cold and sick and said "It is enough!" . . . and when my sister

Abby, (who acknowledged the Southern Con-
federacy when the rebel rabble got back unpur-
sued across the river from Winchester), went
about declaiming out of Isaiah, " To what purpose is the multitude of your sacrifices ; your
country is desolate, strangers devour it in your
presence." . . . We came out of that phase, however, at any rate I did, and concluded that
despondency was but a weak sort of treason ;
and then with the first cool weather came the
Proclamation, like a

" Loud wind, strong wind, blowing from the mountain,"

and we felt a little invigorated and thanked God
and took courage. . . . In Litchfield we followed with great interest the growth of the 19th
Connecticut recruited in that county, all the
little white crumbs of towns dropped in the
wrinkles of the hills sending in their twenty,
thirty, fifty fighting men ; Winsted, Barkhamsted,
Plymouth companies, and companies clubbed
by the *very* little villages, marching under our
windows every day to the camp ground. Almost
all the young men in Litchfield village have
gone ; the farmers, the clerks in the shops, the
singers in the choir. Who is to reap next year's
crops ? Who is to sow them ? Everyone spoke
well of the new recruits. There was not a particle of illusion for them. They understood very
well to what they were going ; disease, death, a

common soldier's nameless grave. They made
themselves a new verse to the marching song :

"A little group stands weeping in every cottage door,
But we're coming, Father Abraham, three hundred
thousand more."

General Tyler went over to Danielsonville
to look at a company just raised in that town,
and was waited on to know if another company
would be accepted. "If it is here this time
to-morrow," he answered in jest. *It was there.*
It is not altogether a question of bounty. A
fine young fellow came into our hotel a day or
two after the bounty-giving ended, to inquire
the way to camp. Charley asked him, "Why
didn't you come before the pay stopped?"
"That's just what I was waiting for," he answered ; and a dozen men went from the village
to whom the bounty could offer not the slightest
inducement. The Congregational clergyman
told us he looked over the growing list of names
with tears, knowing what good names they were
and how ill they could be spared. But the 19th
Connecticut is no better than a hundred other
regiments. There are very few men in the 18th
Connecticut who are not persons of weight and
value in their community, cousin Mary Greene
says. And see how they fight ! Look at the
Michigan Seventh at South Mountain. The
Michigan Seventh was two weeks old. And

yet it is coming to us from over the sea that we can't get men, and if we do they will run ! . . .

The generalship and fighting of the rebels is also certainly very fine—corn-cobs and no shoes are pathetic when one forgets the infamous cause. . . . Their "obsolete fowling-pieces" go off with considerable accuracy, says a malcontent at my elbow.

When we came to town last week the streets seemed full of anxious and haggard faces of women, and when I caught sight of my own face in a shop glass I thought it looked like all the rest. The times are not exactly sad, but a little oppressive. . . . G. and I cannot stand it any longer and we are off to-morrow. We are in the government service now and entitled to thirteen dollars a month !* We are going into exile—a blessed exile.

S. C. W. to G. at Portsmouth Grove.

NEW HAVEN, October, '62.

And now for Miss Wormeley's delightful letter ; my dear, it sounds too good to come true, all of it, and yet I can't help thinking that Providence smiles on the scheme and will bring about papa's consent. . . . We shall have it working beautifully in a short time, I see—and oh, G.,

---

* At the Portsmouth Grove Hospital, as assistants to Miss Wormeley.

what a happy winter we shall have! . . . Abby
remarks in her last to Mary—"Sarah's going
and Jane's (!!) I regard in the light of an
agreeable fiction, but it will do for them to play
at for a little while." . . .

I shall be ready any day after Monday.

A. H. W. to G.

NEW YORK, October 6th.

Jane wishes me to tell you that she leaves
here by the same route that you took for Portsmouth Grove, on Wednesday, 8 A. M. She has
sent word to Sarah to meet her on the train at
New Haven. . . .

Charley proposes that you shall call your
house the (H)'Omestead, in compliment to
F. L. Olmsted.

Charley's determination to join the army Charley
in the field at last had its way, and Mother's joins the
Army.
letter gives us the first news of his commission. Mothers in those two years had
learned that sons were first of all defenders
of the flag, and joining the army had come
to be a matter of course in families where
any sober view of life was taken.

Mother to G.

LIBRARY, No. 8.
. THURSDAY, October 2d.

My dear Georgy : I was charmed to get your pencil note this morning. . . . An hour after you left for Portsmouth Grove, Charley arrived at the door in his wagon, Pico and all, very sorry to have missed you. . . . Oh, Georgy, I do miss you greatly : in the parlor, up stairs, in my bed, morning, noon, and night, and my heart craves you all the while.

Charley has had a letter from Governor Morgan telling him he can have a lieutenancy in an Irish brigade, Colonel Burke. He has gone off this morning full of business, and says he shall accept it at once. There are so many other positions in which he might serve his country that *I* should have preferred for him ! . . . Do let us hear as often as possible, dear G. Tell us just how you found things, and what you have forgotten—your *flask* for one thing. Make my regards acceptable to Miss Wormeley, and always love your loving Mother.

E. W. H. to Chaplain H. H.

December, '62.

Charley, you may have heard, has gone into the service as lieutenant in the 164th, but he was detached at once for staff duty and is aide to General Burnside and a member of good old

General Seth Williams' mess—*just where we would most like to have him.* We have heard from him up to Saturday morning, the day of the battle, and are not yet *very* anxious about him. . . . Georgy and Jane are hard at work at Portsmouth Grove, terrors to evil-doers as well as good friends to those who need it. They and the other ladies have effected many reforms and won the respect and confidence of all concerned except the mutinous convalescents and the lying stewards, whom they pursue like avenging fates.

We were very glad to hear of your work after those dreadful days of the "Second Bull Run." . . . I write principally to ask what I can do to help you take care of the wounded. . . . You know I want to do all I can now that I am unable to be there myself. You must call upon me freely.

On November 8th McClellan had been relieved of command and Burnside had superseded him. On December 13 was fought the first battle of Fredericksburg, with the rebel Lee victorious. Few or no letters mark these anxious months. McClellan relieved of command.

And so the second year of the war came to an end without any sound of public cheer or private rejoicing. There is no mention in the letters of Christmas fun, even for the

children, while our poor defeated Army of
the Potomac was huddled into Fredericksburg with the loss of 13,000 men. As a family we were again scattered, some of us in
hospital work and Charley in the field. One
window, though, was opened Heavenwards,
since for three million slaves, across the
blackness of a civil war

"God made himself an awful rose of dawn."

THIRD YEAR OF THE WAR
1863

CHAPTER XI

CHAPTER XI.

On the 22nd of September, 1862, a gleam of light had shone, the President had issued his preliminary proclamation of emancipation; and now on January 1st, 1863 came the announcement of full liberty to the captives.

Extract from the Proclamation.

"I, Abraham Lincoln, President of the United States, by virtue of the power vested in me as Commander-in-Chief of the Army and Navy of the United States, . . . and as a necessary war-measure, . . . do order and declare that all persons held as slaves (within the states in rebellion) are, and henceforward shall be free."

The passage by Congress of the 13th Amendment to the Constitution followed, extending emancipation to all parts of the United States and its territories.

A. H. W. writes, Jan., '63:

I improved yesterday to my satisfaction in reading the President's proclamation. "The Lord reigneth, let the earth rejoice!"

And so *Abby's* war had ended in victory: ours was carried on for more than two years longer.

The second year of the war closed with Charley's commission for active duty in the field. He must have left at once; two mutilated scraps from a note of Hatty's are the only record. All else is lost.

"Charley appeared just now in full Lieutenant's uniform and looks so tall and brave that I should scarcely know him."

And—

"Charley did not get off this morning; a young scamp of an aide was walking about here in town, with papers directed to Charley in his pocket, and C. spent the day in trying to find him."

The only letter at this time in Charley's handwriting is from the front, to Eliza, January 14, 1863, reporting the 16th New York.

—"The camp is in a pleasant place near White Oak Church. The General and I have established a friendship; he is not too much of a Brigadier for a young cuss of my size. The chaplain took me to see the hospital—new tents, nice large open fire-place, and but five sick men."

Jane, Sarah Woolsey and G. were meantime nicely established at the hospital six
miles from Newport, R. I., with a jolly little
thin board house built for the nursing staff;
their rooms 10 x 10, furnished from home
with every comfort, and work fairly begun.

J. S. W. to A. H. W.

PORTSMOUTH GROVE, January, '63.

Dear Abby: This morning in the grey (I
don't know how she managed to be up and
seeing) Sarah looked in at the ventilator and
announced, "Girls, there's a big black steamer
off the hospital dock.—The soldiers have come !"

She proved to be the Daniel Webster with 290
men from *Fredericksburgh*, many of them ! There
she lies at this writing, two o'clock, no tug having been got up from Newport, and the tide
being so excessively low that she can't move in.
They have boarded her in boats however, and
report the men very comfortable—short, delightful trip from Fortress Monroe, plenty to
eat and no very bad cases on board. . . . Everything is ready for 450. Clean wards, clean beds,
clean clothes and the best of welcomes. Georgy
and I, who have the medical division, will not
profit much. We shall get the sulky old
"chronics" and "convalescents," and Sarah and
H. Whetten will have all the surgical cases ;

Patients
arrive at
Ports-
mouth
Grove
Hospital

but we shall go to see them all the same, and they shall have all our stores, soft towels, jelly and oranges.

Shingling the barracks goes on bravely. I think things will be all so much finished to the satisfaction of Mr. *Jefferson Davis*, by spring, that he will perhaps retain us in office! . . .

7 P. M. The men are all safely landed, housed and suppered, and all the surgeons are busy dressing wounds. They must work all night. The men are bright as buttons and jolly. Tell Harriet Gilman that her shirts are blessing *Fredericksburgh men to-night.*

Dr. Edwards, surgeon-in-charge, in the handsomest way offers to turn *out* anybody we wish and put *in* anybody we wish, so if you know of any first-rate candidates amenable to female influence, forward us their names.

The boxes of home supplies now had Portsmouth Grove Hospital as their principal destination. The following is one of the letters in return for supplies:

The games, as well as the slates, which came in the boxes and barrels, are a great delight. I have just been over to see Fitch and set him up at a *solitaire* board. He was all over smiles, and pegging away with his game in bed.

With another gift of tools, the boys in Ward 20 knocked up a nice little bagatelle board with glass balls and a cambric cover. Ward 6 went over to inspect and imitate. They came back disgusted ; "would scorn to play on such a thing ; would have a board on which a lady could dance a hornpipe, if she pleased." Highly improbable that any one would please to do that, but I promised them that if they would make a first-rate board, they should have all that was necessary. So they went to work, and the result was a beauty. The table is seven or eight feet long, covered with scarlet flannel, and with turned balls and walnut cups, and the men of the ward have enjoyed every minute of its existence for the past month. I have never gone in when there hasn't been a crowd round the table pushing balls or keeping count, and I really think that the health of the ward has improved under the treatment.

Money spent in lemons for bronchitis, oranges for fever patients, mittens and socks for "convalescents" (who have to go on guard in puddles of snow-water) and in games and tools for wretched, bored, half-sick, half-well, wholly demoralized men, may not seem a great investment to the givers ; would not seem so to me, if I did not live in a general hospital, and know where Government munificence stops and where private beneficence may to advantage begin.

The meals in our hospital mess-hall are nicely
served and well cooked. At the beating of the
drum the "convalescents." form in line, and
march, by wards, into the long hall, where three
lines of tables, each 250 feet long, are set. Last
night, when we inspected the supper, there were
shining tins up and down the tables with a very
large portion of rice and molasses, hot coffee,
and plenty of bread for each man, and many
little pots of butter and jam came in under the
Braves' arms, out of their home boxes, to help
garnish the tea.

This morning I was invited by a soldier to
join him in a banquet over a box from home;
"and all I want beside," observed he, "is a little gin." "It is very lucky for you that there
was none," was my answer, "or the whole box
would have been confiscated." "Confiscated,
indeed!" returned the Brave; "I should like
to see *that* thing done. I'm none of your cream
and chocolate men. I'd carry the case up to
Abraham himself!"

The other day Miss —— was washing a boy's
face very gently. "Oh!" said he, "that reminds me of home—" (Miss —— highly grati-
fied); "that's like my sister; she often did that
for me. *My eyes! wasn't she a rough one!* She'd
take off dirt, and skin too, but she'd get the
dirt off."

G. to J. H.

P. G. Hospital.

Thank you, my Colonel, for the doughnuts and comic papers. They are just what the men prize most, and under every pillow I shall establish a little nest of both ! . . . I always accompany a " Life of Headley Vicars " with a piece of chewing tobacco. . . . We are going to have a chapel in two weeks. At present it consists of eight holes in the ground and a tolerable fishing pond, but in one fortnight this will be a church and will stand next door to our house, leaving us no excuse for staying at home in the evening. We have embraced the puddles all along as argument against "protracted meetings." . . . Jane and Sarah and H. Whetten have just been relating their refreshing experiences for the day, in the next room. Miss Wormeley is down stairs getting up her official correspondence with the Surgeon and Q.-M. General. The diet tables are all made out and consolidated for to-morrow, and several reproving notes to ward-masters sent in to meet them at breakfast; and now, nothing comes except the usual burglar and as much sleep as this howling, driving storm will let us have. . . .

From J. S. W.

Portsmouth Grove.

My dear Cousin Margaret: Now that I have been long enough in this place to have learned

tolerably well my topography, the names and
titles of my coadjutors, how to make out my diet
books, etc., . . . I can take breath (and " my pen "
as the soldiers always say in their letters) to say
that we are well and more than contented with
our present position. . . . Georgy already has
her "department" almost completely organized
and supplied, and develops daily an amount of
orderly foresight and comprehensive carefulness which would astonish one who has watched
her somewhat erratic career from childhood. I,
who have always rather held myself up to her
as a model of the non-spasmodic style, find myself in secret and in reluctance borrowing ideas
of *her*. She has found her work certainly, at
least at present. . . . We are nine miles away,
as Sarah pathetically observes, from a spool of
cotton, and of course this has its effect. There
was a time when Newport made it a sort of
fashion, and curious crowds infested the wards
with plum jam and cucumbers, but now "the
season" at Newport is over and the supplies in
a measure fall off. . . . We are fortunate in
having a good and active young man for a
chaplain. He has a large and very attentive
audience on Sunday and at daily evening
prayers, and it is quite refreshing to hear the
full soldiers' chorus in all the good old hymns.
Last Sunday two soldiers were received into the
church and baptized. Mr. Proudfit is a Pres-

byterian. . . . As to our house, it would not
be fair to call it a shanty, as the doctors have
taken so much pains or pleasure in fitting it up.
. . . The outer walls are double and filled in
with paper shavings (I believe), and this, with
large stoves, will keep us warm ; perhaps *too*
warm some fine windy midnight. "Wooden
walls" keep out all enemies according to the
old song, but they don't keep out voices, for
there is Georgy saying (I can hear it as if she
were at my elbow), "I shall never be able to
settle down into the conventionalities of society
after the wandering life I have led these five
years. Once a vagabond always a vagabond ; I
shall marry an army surgeon and go out to the
frontier !" . . . Miss Wormeley, our chief, is
clever, spirited and energetic in the highest
degree—a cultivated woman, with friends and
correspondents among the best literary men
here and in England, John Kenyon and the
Browning family for instance,—a great capacity
for business and not a single grain of mock-
sentiment about her. . . . One good thing has
happened to-day. Miss Wormeley is made
agent of the Sanitary Commission here, with
sole authority to draw and issue supplies, and
we are to have an office full of comforts for the
men at once. . . .

P. S.—All the barracks are to be plastered,
large bath-rooms and steam wash-house to be

built immediately, bad men turned out and good ones put in. " The kid begins *to go*," and I can see by candle-light it's halfpast midnight and time I was dreaming an hour ago.

A little item of interest for those of us who find " washing-day" a nuisance now, turns up in G's ward note-book—the washing-list for her barracks :

" 120 sheets.
    60 shirts.
    70 towels.
    60 pillow-cases.
    Ditto drawers and socks.
    6 washing-machines, 300 pieces to each."

1,800 pieces for her wards weekly. We were pretty clean, you see.

What the children played in those days is shown by the following little letter :

Little May Howland to G.

NEW YORK, January, 1863.

Dear Aunty : Did you get my letter I wrote you from Moremamma's? You must come home now and nurse me, I have the chicken pox. . . . The children play that one is you, and the other Aunt Jane, and they play that the logs of wood are the soldiers. They get bits of ribbons. for

cravats. I am going to crochet a pair of slippers
for the soldiers. I may as well scratch out that
I have the chicken pox, for the doctor has just
been here and said that I can go out. . . .

A. H. W. to G.

Charley sends his "regrets" from Headquarters for the Bond wedding. We get his
letters with wonderful despatch. A letter written Saturday *night* delivered here by twelve
on Monday! General Williams had reached
Falmouth again and will be very busy. The
four grand divisions being abolished, the eight
corps commanders report directly to Hooker,
which doubles the work of his A. A. G. Charley is to have an office tent and one branch of
the business to be assigned specially to him.
General Williams will employ several such aides
or clerks. . . .

I have ordered for you ten copies of the Independent for three months, ten of the Methodist
and ten of the Advocate. . . .

Our service at Portsmouth Grove lasted
only about five months. Sarah was the first
to be called home, the family greatly alarmed
over an outbreak of smallpox of the worst
variety, with a number of deaths among our
men. S. had to obey the call, leaving me

(G.) in charge of her wards and this scrap of a note: "Number 41 ought to have soda-water and egg beaten in wine every day— Eastman, near the door; be good to him and to D. and C. and M., and read the Pickwick Papers to the poor fellow who blew himself up with gunpowder."

S. came back for a little while, later, but our "staff" was broken up; Jane and I yielded to the home demand, went back to New York and did not return.

S. C. W. expressed our common sentiment: "Civilization is even more revolting than I supposed, and I pine all the time for our beloved Bohemia."

G. writes to mother from Fishkill: "If you have any difficulty in deciding what we shall have for dinner, the Surgeon-General's diet-table for each day will be found among my papers; what is good enough for our soldiers will be even too good for us."

Portsmouth Grove was before long turned into a convalescent camp.

C.W.W. on staff duty at Battle of Fredericksburg   Charley was all this time at the headquarters of the army, assigned to duty on the Adjutant-General's staff. He has kept some of his original dispatches, sent to General

Burnside from the fighting front at the *first battle of Fredericksburg*, because, as he says, he "was so green and young at that time." He writes: "The first time I went under fire I had a tremendous responsibility put upon me, to send back half-hourly reports to the commanding general, Burnside, of the way the battle was going. Later I had a thousand other quite as important duties, but this *first* plunge into the uproar of a great battle I can never forget." And *we* had been quieting our anxieties with the idea that "aides at headquarters were never much exposed!"

We have two or three of these hasty dispatches in Charley's handwriting:

"HEADQUARTERS ARMY OF POTOMAC,
April 30.

Major General Howard: I have the honor to enclose to you the accompanying statement concerning the position and forces of the enemy.

Very respectfully,
Your obedient servant,
CHAS. W. WOOLSEY,
Lt. and A. D. C."

Copy of telegram:

"The Major General commanding directs that General Sedgwick cross the river as soon as

indications will permit, capture Fredericksburg,
with everything in it, and vigorously pursue the
enemy.

(Signed)   BRIG. GENL. VANALEN.
Per CHARLES W. WOOLSEY, *A. D. C.*"

Then a list of countersigns for the month,
under Hooker, and best of all, a copy of this
original paper written by Charley June 4th:

"*Major General Meade, commanding 5th Corps.*

General: I have the honor of transmitting
to you herewith a copy of a telegram just
received from the President respecting sentences of Daily, Magraffe and Harrington.

(Signed)   C. W. W., *A. D. C.*"

—and Charley had the pleasure of hurrying
to Meade's headquarters with the *reprieve*
of these men from sentence to be shot.
These are among the very few papers connected with Charley's position at headquarters which are now in our possession, many
others having been lost in the Morrell fire.

Memorandum by C. W. W.

While in camp before Fredericksburg,
"Snowden," the Seddons' house, was in full
view on the other side of the river, inside the
rebel lines. When the town was taken by us a

guard was stationed at the house for its protection, but the people in it were suspected of signaling, by lamps at night, to confederates in our (then) rear—the side of the river we had left. I was sent to Mrs. Seddons with a letter containing a word of advice to her in this connection—it was probably a threat of very severe punishment if anything further occurred to excite suspicion. I do not remember seeing the letter, but I took her reply, which she wrote while I waited. It is very plucky and to the point, unswerving in her loyalty to the rebel cause, and has quite the story-book smack to it.

Here it is :

"I, Mrs. Seddon, utterly deny and challenge the proof that any signals of *any kind* have been made from this house 'to parties on the other side of the river.'

While Federal guards protect my property my hands are bound to refrain from serving a cause to which I would willingly sacrifice my life, but not my honor.

Respectfully,　　MARY A. SEDDON."

SNOWDEN,
March 13, 1863.

The term of service for which thousands of men had enlisted was now ending; the old army organization was expiring by its own limitations. There were in this army, as in all others, mercenaries and shirkers, but the bulk of the volunteer forces was of splendid and steadfast purpose. Early in the war this was seen with many of the three months' men; for example, the 2nd Connecticut, F. B.'s regiment. They kept their faces to the foe, and though their time was more than up, and they might have gone home with honor before the First Bull Run fight, they marched as a matter of course into that disaster, many of them never seeing again the wives and mothers who had believed the days of danger and separation ended. The spirit of the veterans of two years is shown in the history of the last few days of *our* 16th New York. Its time of service expired May 10, 1863. The terrible Chancellorsville campaign was its last and severest test, a few days only before the regiment was mustered out.

The 16th New York's last battle.

Lieutenant Robert P. Wilson of the 16th, at this time Captain and A. A. G. on the brigade staff, wrote:

I did not think we were to be attacked. It was so late, we were all so tired, the day had been one of such constant fighting, that I could not believe another engagement imminent; but as I was returning towards the General I saw him take off his hat in rear of a New Jersey regiment and cheer them on. The whole thing flashed upon me at once. I drew my sword, and felt that *the test had come.* . . . I never felt prouder than when I saw the brave men of the 16th—each one of whom I knew—steadily advancing through the woods to what we knew was all but certain death. Their term of service nearly expired, their lives dearer than ever now, their hopes of home strong; yet, flinging all these aside, thinking of nothing but duty and honor, they coolly dressed their line and as willingly entered the woods as if friends instead of foes lay behind. . . . For a moment we were irresistible and the rebels ran, but now from behind the rifle-pits in our front, which we had thought unoccupied, there rose up like magic a fresh line and into their very hearts at point-blank range poured the deadliest volley I ever saw. Our whole line melted before it. . . . The *brigade* when rallied was a sad sight : 687 men were gone, and but a remnant of each regiment was left to tell the fearful tale. . . .

E. W. H. to A. H. W.

May 9, 1863.

Dear Abby: The loss of the 16th alone is placed at 20 killed, 83 wounded, and 64 missing —probably badly wounded and left behind. A frightful proportion : nearly half I should think. What a little handful are left to come home next week !

Colonel Woolsey Hopkins, Assistant Quartermaster-General of Division, writes at this time to E. W. H., on the disbanding of the division.

STAFFORD COURT HOUSE, VIRGINIA,
May 9th, 1863.

My dear Mrs. Howland: This has been a sad day to me. We were ordered to a review of the 1st division at 2 P. M. We rode silently and slowly to the field, and then down the front, stopping at regiments of 200 and 300 men. General Slocum would make some remark to the Colonel, and move slowly on. Thus we passed the infantry and artillery. The General then ordered all the commanding officers to the front, where he very feelingly addressed them ; thanking them for their services, and urging them to encourage their men. . . .

There was a sad, proud look, in men and officers, as of those who had just looked death in the face, as he seized companions on the right and left of them. The tattered flags riddled by bullets brought tears to my eyes, and that choking sigh that came when I saw the 16th without our dear Colonel.

One of the last acts of the 16th N. Y., be- <small>Sword and Bible.</small> fore being mustered out of service, was the presentation of a superb sword, with sword-belt and sash, to their old Colonel, J. H., "as a mark of their regard for him as a man, a Christian, and a soldier."

At the same time the enlisted men of the regiment, of their own motion, sent to E. W. H. a beautiful folio copy of the Bible, very valuable in itself and made still more so by the addition in binding of a full list of the donors' names.

The following letter, written while the regiment was still at the front, accompanied the gifts :—

HEADQUARTERS 16TH N. Y. VOLS.
CAMP NEAR WHITE OAK CHURCH, VA.,
April 25, 1863.

Col. Joseph Howland.

Dear Sir: The officers of the Sixteenth New York Volunteers desire to present you with the accompanying sword as a testimonial of their appreciation of the gallantry and ability displayed by you while in command of the regiment during the Peninsular Campaign.

The enlisted men of the regiment, feeling that Mrs. Howland has laid them under a deep debt of gratitude by her many contributions to their comfort and by philanthropic labors in the hospitals, send the Bible for her acceptance.

Very respectfully,

W. B. CRANDALL, ⎫
PLINY MOORE,   ⎬ *Committee.*
R. W. WILSON, ⎭

J. S. W. to a friend in Europe.

WASHINGTON, May 25.

Wash-
ington
in 1863.

We have just been spending a month in Washington, my first visit since the war, and the city certainly looks like war-time, the white tents showing out of the green of all the hills, headquarters' flags flying above all the remaining bits of wood, and everywhere on the highish places, the long, low, dun banks of earthworks you get to detect so soon, looking like a western river levee. Then it is strange not to be able to go in the ferry-boat to Alexandria, or take an afternoon drive across the bridges into the country, without producing a document which sets forth over your names in full,—men and women,—that your purpose is pleasure visiting, and that you solemnly affirm that you will support, protect and defend the Government, etc., against all enemies, domestic or foreign, etc., any law of any State to the contrary notwithstanding, so help you God. It was odd, too, at the opera one night, to see an officer of the Provost Guard come into the theatre between

the acts and accost the gentlemen in front of
us: "Sorry to trouble you, Major; your pass if
you please"; and so, to every pair of shoulder-
straps in the house. Then there are the great
Barrack hospitals and the dwelling-houses
turned into hospitals, the incessant drum-beat
in the streets and the going and coming of
squads of foot and horse, the huge packs of
army-wagons in vacant lots, the armed sentinels
at the public buildings, and all the rest of it.
Washington certainly shows the grim presence.
It is a calumniated city in some respects. It is
as bright and fresh this springtime as any
town could be. The sweet, early, half-southern
spring is nowhere sweeter than in the suburbs
of Washington; on the Georgetown Heights,
as we drove with Dr. Bacon up the river-edges
to the Maryland forts or the great new arch
"Union" of the new aqueduct, or down the
river-edges by the horrible road, or went on a
little breezy rushing voyage in a quartermaster's tug to Mount Vernon to see Miss Tracy,
the lady who lives all alone with the Great
Ghost,—all these little excursions are most
charming. . . . But some days of our visit
were dark ones,—the three or four inevitable
days of doubt and lying despatches at the time
of the Chancellorsville battles; then the days
when the truth came partially out (Mr. Sumner
told one of our party last week that it has never

yet come out) ; then the days when the wrecks
drifted in, hospitals filled up and our hotel,
being a quiet one, became almost a hospital for
wounded officers. In the evening we used to
hear the tugs screaming at the wharf ; soon
after, carriages would drive up, a servant get
out with one or two pairs of crutches, then a
couple of young fellows, painfully hoisted upon
them, would hobble in. Some were brought on
stretchers. Then one day came our friends,
Frank Stevens, 1st New York, shot through the
knee, and Captain Van Tuyl, shot through both
legs ; then Lieutenants Asch and Kirby, one,
arm gone, one, leg gone ; then Palmer and Best
of the 16th, etc. Stevens was left on the field at
Chancellorsville, taken prisoner, sadly neglected. But it is astonishing to see the cheerful
courage of these young men. I went to see
Captain Bailey, 5th Maine, with superfluous
condolences. " In six weeks I shall be in the
service again ; if they can't make me a marching
leg I'll go into a mounted corps; you don't
suppose I call *that* a 'disability'!" pointing to
where his right leg used to be ; lying, pale and
plucky, encouraging three other more or less
mutilated men in the same room with him ; and
much more in the same strain, like the music of
Carryl, "pleasant and mournful to the soul."
We saw a long train of rebel prisoners come in,
not by any means, I am bound to say, ragged

or gaunt or hungry-looking ; dirty, of course, with queer patchwork quilts in many cases for blankets ; some without shoes, some without hats, but fighting men, not starvelings, every one of them. Our friend Major Porter came up on the tug with one detachment. They opened their haversacks and ate their rations, which consisted in every case of crackers and sugar. One young fellow brought his blanket and spread it by Major Porter, to take a nap, saying, "Would you please wake me up, sir, when we pass Mount Vernon ? I'd like to take off my hat when we come to the place where Gentleman George Washington lived." . . . None of us know much about the retreat and the "reason why." The President was anxious and restless in those days, and went down to the tugs two or three times to see and talk with wounded officers. Georgy met him by chance one morning in the White House garden, and found him greatly changed since last summer. He was walking slowly, eating an apple, dragging "Tad" along by the hand and gazing straight before him, afar off,—older, grayer, yellower, more stooping and harassed-looking. . . .

Jane's letter, given above, happily contains also extracts from one of Charley's, after the Battle of Chancellorsville.

He writes May 8th : " We have forced the
enemy out of their works and made them fight
us in the open, but instead of their 'ignominiously flying,' *we* have retired in good order to
the other side of the Rappahannock, and are
in our old camp again, bitterly regretting that we
pulled down our chimneys when we went forward. And why did we come back? Nobody
knows. It was *not* the storm, for when the
order was given it was fine weather. Our position was strong. Everybody thought we could
hold it for any length of time. I have been on
the go of course, day and night ; no rest for the
A.D.C. On Thursday night (April 30) I was
sent to Potomac Creek to look for a missing
battery ; then to the bridges to report progress ;
was on duty the rest of the night opening despatches, and back and forth all next day with
orders to Gibbon. At 11.45 Saturday night I
delivered to Sedgwick General Hooker's orders
to cross the river at once, march on Fredericksburg, capture everything in it and march by the
flank road to Chancellorsville. The night march
began immediately. At 10.30 next morning I
found Sedgwick in one of the houses in the town
and gave him the General's order to attack.
He charged on the heights splendidly. Later
in the day I took the order to General Gibbon
to hold the town, and then went to Sedgwick,
three miles beyond the town, to report progress.

He was resting on the hills we have been looking at all winter. I reported to General Hooker
up the river. The General said to me, "Mr.
Woolsey, you will remain with me and take in
all despatches that come." So I saw only
Meade's fight, and was favored with communi-
tions from "Father Abraham," (who knew very
little of what was going on) ; from Peck, who
ought to have walked into Richmond, and from
corps commanders. On Tuesday night the
army re-crossed about dark, the General started
off suddenly and the staff scattered. He was
just in time, the Rappahannock was rising, the
pontoons shifting. I had to jump my horse
from the last boat and wade him 20–30 feet,
quite deep. The crossing of the artillery and
infantry was tediously delayed. After some
search I found General Hooker on the back
porch of a little house high up on the river's
bank ; the front rooms were filled with wounded.
There were only three or four men with him; he
looked very dejected and sad. The wet troops
outside were toiling by in the mud and dark, in
full retreat. The General and Butterfield nodded
in their chairs before the fire. It was a melan-
choly sight. The General sent me repeatedly to
report from the bridges. 'Tell them,' he sent
word, with great solemnity, 'tell them that the
lives of thousands depend upon their efforts.'
All night and all the early morning the troops

came slowly in. It was with great difficulty that I could stem the crowd on the bridges to get back with messages 'to Meade, who was covering the rear. He expected to be harassed, but I do not know of a shot being fired. We are all very much disappointed, but do not believe that we are demoralized. I have heard hard things said of Hooker. Some of the headquarters men use his name in a way that ought to be punished as rank insubordination. The congratulatory order is the subject of many sarcastic remarks. On authority I may state that this army will be filled up with conscript men, and I am disposed to think that Providence never intended the A. P. for anything but an army of observation. Let Hitchcock succeed Halleck and Dan Sickles Hooker, and I think we may all go abroad to live, with a clear conscience."

About this time President Lincoln left Washington to visit the commanding General at Headquarters, going by steamer to Aquia Creek. Charley, who must by this time have received his first promotion as Captain, was detailed to escort the President to the front, and arrived at the banks of the Potomac with a headquarters' ambulance and a fine led horse in charge of a lieutenant and

guard. He met Mr. Lincoln, presented his
credentials, offered the ambulance or horse,
and asked for orders. " Well, Captain," the
President said, *"You* be boss," and seated
himself in the ambulance, where by his side
Charley had the honor and pleasure of a
friendly talk during the long drive back to
the army headquarters.

F. B. having been on duty as Chief Medi- New
cal Officer of Provisional Brigades for months Orleans
in Washington, was now, in the early part of
June, '63, relieved from this duty, with orders
to report to General Banks, commanding the
Department of the Gulf. General Casey, on
whose staff he was while in Washington,
thanked him for his services in a highly complimentary general order, and he left for
New Orleans, where he organized and took
charge for nearly a year of the great St.
Louis Hotel Hospital. After this he was
made medical inspector, and then medical
director of the department. He resigned
late in the summer of '64, after nearly four
years' service, to accept the Professorship
of Surgery in Yale College. The following
letter was written in '63 while he was still in
charge of the New Orleans Hospital:

F. B. to G. M. W.

July 6th, 1863.

My present experiment is trying whether I am equal to that American standard of ability "to keep a hotel,"—the St. Louis Hotel, to wit. It is a fine building over in the French quarter of the city. Chocolate-colored old gentlemen with white moustaches, much given to wearing of nankeen and seersucker and twirling of bamboo sticks, (whom tortures could not compel to speak three words of English, nor a general conflagration drive across Canal street into the American region,) prowl thereabout, and scowl French detestation at the interloping Yankee as he passes in and out of their national hotel. The rattle of dominoes, upon marble tables in *cafés* all about, is incessant, and on Sundays rises almost to the sublime.

The St. Louis was a good hotel, but makes a bad hospital. I remonstrated as stoutly as I could against its being taken for the purpose, but, with a fixity of will which I would have preferred to see exercised in some other direction, the order came for the St. Louis to be a hospital, and for me to be Surgeon in charge. So now, making the best of it, though my rooms are mostly small and my passages narrow, I have a superb marble entrance with two big lions, one *dormant*, one *couchant*, "to comfort me on my entablature." . . .

The labor of starting the Hospital has been immense, . . . for nothing about the house that could be disordered, from the steam-engine in the cellar to the water-tanks upon the roof, was in working order. . . . On the 16th I had to receive a steamboat load of patients, all of the poor fellows wounded, from Banks' second assault of Port Hudson ; hourly, for the past week, we have been painfully expecting another such arrival from his *third*. . . .

Thank Heaven, the patients have done well ! I am going to send as many North on furloughs as possible, convalescence is so slow and uncertain in this climate.

How wonderfully cheerful these wounded men always are ! You should see one of our pets, a young fellow about twenty-one years old, from a New York regiment, Kretzler by name. Right thigh amputated, right fore-arm the same, shell wound as big as my two hands in the left thigh, ugly wound under the jaw, scratches about left hand and arm. He never complains of anything, takes all the beefsteak and porter we can give him, insisting on helping himself to the latter and drinking it from the bottle. He sits up in his bed a large part of the time, smoking his pipe with an expression of perfect serenity. When I ask him how he does, it is always "bully," with a triumphant air. Passing near his room the other day, I heard him

singing "The Star-Spangled Banner" in a
robust style, with the remark in conclusion,
"There, guess them Rebs won't like that much,"
alluding thereby to a lot of hulking scoundrels
of Texans, prisoners, wounded at Donaldson-
ville, and lying in a room within ear-shot of
him, as well as to some female visitors of theirs,
who, having no longer the salutary fear of Ben.
Butler before their eyes, were making their
sympathies a little too apparent. This kind of
cats I pretty uniformly exclude now, and as a
consequence, when they find themselves baffled,
I have some highly dramatic interviews with
them, almost at the risk of my eyes, I sometimes
feel.

I reluctantly confess that I am subjugated
and crushed by a woman who sings The Star-
Spangled Banner copiously through all the
wards of my hospital. . . . She weighs three
hundred pounds. She comes every morning,
early. She wears the Flag of our Country
pinned across her heart. She comes into *my*
room, my own office, unabashed by the fact that
I am the Surgeon in charge, and that an orderly
in white gloves stands at the door. She looks
me in the eye with perfect calmness and intre-
pidity. She takes off her sunbonnet and man-
tilla and lays them upon my table, over my
papers, as if they were rare and lovely flowers
of the tropics. She knocks off three of my pens

with her brown parasol, worn out in the joint,
and begins to exude small parcels from every
pocket. . . . She nurses tenderly, and feeds and
cries over the bad cases. Poor Martin Rose-
bush, a handsome, smooth-faced, good boy from
New Hampshire, desperately wounded and
delirious, would start up with a cry of joy when
she came, and died with his arms around her
neck, calling her his mammy.

Jerry Cammett, a peaceful giant, grown as
they grow them in Maine, with pink cheeks,
bright-yellow beard, and handsome blue eyes
as free from guile as a baby's, lies with his right
thigh amputated. After each visit she makes
him, I hear the effect it has upon Jerry in about
three hours of steady quiet whistling to himself
of funny, twiddling Methodist hymns.

Of course I do not encourage the visits of
this creature with the Flag of our Country and
the National Anthem. On the contrary, they
encourage me.

So do those of " Olympe, sare, natif to ze
citie." She is a stately, sybilline old black, or
rather brown woman, everything in her appearance indicating great age, except her intensely
black and glittering eyes, which still show the
fire of youth. She wears a most elaborate tur-
ban of Madras handkerchiefs, a dress of fine
and exquisitely white muslin, handsome pearl
drops in her ears, and around her wrinkled neck

a string of large beads of that deep yellow, almost tawny gold, which comes with ivory and palm-oil from the African coast. She brings little parcels of extremely nice lint, small pots of jelly, and bottles of orange-flower syrup, all made, she would have me know, with her own hands in her own house; this she says with great dignity, and shows me how carefully she wraps them up so that the Confederate ladies, her neighbors, shall not know that she brings them to Union soldiers. I fancy that if one should sit down with this old lady, and, in French, talk oneself into her confidence, she would prove immensely entertaining and instructive.

Captain Charles Rockwell's appearance was a very pleasant surprise to me. I hoped that he would be assigned to duty in the city here, but, the day after his arrival, he was ordered up to Port Hudson. . . .

July 10th.

P. S. Let us have a season of felicitation over Vicksburg aad Port Hudson, from both of which we have got the good news since I stopped writing.

The rage and incredulity of the Secesh are really comical, and fill my soul with an infinite peace.

Now send us good news of what cometh to Lee of the wicked raid, and all may be well.

CHAPTER XII.

The Army of the Potomac, after the Battle of Gettysburg. wretched retreat at Chancellorsville, had lain along the Rappahannock, scouting here and Mother at the Front. there, burning rebel sloops and bringing in "contrabands," till Lee, who had not followed up his victory at once, put his forces in rapid march up the valley for the invasion of Pennsylvania, part of his army reaching and occupying Gettysburg June 26.

The Army of the Potomac made quick marches to overtake the enemy, but by the 27th of June were only a little to the northwest of Baltimore. At this point Hooker was relieved from command, on June 28, and Meade put at the head of the Army, which he at once put in motion.

Charley continued always with General Seth Williams, but was in every action assigned to duty on the commanding General's staff. He was transferred in this way to duty as "aide" to General Meade on the field, for the frightful battle which was

approaching.   On the night of June 30th the
two armies faced each other in the immediate vicinity of Gettysburg, and on July 1st
the fight began,—one of the decisive battles
of the war.

It had been raging for three days.   We
at home knew that Charley was in the
thick of it, and were most anxious and
ready to believe the worst, when a telegram to me (G.) came from our old commander, Mr. F. L. Olmsted, saying, "If you
are going to Gettysburg let me know."   We
jumped at the conclusion that *he* knew of
bad news for us from Charley, and Mother
and I started at once to go to him,—Uncle
Edward taking us as far as Baltimore.   There
the news reached us that Charley was safe,
and the rebels, repulsed at every point, were,
at that date, July 4, in rapid retreat towards
the Potomac. which they reached and re-
crossed July 13th, with the loss only of
their rear guard of 1,500 men captured.
They left all their dead and dying in our
hands at Gettysburg.   7,000 of the dead of
both armies were buried on the field at once;
and all buildings on the hillsides and in the
little town, both private houses and shops,
were full of wounded men.   That July 4th

saw also Pembroke's entire army of 31,000 surrender to Grant at Vicksburg; and Charley was safe! So it was a day always to remember with wonder and solemn thankfulness, though with horror at the suffering and distress all about us.

A month later I wrote a little account of our three weeks stay at Gettysburg to F. B. in answer to his New Orleans letter of July 6th, already given.

G. M. W. to F. B.

FISHKILL, Aug. 6, '63.

Mother and I were in Gettysburg when your letter came, having hurried on immediately after the battle, under the impression, due to a mistake in telegraphing, that Charley was hurt; and, being on hand, were fastened upon by Mr. Olmsted, to take charge of a feeding station and lodge for the wounded men. So there we were, looking after other people's boys, since our own was safe, for three weeks, coming as near the actual battle field as I should ever wish to. You know all about that fighting, how desperate it was on both sides; what loss, and what misery; the communications cut, no supplies on hand, no surgeons, or so few that they were driven to despair from the sight of wretchedness they could not help,—20,000 badly wounded soldiers

and only one miserable, unsafe line of railroad
to bring supplies and carry men away. We
were twenty-four hours in getting from Baltimore to Gettysburg, when in ordinary times we
should have been four. This was the only excuse I could think of to give the wretched rebels
who, two weeks after the battle, lay in the mud
under shelter tents, and had their food handed
them in newspapers : " I am sorry, my man ;
we are all distressed at it; but *you* have cut our
communications and nothing arrives."

Never say anything against the Army of the
Potomac again, when so few of our men, after
their marching and fasting, overtook and over-
came Lee's fatted twice-their-number. I saw
but very few who were *slightly* hurt among the
wounded, and we fed all the 16,000 who went
away from Gettysburg. So brave as they were
too, and so pleased with all that was done for
them—even the rebels. We had our station
with tents for a hundred, with kitchen, surgeon
and "delegation," right on the railroad line between Gettysburg and Baltimore, and twice a
day the trains left with soldiers,—long trains of
ambulances always arriving just too late for the
cars, and no provision being made to shelter
and feed them except by the Sanitary Commission. We had the full storehouse of the Commission to draw upon, and took real satisfaction
in dressing and comforting all our men. No

man of the 16,000 went away without a good hot
meal, and none from our tents without the fresh
clothes they needed. Mother put great spirit
into it all, listened to all their stories, petted
them, fed them, and distributed clothes, including handkerchiefs with cologne, and got herself
called "Mother,"—"This way, Mother," "Here's
the bucket, Mother," and "Isn't she a glorious
old woman?"—while the most that *I* ever heard
was, "*She* knows how; why, it would have taken
our steward two hours to get round; but then
she's used to it, you see;" which, when you consider that I was distributing hot grog, and must
have been taken for a barmaid, was not so complimentary! Then those rebels too, miserable
fellows; we hated them so much when they were
away from us, and couldn't help being so good to
them when they were in our hands. I am, or
should be, angry with myself in that I felt worse
when Lieutenant Rhout of the 14th South Carolina died on my hands, singing the Lutheran
chants he had sung in his father's church before
they made a soldier of him, than when E. C.
writes me that "Amos" was their oldest son,
and that she and his father were over sixty. . . .
I am glad we helped those rebels. They had
just as much good hot soup, when our procession of cans and cups and soft bread and general refreshment went round from car to car, as
they wanted; and I even filled the silver pap-

cup that a pretty boy from North Carolina had round his neck, though he was an officer and showed no intention to become a Unionist. " Yes, it was his baby-cup," and "his mother gave it to him ; " and he lay on the floor of the baggage car, wounded, with this most domestic and peaceful of all little relics tied round his neck.   We had lovely things for the men to eat —as many potatoes and turnips as they wanted, and almost " *too* much cabbages "; and custard pudding, and codfish hash, and jelly an inch high on their bread, and their bread *buttered*— "buttered on *both* sides," as the men discovered, greatly to their amusement one night, consider- ing that the final touch had been given when *this* followed the clean clothes and cologne,— "cologne worth a penny a sniff." "I smell it up here," a soldier called to me, poking his head out of the second story window, while I and my bottle stood at the door of his hospital.

If at any time you would like to swear, call your enemy a Dutch farmer—nothing can be worse, or, if he is a man of decency, make him feel more indignant. The D—— farmers of Gettysburg have made themselves a name and a fame to the latest day, by charging our poor men, who crawled out of the barns and woods where they hid themselves after they were wounded, three and four dollars each for bring- ing all that was left of their poor bodies, after

defending the contemptible D—— firesides,
down to the railroad. We found this out, and
had a detail from the Provost Marshal to arrest
the next farmer who did it, and oblige him to
refund or go to prison. The day before we
came away a sleepy-looking, utterly stupid
Dutchman walked into camp, having heard we
had "some rebels." He lived five miles from
the city and had "never seen one," and came
mooning in to stare at them, and stood with his
mouth open, while the rebels and ourselves were
shouting with laughter, he "pledging his word"
that "he never saw a rebel afore." "And why
didn't you take your gun and help drive them
out of your town?" Mother said. "Why, a fel-
ler might a got hit;" at which the rebels, lying
in double rows in the tent, shook themselves
almost to pieces.

It was a satisfaction to be in Gettysburg,
though I confess to a longing to shut out the
sight of it all, sometimes. The dear fellows
were so badly hurt, and it was so hard to bear
their perfect patience ; men with a right arm
gone, and children at home, and no word or
look of discontent.

The authorities want us to go back again, and
look after the special diet in the new and fine
General Hospital for 3000 men, too sick to be
moved. We can't do so, though, as Jane and I
have promised to spend the winter at Point

Lookout in the Hammond Hospital. Look with respect upon your correspondent; she is at the head of the Protestant half of the women's department of that hospital. The Sisters run half the wards, and I expect to have fun with their Lady Superior and to wheedle her out of all her secrets, and get myself invited out to tea. Why shouldn't she and I compare notes on the proper way to make soup? I will call her "Sister," and agree to eat oysters on Friday,—(they are particularly fine on the Maryland shore).

It will be rather jolly down there, particularly as the surgeon in charge is delighted to have us come, and we shall ride over him just as much as your dear old women, black and white, do over their particular conquest. As for gardens of oranges, and flowers—well, we shall have beds of oysters, and, as it is a military station, there will be a band there to keep up our spirits; which reminds me to give the Baltimore fireman his due, who, being one of our friends at Gettysburg, secured two bands before we came away and marched them down to camp to serenade us, which they did standing at the mouth of the long tent and refreshing themselves afterwards with gingerbread and punch, unmindful of the fact that the jolly Canandaigua "delegation," finding its fingers inconvenienced by the sugar on them, just dipped their hands in the claret and water without saying anything! It

will be a long time before Gettysburg will forget the Army of the Potomac. Their houses
are battered, some of them with great holes
through and through them. Their streets are
filled with old caps, pieces of muskets, haversacks, scraps of war everywhere, and even the
children fling stones across the streets, and call
to each other, " Here, you rebel, don't you hear
that shell?" and one babe of four years I found
sitting on the pavement with a hammer peacefully cracking percussion caps from the little
cupful he had. . . .

What a good thing the public burying of the
colored Captain has been, down where you are
in New Orleans. Send me some more accounts
of your hospital.

I have your great-grandmother's little note
book, Una,—kept while at Gettysburg, with
such entries as these :

"*Myers :* Wrote a letter to his father for
him ; only son—leg badly wounded."

" *Chester Gillett :* Wrote to his brother ;
right leg wounded on the 1st of July, amputated on the 8th."

" *Henry Rauch :* Lieutenant, Rebel Army—
Came into the tent July 16th, died 17th ; his
father is old and blind."

" *Young Sloat:* Died of lockjaw ; wrote
to his mother."—You can imagine what a
tender letter that was, from a mother to a
mother.

23,000 rebels were wounded in those four
July days, and 13,713 loyal men.

I (your Aunt G.) being urged, wrote later
a little pamphlet giving Mother's and my
experience at the front, and called " Three
Weeks at Gettysburg." It was meant to
"fire the hearts" of the sewing circles,
which, all over the country, were keeping
up the Sanitary Commission supplies. The
Commission ordered 10,000 copies for distribution, and I went off to Point Lookout
Hospital, leaving Abby all the work of getting it printed.

A. H. W. to Harriet Gilman.

FISHKILL, July, 1863.

Mother
at home
again.

It took so long for letters to come from
Gettysburg, and Mother and Georgy had so
little time to write, that we didn't hear often.
They have come *themselves* at last ; arrived Tuesday, midnight. . . . Georgy came up here this
noon, and we have been sitting together talking
over all the strange scenes in those tents by the
railroad, where 16,000 men have been fed and

comforted in the last three weeks. Just imagine
Mother in a straw flat and heavy *Gettysburg* boots,
standing cooking soup for 200 men at a time,
and distributing it in tin cups ; or giving clean
shirts to ragged rebels ; or sitting on a pile of
grocer's boxes, under the shadow of a string of
codfish, scribbling her notes to us.

She has many a memento of that strange battle—one, of a rebel lieutenant who died in her
care ; and a score of palmetto buttons from rebel
coats—dirty but grateful, poor wretches ; etc. . . .
They say that the *women* of Gettysburg have
done all they can, given the wounded all that
the rebels had not taken, and have boarded the
Sanitary and Christian Commission for nothing.
At one house, where Mother and G. got their
dinner one day, the woman could not be induced
to take money. " No, ma'am," she said, " I would
not wish to have *that* sin on my soul when this
war is over."

We may go to Brattleboro for a month. But
if Charley holds out the hope of his coming
home, it won't be worth while to go away. . . .
We have not heard anything recently from " the
army,"—I mean *our* modest portion of it in the
form of Charley. He and all of them I am
sure must be mortified at this escape of Lee at
Gettysburg, scot free. He lost many men, but
so did we. Pennsylvania is safe from " the
invader"; but, dear me, our army has begun the

hateful scramble all over Virginia again. . . .
Charley wrote that "Halleck urged forced
marches after the retreating rebels and an immediate attack, as he had positive information that
Lee was rapidly crossing the Potomac." Charley adds, "but we have had nothing but forced
marches since we left the Rappahannock, and
we *know* that Lee *isn't* crossing and cannot cross
rapidly." [He did, though.]

The
Draft
Riots.
 The enormous losses of the war now made
a draft necessary to fill up the depleted
regiments. Many thousands of the discharged two-years' men re-enlisted for the
war; but idlers, and the evil-minded, re-
sisted. There were serious outbreaks in
Boston and other cities, but in New York
the disorders were outrageous. Mother and
G. were still at Gettysburg at that time;
Abby and Jane away from home, and Hatty
and Carry alone in the house. C's letter
seems written in haste with a poker:—

C. C. W. to A. at Fishkill.

10TH ST., NEW YORK, MONDAY, July 13, 1863.

Dear Abby: It has come—resistance to the
draft! The city is in a tumult and Uncle
Edward wishes us to go out to Astoria in the 6
o'clock boat. The regulars are all out and the

streets are full of rioters. The gas house on
23rd Street is blown up and 10th Street full of
black ashes,—our door-steps covered. They say
they will blow up the powder-mill in 28th
Street, where the Gilmans live, and we have
told them (if they will) to come all here.
Hatty G. was in a minute ago, and Mr. Prentiss. There has been a great noise in town all
day. The carriage is waiting, but I was afraid
you would feel anxious. We would like very
much to stay, but Uncle E. insists.

C. C. W. to A.

ASTORIA, July 15th, 1863.

We left in such a hurry we had no time to
leave directions for the servants, except to close
the house early, and be very particular about
fastening the doors and windows. . . . While
driving out here we heard distinctly the cannon
at Harlem. We have had no real trouble here
from the mob, but were *threatened* last night and
the night before. About two hundred men and
boys, principally from Harlem and the upper
parts of the city, were careering round the village. They went to Mr. M—'s, and made him
come out and speak against the draft, and announced their intention of visiting Messrs.
Wolcott, Woolsey and Howland among others.
Groups of them were gathering in the afternoon
as we drove through the village. Uncle Edward

was a good deal excited as night came on, and
had a man placed in the stable with directions
to cut the horses loose should any alarm be
made. Robert had his carriage, or rather his
horses, harnessed and ready to pack the children
in. Uncle Edward had a pile of fire-arms loaded
and placed conveniently near the window.
Aunt Emily put her rings on and her valuables
in a safe place, and we pocketed our purses and
laid Mother's camel's-hair shawls, which we
brought with us, where we could easily seize
them in case of sudden chill, caused by the
draft ! . . . But nothing turned up, and things
have quieted down. The militia regiments are
(five of them) coming home ; the 7th has already
arrived.

Hatty adds :—

One of the Ball & Black firm came the next
morning to ask Uncle E. if he could hide some
treasure on his place. He lives in 86th Street
and his house had been threatened. Uncle E.
said he might take his three or four trunks
through the woods to the "black lodge," but of
course it was at his own risk, as no one was to
be trusted on the place. They were all kept
safe in Margaret's hands, and he came back and
got them in a few days. Isn't it shameful that
the fiends should have sacked Mrs. Gibbons'
house ?—everything destroyed and all her little

things carried off. Uncle E. is perfectly indignant and in a state of suppressed rage at the Irish, but he agrees with Aunt E. in not allowing a word said against them at table, or within reach of any of the servants' ears.

Mrs. Gibbons was a victim to the low pro-slavery roughs, the dregs of the democratic party in New York, round whom all the worst elements of the city rallied. She was too well known as a pronounced abolitionist to escape. She had been, as she wrote Abby a few days before the riot, six months at Point Lookout Hospital, "a long time for a person of my age"; adding that she must come back where she "could enjoy home, and work too." Her "home" was gutted by the mob!

Joe at once went down from Fishkill to New York, to offer his assistance to the authorities, at the time of the riot. His train was surrounded at Manhattanville by a crowd with clubs, searching for soldiers. Being in citizen's dress, with his uniform in a portmanteau, he escaped, crossed a field and found a place at the nearest stage-line on top of an omnibus crowded with roughs, one of whom clapped him on the back and said, "You're a fancy looking sort of a chap; what would *you* pay for a substitute?"

Joe turned and looked at the man, saying, "I don't need to pay for a substitute, I went myself;" and then, by a happy inspiration recognizing the unmistakable look that old soldiers, even bad ones, brought home from the army, added, "Do you know I believe I have seen you before! weren't you encamped on Cameron Run in the winter of '61?" Sure enough, he had been, with the Irish 69th, and they fell into old-time army talk till, presently, the rough threw his arms round Joe with a half-tipsy hug, and said to his fellows, "Take good care o' this gen'lman, he's a partic'lar frien' o' mine."

As they got near the city some row down a side street attracted the attention of the gang, and they all climbed down from the omnibus and disappeared. Then the driver turned and said to Joe, "Well, you had a *mighty narrow escape,*" adding that they were one of the roughest gangs in the city and capable of any crime.

St. Luke's Hospital and Dr. Muhlenberg.

Little Georgy Howland's peaceful christening in the Chapel of St. Luke's was a pleasant picture connected with the old building in 1862. In 1863 the hospital saw a different sight. The riots reached even that sacred spot. One hundred beds were at the time filled with wounded soldiers. The first alarm was the burning, that morning, of the Colored Orphan Asylum, corner of 5th Avenue and 44th Street, by the mob. At noon a stentorian voice called from the basement of St. Luke's, "Turn out; turn out by six o'clock, or we'll burn you in your beds!" "as a huge, hatless laborer, with his sleeves rolled up to the armpits, bare-breasted, red with liquor and rage, strode up and down the hall."

But a wounded rioter (shot, with a brickbat in his hand), was about this time brought by a crowd to the hospital door, promptly admitted, and kindly cared for. Dr. Muhlenberg, leaving the man's bedside, went down alone to face the crowd, going right in among them, "in simple dignity," and telling them that to every wounded man needing help those doors were freely open;— "would they threaten this house with fire and storm?" Cries of "No, no; long live St. Luke's," came at once, and the crowd formed themselves into a vigilance committee, and protected the hospital from all harm.

The Rev. Dr. Muhlenberg, at the head of this great charity founded by himself, was an elderly man then, with a noble face, white hair and wonderful dark eyes. As he braved alone that howling mob of men and women, and by his personal magnetism quieted their rage, it was like the picture of the working of a miracle by a mediæval saint.

Mother and G. came home after the riots from Gettysburg and longed for their hospital life again. Georgy did not long keep out of it.

G. M. W. to Mother.

FISHKILL, August 5.

Dear Mother : Thank you for your nice note which came last night. . . . No wonder you regret Gettysburg. You will be gladder all the time that you went there and did what you did ; and you will be ready to give me great praise, I hope, when I tell you that I have given up all idea of going back there, and have accepted in place of it Mrs. Gibbons' offer of the position she is giving up at Point Lookout Hospital ; securing, before I go, the month you want me to have in the country, as we need not go to the Point before September. After the intense satisfaction you have experienced at

Gettysburg, you cannot, my dear and patriotic
Mamma, be otherwise than delighted at the prospect before us, while you must regret that I
cannot also pull the special diet of Gettysburg
through. Mrs. Gibbons will, I suppose, have
got all things about straight at the Point, so that
with little effort we can keep them going. It will
be an easy and pleasant position; better, "till this
cruel war is over," than sitting at home thinking what we *might* be doing. The surgeon in
charge is "delighted" to think that we will
come. . . . I shall hanker for our old life at
Gettysburg and wish you and I were going
back to run the new concern. However, there
will be the satisfaction of taking the wind out
of the "sisters'" sails. I dare say they will
have made headway during this interval, and
when I arrive with three feathers stuck in my
head, "O won't I make those ladies stare." . . .
We shall collect at home once more, Charley
and all, before the winter, as you will not of
course go to Brattleboro now till he arrives. . . .

Charley came North at this time on short
furlough, and the family were reunited for
twenty days before scattering again, Jane
and G. to Point Lookout Hospital, Charley
to the front, and Mother and the other home
ones to rest, in Brattleboro, Vt.

The Army of the Potomac had followed the retreating rebels from Gettysburg south again into Virginia, and by July 31st both armies were again on the Rappahannock, where cavalry raids and skirmishing all along the lines went on.

E. W. H. to Mother.

FISHKILL, August 24.

We ought soon to hear from Charley, and if Mr. Hopkins' rumor is true we may feel at ease about him for the present, for Meade won't attempt a movement without the conscripts. Do you see that Charley himself is one, although in the service already? Let us know how he got down to camp after his furlough with all his traps, and send us all his letters. . . .

Point Lookout Hospital

Mrs. Gibbons remained after all at Point Lookout, and we were quickly established in our half of the Hammond General Hospital and "supplies" were laid in. One list is before me of the twenty boxes and barrels received from home and the twenty-four Boston rocking chairs. These we found mines of comfort wherever we went.

The Point was a delightful place, the Chesapeake Bay and the Atlantic Ocean meeting and rolling in opposing breakers at

our feet. Every morning we watched our
little darkey tuck up her skirt and take her
bucket and her chance of catching a wave
or two for our bath tubs, and all day the salt
wind was a spur to work. Ten women
nurses reported for duty to Mrs. Gibbons.

The Brattleboro Hospital was also full of
returned soldiers, and Mother, who was longing for Gettysburg, took a little consolation
in visits there.

A. H. W. to H. Gilman.

BRATTLEBORO, September 17.

I hope soon to hear of the girls' arrival at
Point Lookout. Georgy wrote us of her night
at your house and how good you all were to her
and to her *soldiers* too.

Mother is much interested in the hospital
here and has been up several times; is interested in the worst way, that is, without the
opportunity of doing anything. The wards are
thrown open every afternoon from two to five,
but visitors are few, and even the kind words
she can take, and those of other ladies from this
house, seem valued. The men said, "You are so
different, ladies, from *some* that come here, who
only walk through and stare at us as if we were
wild beasts." One man was almost convulsed
at seeing Mother, and, with tears, would hardly

let her hand go. "I knew you, ma'am, the minute you came in. You were at Gettysburg, and were the first one that dressed my arm." And there the poor arm still lay, useless and swollen, and constant streams of cold water necessary to keep down inflammation.

The same wretched want marks this hospital as all others: the little attention paid to the food of the sick men. Typhoid patients are starving on pork slop, or eat smuggled sutler's pies of the toughest sort, from a craving for food of some kind. Some of those alphabets for "spelling games" which Mother took up were a great amusement to them, and to-day in the book-store Mother saw one of the soldiers trying to buy some more. None were for sale, but Mother promised him some, and at the printing office ordered, for a very little trifle, a hundred alphabets, which she will give them. . . . We hear that Joe was drafted in Fishkill, and as *colored!* the "colonel" before his name which the enrolling officer inserted, being so understood. He feels himself a thorough *black Republican* now. The villagers met him at the depot one day as he came up from New York and informed him he was drawn, and he had to make them a speech, telling them what an honor he should consider it, if he were well enough, to go, but he should find a substitute (which he has done, a "veteran"), etc., etc. They called

out now and then, " That's so ! that's right, we
knew you would take a proper view of it ! " . . .

When the substitute was ready to leave
for the front, he came to say goodbye, " a
little the worse for wear," and assured Joe
with a beaming smile, " Kurnel, you're a
noble man, and I'll exhonorate your name ! "

A. H. W. to H. G.
BRATTLEBORO, September.

We have had our first letters from the girls
at Point Lookout, and everything promises
pleasantly. The only grievance is the chaplain,
whose face is "as hard as a wooden chair," and
who looks as if he had fought through life, inch
by inch. He is fanatically Episcopal, though
his sermons were practical and good, and he
has the melodeon (paid for by general subscrip-
tion) picked up and carried off and locked in
his own room after every Sunday service, that it
may not be used at the Methodist prayer meetings which the men choose to have ! Georgy
says they have grand good singing, whether or
no, without it. . . . There is a little of almost
every phase of the war there, except the actual
fighting. They have the prisoner's camp, the
New Hampshire brigade to guard it, with their
splendid drill, dress parades, officers' wives,
hops, etc. There are the hospitals for each, the

General Hospital, and lastly the large Contraband camp. Jane's first letter was long and interesting, as she was much at leisure, but we do not expect to hear at great length hereafter. . . . Charley, always at Headquarters Army of the Potomac, writes us to-night that they have sent off two corps to West Tennessee, and that he thinks the ultimate use of the balance will be within the defences of Washington. Is not Rosecrans' crushing defeat a sad blow? . . .

J. S. W. to J. H.
POINT LOOKOUT HOSPITAL,
September.

Eliza's help and all her little nice things were, and are, invaluable to us. . . . Things promise pretty fair here in every respect. The surgeon in charge is civil and ready to support us in everything necessary. The post is a queer one, hospital, military encampment, Contraband camp, rebel camp, Roman Catholic element and divided jurisdiction of Mrs. Gibbons and Miss Dix. Quite a mixture. We shall be involved in no gossip or small quarrels, but do our work as we find occasion, without partiality and without hypocrisy. . . . John, our man servant, is a nuisance. He interferes right and left, upsets everybody in a mistaken idea to serve *us*, and volunteers his views on all subjects. He would be in the guard-house in a week if he didn't go home to-night. . . .

Women were only recognized, in connection with the *regular army* service, as washerwomen, and were so entered on the payrolls, and detailed to the nursing department when needed. As Point Lookout was a regular army hospital, we were obliged by army regulations to be mustered in, and paid $12.00 a month. But we were hardly well established and in good working condition, when the following general orders were received and issued by the Surgeon-in-charge. The Point became a camp for rebel prisoners, and our connection with it ceased.

SURGEON-GENERAL'S OFFICE,
WASHINGTON, Sept. 26th.

Surgeon Heger, U. S. A. Sir : The Secretary of War has directed the transfer of seven hundred wounded *prisoners* from Chester, Pa., to Point Lookout General Hospital. . . .

Upon their arrival you will discharge the female nurses (both of Miss Dix's and Mrs. Gibbons' selection) reserving only one suitable person in low-diet kitchen and one in linen room. By order,

C. H. CRANE, Surg. U. S. A.

POINT LOOKOUT, MD., Oct. 7th, 1863.

Special Order No. 123 :

The female nurses will be relieved from wards 6, 7, 8, 9, 10, 11 and 14, and they are strictly enjoined to abstain from any intercourse with the Prisoners of War.

A. HEGER, U. S. A.

Circular, No. 17.

POINT LOOKOUT, Oct. 7, '63.

Miss G. Woolsey: In accordance with instructions received from the Surgeon-General's Office, dated October 7th, 1863, the discharge of the female nurses on the 5th inst. refers only to their discharge from the *Hospital*, not from the service at large. . . . Enclosed please find certificates of pay.

By order of the Surgeon-in-Charge.

W. H. G., Assist. Surgeon.

A. Heger, Surgeon-in-Charge Hammond General Hospital: Sir :

I have the honor to enclose four duplicate certificates of pay, for myself and my sister, Miss Jane S. Woolsey. Will you be kind enough to make use of them for the benefit of the hospital fund ?

G. M. WOOLSEY.

POINT LOOKOUT, MD., Oct. 7, 1863.

Madam : The transfer of the certificates of pay of yourself and sister to this Hospital is received, and in the name of those poor soldiers who shall enjoy the benefits of your gift, I tender you many thanks for it.

Very respectfully,
Your obedient servant,
A. HEGER.

On our retreat from Point Lookout, via Washington, it was suggested to Mrs. Gibbons, who was with Jane and me at the Ebbitt House, that there was work to be done at the large barrack hospital established on the Fairfax Theological Seminary grounds near Alexandria; and through Mrs. Gibbons an introduction was secured for us to the surgeon, Dr. David P. Smith, who called to talk matters over with us. We followed up the conversation with an inspection of the hospital, and were put through a catechism by Dr. Smith as to what we thought we could do, if we came and took charge. The result was that he told us he should like us to try it, and we moved over the river and were installed as Superintendents of nursing, and quartered in the house of the Chaplain and his wife. Here Jane

[marginal note: Fairfax Seminary Hospital]

and I found ourselves in absolute control of
our own department, and most cordially sustained by the surgeon-in-charge. An office
was assigned to us in the Seminary building,
where there was room enough for barrels
and boxes of stores, a long table for office
work, and a huge open fire-place where we
kept a blazing wood fire, tempering it with a
wide open window towards the hills and
the distant view of the dome of the Capitol.
The hospital filled up rapidly and supplies
from home began to arrive.

J. S. W. to A. H. W.

FAIRFAX SEMINARY, VIRGINIA,
MONDAY NIGHT.

Please present my grateful acknowledg-
ments to the Society for the barrel of shirts, etc.,
received Saturday P. M.   They are always very
valuable.   Cases come up every day for such
charities.   Last night, for instance, a modest
note was handed in at my door, signed Crawford, saying, "I am discharged for disability
and am going a day's journey home in the morning. I have no means of procuring clothes
and must leave the hospital clothes behind me;
could you let me have a shirt?"   Another man
brought the note while "Crawford" waited at
the foot of the stairs.   I asked if he could come

up. "Yes," the friend answered; "he ain't lame." So he came up to the door. It appears he was very modest; a tall, gaunt, bright-eyed man, not old, but with greyish hair. His left arm hung at his side,—elbow shattered and three-fourths of his hand cut out,—frightful looking; health broken, means of support all gone, but as cheery as possible. He got his shirt and a pair of socks besides, for which he was modestly thankful. Another man with one leg, got one, and a broken-down rheumatic at the High School another. . . . I shall give the woolen shirts to discharged-for-disability men, and poor men with large families. There was one such case I had almost forgotten—a drafted man, of the draft before the last—who has not been assigned to any regiment and can draw no pay or clothes. He got no bounty and came out, leaving seven children behind him. The chaplain knows his story and says he has done his duty bravely and cheerfully. . . . So *he* got a shirt. . . .

We are slowly working up new diet-tables.

J. S. W. to J. H.

FAIRFAX HOSPITAL.

We are trying to get the regimental hospitals in the neighborhood—poor places at best—emptied into this or some other General Hospital. There is a great deal of bad sickness among the new recruits. Six men have died of typhoid malaria this last week in the 2d Connecticut Artillery, near here—new men all but one, but good healthy, decent, Litchfield County men. Some of the hospitals in Alexandria are to be broken up and the sick will probably be sent in to us. We hear more of the army via New York than in any other way. We had pressing invitations! to the Great Ball, to join a party in a special car and all that, which we think we see ourselves!

The country, the air and the weather are as sweet as sweet can be, with a sort of barren sweetness. You know what the country is. From our uncurtained windows' height we see the shining river and the bluish-purplish fields and shores and the trees still left standing, with the sort of look of spring, 'not now but presently,' in them.

I hope your lame leg has forgotten its bruises by this time, and you won't have to apply to Palmer. Three Palmer legs go up and down stairs daily under our ears, and do wonderfully well. The legs are heroic ; the men are not— being addicted to poor whiskey and indifferent witticisms. . . .

Your cheese is lovely and has already gladdened the stomachs of fifty braves. Eliza's rugs are very uncommonly nice and useful. They are the only vestige of carpet we have.

E's jelly is famous. It rejoices the heart of poor Clymer, a man with half his face torn away by a shell, one eye gone. He can only eat soft things, and thought "if he had some acid jelly it would taste first-rate." . . . Nothing we have to distribute can possibly go astray or be stolen.

I'll remember that G. owes $11.00 for a chair, which came safely. The man it was meant for, first, died last night, after a wonderful fight for his life.

Our Surgeon in charge at Fairfax, Dr. David P. Smith, had a lurking distrust of his "contract surgeons" and implicit confidence in his two women Superintendents, and the most friendly relations with them. I remember a "general order" which came to me one morning from his office: "The Surgeon in charge requests that his aide, Miss G. Woolsey, will report to him any case of smallpox she may find in the wards in her rounds;" and daily bulletins, such as the following, came to our office door:

My dear Miss Woolsey :

3 P. M.

I don't just see the force of your requisition for hatchets, unless it be to endeavor to let a little common and uncommon sense into the brains of "them officers?" . . .

I send up my General Orders for your edification.

Mayn't I take my coffee with you this evening?
Very respectfully.

G. to A. H. W.
FAIRFAX HOSPITAL.

To-day (Monday) the Pierson box has arrived. . . . I gave Nurse —— one of the two little brooms in it, with an exhortation to have a man detailed to attend to the little tables by each bed, and to brush them off with the nice new brush, every day. So that if the frantic little tables in Ward G improve, and banish their bits of bread-crumbs, dirty newspapers and stale tobacco scraps, it will be entirely owing to Mr. Pierson's broom.

Mr. Prentiss' note (with the extract from the *North American* about the Gettysburg tract) is amusing. However, I don't equal the celebrity of "A Rainy Day in Camp." Miss Dix has a standing *mis*understanding with the Surgeon in charge; in short, she hates him. He is a genius, a remarkable man in his profession. Miss Dix writes him a highly dignified note assuming command of him and his, and then, either to show her willingness to labor for him as a human being, or else to intimate that she considers him a fit subject for "tracts," she encloses

"A Rainy Day in Camp." He told us of it!
We told *him* nothing! We never let on!

Tell Mary that when *I* am used to box the
ears of refractory surgeons, she may look upon
me as an equal.

Chaplain Hopkins, whom E. and G. left
two years before at his work in the Alexandria Hospitals, still toiled on with the
utmost faithfulness, and now and then when
a half hour of leisure came, galloped his
pony out to the Seminary, and by our bright
fireside made a link for us to home and civilization. He brought us good cheer, and
we shared our supplies with him.

He was our most willing agent, shopping
for us in Alexandria and Washington when--
ever we needed extras for our hospital, and
we needed them in considerable variety and
quantity. From a large package of hastily
scribbled notes sent in to the Chaplain's hospital from our's, and full of commissions,
these few will show what demands we made
on our comrade in the service.

Dear Harry.

Don't forget to get me the boards for filing
away all the hospital accounts, double, with
elastic straps. The Surgeon in charge has, in

the handsomest way, laid the hospital at our feet, and implored us to buy every thing, including the kerosene oil, and to keep all the accounts *strictly*, and save him all trouble. So send out some boards to keep the nasty accounts straight with. Also send me some note paper.   G.

To the Same.

Will you be kind enough to ask at some beer shop, if you don't mind going to such places, what the price of porter is by the cask? I don't mean bottled stuff, but a cask full of the unpleasant thing, and whether they can get me some in a day or two. I don't want to ask the Sanitary Commission for any more, as they have sent me five casks already; and besides they are having a "convocation of women." Fifty delegates from the sewing circles, East and West, have assembled to talk it all over, and shake hands, saying "Courage my sister," or (which is quite as likely) to make faces across the table from East to West. Send me word about the something to drink as soon as you can.   G.

To the Same.

If you have time, will you send me by the ambulance a box of brandy? We are ordered to receive 275 patients to-night from the A. P.

G.

Chaplain Hopkins to G. M. W.

ALEXANDRIA, FRIDAY MORNING.

Dear Georgy :—I take you at your word and send for the chairs and crutches. Nothing ever sent to the hospital did half the good that those two dozen chairs have done, which you and your Mother gave us more than a year ago. These go to Fairfax Street and Wolfe Street. . . . With a good morning to Jane. In haste, Yours,

HARRY.

Rev. Henry Hopkins writes to me now, 36 years later, from his post, at the head of important religious operations in Kansas City:

No picture from any scene of my life is more vivid in my recollection than that of Jane, of beloved memory, as I saw her sometimes at Fairfax—her illuminated face with the wonderful eyes, and the wonderful smile, her fragile form wrapped in the ermine-lined cloak she used to wear. Do you remember the night when a sudden snow storm in the evening prevented my return to the city, and I slept on the floor in your office with your two ermine cloaks [they were rabbit, but never mind] for a covering—after the sentinel and I, making a chair of our hands, had carried you two through the deep snow to your house? And the afternoon, just before I left Alexandria for the field, when we three sat on the grassy slope south of the buildings, and you two gave me your blessing as I went to try the new scenes?

The further history of life at Fairfax, is beautifully given by your Aunt Jane in her pamphlet, printed for her own family, and called "Hospital Days." You have it. She remained in charge at this hospital till the close of the war.

Charley was in camp near enough to the hospital for us to get an occasional note on a mutilated scrap of paper, and to allow of mutual aid in emergencies, should they occur.

One morning in November, 1863, the poor boy hobbled into our office crippled, and suffering severely with inflammatory rheumatism. We tucked him up for the night by our bright fire, and next day I took him home to New York, where he was nursed by Mother back into what *he* considered good condition, and left for the field again, only half fit for it, as *we* knew.

That rheumatism has never left him.

Gentlemen's sons in those days left the soft beds and luxurious surroundings of their own homes, and went cheerfully out to lie down in mud puddles, to crawl at night under gun-carriages, or to spread their blankets under the sky in pouring rains, for such sleep as they could catch.

H. R. W. to Jane and G.

NEW YORK, Dec. 2, '63.

Dear Girls :—Charley's rheumatism is better and yesterday he walked without his cane. When he gets on the doe-skins (the triumphs of art that Mother is now at work upon) and his india-rubber knee-cap, I think he will be all right. At any rate, well or not, I suppose it is better for him to go to Washington, for he worries, now that the army is moving and he not with it, and his leave expired. . . . He is pounding away at a new camp-bed he is making. . . . I consider him a fit subject for the hospital, and to be doctored accordingly. . . . Our Church Sewing Society for the army had its first regular meeting yesterday. Abby is treasurer, and Mother, having been put into the president's chair, got out again, not liking the conspicuousness, and was immediately pounced upon for the purchasing committee.

E. W. H. writes:—Charley is doing up all his errands (very fatiguingly) and announces

his intention of going back, leg or no leg. . . .
We are waiting very anxiously now for every
mail and the news from Grant and Burnside—
and if Meade is also fighting, as last night's
Post thinks, it would seem that the great crisis
has really come.

I go to cut out army shirts.

There had been some heavy cavalry fighting along the Rappahannock about Nov. 7th,
and again on the 26th, and the rebels had
been driven and 2,000 prisoners taken, but
there was no following up of the victory.
Charley, happily for us, was at home then
and out of the horror of war ; but at the front
again, soon.

C. W. W. to J. S. W. at Fairfax Hospital.

GENERAL MEADE'S CAMP,
NEAR BRANDY STA., Dec. 7th, '63.

C. W. W.
back in
Camp
again.

Dear Jane :—The train which left at 11 yesterday morning brought me through all right
last night, by dark. A telegram from General
Williams, sent to the conductor and meeting me
on the train, said, in reply to one from me, that
the ambulance would meet me at Brandy Station.
The conductor had had some difficulty in finding me on the long train, but at the railroad
bridge I heard " Woolsey " yelled at the door

instead of "Rappahannock Station,"—which proved successful. I find that no movement of importance is on foot, and winter quarters somewhere (not here) confidently looked for this time. I hear a great deal said in justification of General Meade's retrograde movement. The War Department is entirely responsible for the failure of the last campaign,—having ordered it, but not allowing General Meade to attack in his own way. We might have had a great battle and carried the rebel position with very great loss, but nothing but the position would have been gained. The rebels behind their strong works could have been very little damaged and would have had only to fall back, if we had assaulted.

We are camped in the woods near John M. Botts' house, and are in this way shielded from the winds. There is no news.

FOURTH YEAR OF THE WAR

1864

CHAPTER XIII.

By 1864, operations against Richmond hav- General Grant in command. ing been practical failures, a general feeling of distrust as to the officers in command prevailed, and the necessity for a reorganization was apparent. General Grant's splendid victories at the West had given the deathblow to the rebellion along the Mississippi, and public opinion selected him for supreme control of the National Army. He was called to that position, and established his headquarters with the Army of the Potomac, in the field, issuing his first General Order March 16, 1864.

Work for the soldiers was still going on The Sanitary Commission Fair. all over the land, and in the spring of this year all New York was given over, body and soul, to the raising of money for the Sanitary Commission through a monster Fair.

Home letters sent to Jane and G. at the Fairfax Hospital were full of it, and it helped as a distraction for thoughts which otherwise would have been gloomy and anxious.

Mother to Jane and G.

8 BREVOORT PLACE, March 9, 1864.

My dear Girls: We are all sitting together at the round table, Abby looking over the old letters from Point Lookout, and reading an incident occasionally aloud ; Carry composing an address on her Bloomingdale orphans for their May anniversary. It is too amusing to have Caroline Murray and all those old lady-managers deferring to our Carry on all subjects connected with the asylum. . . . Mary is very much engaged in her arrangements for the floral department at the Fair, and very much interested in it. All the ladies are agog for novelties. They will be charmed with an occasional communication from the Hospital at Fairfax ! We are to have a daily paper too, which is to beat the " Drum Beat"—" The Fair Champion." Do send in poetry and prose and as many incidents as you can; get your doctor and the soldiers to send me an article for it, or letters for the Post Office. Send whatever you have to *me*, that I may have the pleasure of handing it to the committee on *literature!* Abby says, " Georgy, may I write out the German soldier-boy's dream, or any other extract from your old letters that is not too stale?" I am sure you will say yes. Abby is getting quite warmed up about the Fair; it is difficult not to feel so when everybody else is full of excitement about it. She is making a beautiful silk flag, a dozen or two of the new style of tidy-covers of muslin or embroidery edged with lace, beside lots of other little matters. Mary's idea of having garden hats of white straw, with broad ribbons, and their ends painted in flowers, is a pretty one, to be hung in her arbor of flowers. She is also painting a lot of little wooden articles. Every thing of hers is to be of the garden style. We find a use now for all our old flower baskets, rustic stands, etc., and a huge pile of them now stands ready to be carried to the flower department. My chair, the cover for which I was obliged to give up working, is under way, also three silk comfortables, all spandy new, none of your old gowns, lined with silk and beautifully quilted in scrolls and medallions by a Fishkill woman, and trimmed with ribbon quillings; also one dozen ladies' dressing-sacks of various styles; also, one India satin sofa cushion, one embroidered worsted do., four elegant toilette cushions, one doll's complete street dress, (even to an embroidered pocket-handkerchief), one doll's stuffed chair, and other articles "too tedious to mention," are all under way. I dare say we shall all do our full part, both in making and purchasing.

Mrs. Chauncey has already sold her baby-house, Sarah Coit tells me, for five hundred dollars! Kate Hunt has received her Parisian purchases for the Fair, for which she expects to realize a very large amount; says she is furnishing things to the amount of a thousand dollars! Eliza is coming down to-morrow. . . .

H. R. W. to J. and G.

FISHKILL, SUNDAY.

My Dears: We came up here last Thursday, and you may imagine it was somewhat of a relief to get Mother away from the everlasting Fair business that, for the last few weeks, has completely run her off her feet. . . .

New York is really in a disgusting state of fashionable excitement; nothing is talked of, or thought of, or dreamed of, but the big Metropolitan Fair! Mrs. Parker has her thousand dollar tea-sets to dispose of; Kate Hunt, her two hundred dollar curtains; Mrs. Schermerhorn, her elegant watches; and Mrs. Somebody-else, the beautiful jewelry sent from Rome for the Sanitary Commission. . . .

Mary, and Edward Potter have been very busy with their floral department, and Mary has made some "sweet" things, one very pretty garden hat, a pure white straw with wide white ribbon streamers and a bunch of large pansies painted on the end of each, exquisitely painted, and to bring in thirty dollars or more. . . .

All the committees are at swords' points, of course; the Restaurant ladies wish flowers in their department, to which Mrs. George Betts, chairwoman of the Floral Committee, says "as sure as they do, I will have oysters on the shell in mine, and call them seaweeds." . . .

A. H. W. to Jane and G.

WEDNESDAY, March 30th.

I came from Fishkill yesterday afternoon with a trunk full of finished elegancies for the Fair. . .

They have put up a tremendous and expensive building in 17th Street, reaching from Broadway to Fourth Avenue, which we saw yesterday for the first time. It is a long barrack, with the end buildings one story higher, truss roof, huge oriel windows, and fine planed plank throughout. This is supplementary to the other structures on 14th Street. . . .

"Taps," Mary's army poem, is really coming to something. Robert sends word that he has an appointment this afternoon to go to see about the illustrations for it with Mr. Potter. If it isn't ready for the *first day* of the Fair, it will still be in time. A discharged one-armed soldier, James Nichols, 5th N. H., has offered himself very promptly, as salesman. . . .

E. W. H. to G. M. W.

FISHKILL, April 26.

I am thankful the Fair is over, particularly on Mother's account, for she used herself up completely day by day, and would have given out entirely if it had lasted another week. Abby and Mary and in fact everyone who has had anything to do with it, is tired out, and there are still the auctions to arrange for and attend, and I have no doubt our whole family will help in them.

I wish we could have brought Mother again to the country, for it is delicious here and the spring is opening beautifully. Is there nothing you want in the way of wines and brandies, etc., in view of the coming campaign? There must be, and *we* wish to send it.

A. H. W. to Jane.

8 BREVOORT PLACE. SUNDAY.

A Characteristic Scene at Home and its sequel.

We three girls had a glorious time on Thursday afternoon, at a banquet given to William Wheeler's Battery. We came away enthusiastic in our admiration for him. Imagine this handsome, manly, gallant officer, loved by the men, cheered uproariously by them at intervals of five minutes all the afternoon, and *à propos* of nothing,—"Three cheers for Cap'n Will Wheeler." He is as free with them in the German language as in English. There was also a distribution of beautiful bouquets which the Wheelers had been busy tying up all the morning, 60 or 70—one for each man.

The Battery has re-enlisted for the war; their 30 days' furlough is up, and they go back to Tennessee. . . .

Old Mr. Boorman, the Wheelers' uncle, made a speech *that* afternoon—feeble and pale and broken as he is. He told the men he " remembered the Captain as a baby, he remembered the Captain's *Mother* as a baby, and he remembered the Captain's *Grandmother* as the prettiest little girl they ever saw. She is not on earth now, I shall go to her soon, and—boys, if any of you ever desert that flag, I'll send Grandmother to haunt you all the days of your life!"

The Captain never came home. So many captains never came home. By August he had been killed, while his brother John, hungry and bare-foot, was a prisoner at Macon. Abby says, "how characteristic the history of these two young men is of the spirit of the times, and the conduct of the war."

At midnight, May 3d, '64, the Army of the Potomac crossed the Rapidan, and Grant's campaign against Richmond began. Charley as usual served as aide on the personal

Battles of the Wilderness.

Charley with Grant.

staff of the commanding General, through the frightful battles of the Wilderness, Spottsylvania, Cold Harbor, and all that they involved. Fortunately, a few of his hurried notes to Mother, written on the field to quiet her fears, had been copied to send to friends, the originals (afterwards burned) being too valuable to risk in the mails. The first day's fight, of the twelve continuous ones in the Wilderness, was over, and at midnight, tired enough, no doubt, he writes :

C. C. W. to Mother.

FIVE MILES SOUTH OF GERMANNIA FORD,
May 5th, 11.30 P. M., 1864.

Dear Mother : To-day we have had probably the hardest fight of this campaign. The battle was principally fought after 4 P. M., (our troops attacking,) and raged until dark. Our losses have been great, for the fighting on both sides was desperate, but all goes well and Generals Grant and Meade are in good spirits and confident of completely finishing up the thing this time. The ground is the very worst kind for fighting, a perfect wilderness of dense forests and underbrush, where you would suppose it impossible for anything to get through. Hence there has been no opportunity for the use of artillery, the infantry has done it all.

The cavalry also has been successful on the left flank, driving the enemy splendidly.

A despatch I took to General Meade from Sheridan about 4.30 this P. M. pleased him greatly, " The cavalry bricks are driving them ; three cheers for the cavalry," he said. The lay of the land and the underbrush render it entirely unnecessary that the army headquarters A. D. C.'s should be up with the troops on the actual line of battle, and on this account scarcely any of us have been under fire. We communicate chiefly, you know, with the Corps headquarters, which are always in the rear. We have been going about all day, but shall have a good rest to-night, grateful to many a tired fellow. Of all the movements, of course, I can tell you nothing now. With Burnside and part of the Sixth Corps we shall have from 35,000 to 40,000 fresh troops to-morrow. Everything is working well, but it is a matter of great regret to Meade's "company," his A. D. C.'s, that we have seen, and can see, so little of the front. Carry's note reached me this morning, when the musketry was very loud. Hooray for the American Eagle ! With much love to all.

Aff'ly, dear Mother,

C. W. W.

Five Miles South of the Ford,
Friday, May 6, 1864, 5 a. m.

No mails go out, but I shall write each day. I wrote yesterday, but it could not go. The infantry has begun again with light. Burnside will go in to-day. We are sure of the best result with all these fresh men. Everything is going well.

May 7th, 3 p. m.

This goes by a special messenger, and I cannot tell you more than that everything is going well, and that I am all right. The enemy has fallen back and the prospect is very cheering. The roads and thick underbrush are such that the corps headquarters with which we aides communicate must be farther to the rear from the line of battle than under ordinary circumstances, and on this account we can see but little of the fighting in the front.

May 7th, Saturday, p. m.

All right along the lines, and with

Yours aff'ly.

Spottsylvania C. H., May 8th, p. m.

The infantry fighting is over, for some time probably. We are apparently pushing hard for Richmond, and all goes well. Don't have any fears for my safety, for I have not yet been to the extreme front. No Headquarters' aides are sent, and no mishaps as yet. This goes via train of wounded to Fredericksburg.

Aff'ly,   C. W. W.

A. H. W. to Rev. Dr. Prentiss.

8 BREVOORT PLACE, THURSDAY, May 12.

My dear Mr. Prentiss : The mail that has come through from the army has brought us, just now, a note from Charley, dated Tuesday, 10th, written, of course, before that horrible conflict began again Tuesday evening. How thankful we are—to hear so promptly—when so many are in suspense or grief. Here it is :

NEAR SPOTTSYLVANIA C. H., May 10th.

To-day for the first time we are going to send a mail through if possible, via Fredericksburg. You have no doubt received some, if not all, the notes I have sent you, and the papers have given you an account of our successful advance. It is by no means probable that we could have got to Richmond without hard fighting. This we have had, but we have beaten the enemy back in each instance, and his army is very much cut up. Our own is rested and in good spirits and admirably disposed. There is no enemy on our right, and the cavalry are probably doing great damage to their railroad communication. The rebel cavalry have been plucky, but have invariably been driven with loss. You may expect to hear of the destruction of the rebel army very soon. Our scouts do good service and information has come in from the rebs which is very cheering. The weather has been delightful, except at times too hot for the infantry. With love to all,

C. W. W.

Another note says—on Monday:

" Our losses have been large, in all the battles, but not extraordinarily so. The fighting has usually been only part of a day, and still through the thickest underbrush. We lose a great deal in General Sedgwick's death, but Wright is an able soldier."

C. W. W. (Copy.)

In Front of Spottsylvania.
Wednesday, May 11th,

Dear Mother :—I have written you up to yesterday A. M. Last night at 5 there was to have been a general attack along our lines, but the report came in that the enemy was massing on our right and trying to turn it, and the attack was suspended. A sharp fight however took place before dark, when Upton distinguished himself, taking 1,200 prisoners and driving the enemy from a breastwork five feet high. There is now better opportunity for the use of our artillery and the batteries were firing sharply up to dark. As we cannot see the enemy's line, all this counts for but little, and is successful only as *demonstration.*

Burnside was engaged yesterday, during the day, but we could not hear his musketry—his guns we heard distinctly toward dark, coming from the enemy's rear, almost, Burnside having got well round on their right flank. General Meade, I think, does not consider it at all probable that the rebels would try to turn our right. To me, it seems the absurdest thing possible. The enemy to do it must withdraw troops from his right or centre, weakening his line too much, when ours is so long and so strong on our left.

Yesterday P. M. I took to General Meade the rumor that we had possession of Petersburgh, &c., &c. This was at once published to the troops, but cheering was strictly prohibited, as this would discover to the enemy our position. Since yesterday A. M. our right and left have advanced.

Our headquarters' staff are all right. General Grant camps near us and is on the field with us. He says very little and smokes a great deal.

Everything is quiet this (Wednesday) morning, except the skirmishers, and it is rumored that the enemy is falling back. All is going well.

Don't say "why don't they push into Richmond."

Wait and see !

I do not think I have said anything contraband. Very aff'ly yours,

C. W. Woolsey.

Mother to J. and G. at Fairfax.

NEW YORK, THURSDAY, May 12th.

What awful carnage is going on from day to day, and what an immense amount of suffering, in the heaps of wretched wounded men. I am glad so many of our surgeons have gone on, but what are a dozen of them among thousands of sufferers? I do not believe they have anything like half enough for the demand. I wish *I* were a man! I would be there to do my little all, and I think I could beat some of those old fogies in dressing wounds, if not in sawing off limbs! Dr. Buck went on Monday to Fredericksburg [which on May 9th part of our army under Burnside occupied as an hospital].

We have more pencil notes from Charley—up to Tuesday 10th; after this the great battles of that day came off. All was well up to that time. I enclose copies of his notes. What terrific fighting there has been! and oh! the dead, the dead, the maimed, and worse than dead! and the desolate homes throughout the land. Peace and freedom dearly bought—if indeed we get them in the end,—which is not yet. . . . Mary is making her arrangements for the country, and a little previous visit to Eliza for a few days; was to have gone to day to Fishkill, but one of her headaches has put a stop to it. She came over yesterday and drove us to the park.

It is perfectly beautiful there, and so filled with gay vehicles of every description, and happy faces, you would not dream of war and bloodshed in the land. So goes the world, and *we* a part of it. A telegram from Charley just arrived dated 8th—older than his notes; could not be sent I suppose. We are very fortunate in hearing from him so often in such a state of things; he is very attentive about writing to us under all circumstances. . . . The big box stands ready for your duds; if there is anything else you need, say so *at once*, "or forever after," etc., etc.

C. W. W. to Mother (Copy).

HEADQUARTERS, A. P.
FRIDAY, May 13, '64.

Dear Mother :—The enemy has been badly whipped and has fallen back again. We still have communication with Washington through Fredericksburg, but this is not intended to be our base, we only make a convenience of it for the wounded and for some supplies. Hancock and Wright and Burnside report the enemy as having withdrawn, maintaining though, a thin line in front of Burnside. Hancock's attack was by far the most brilliant thing so far, in this campaign. We have certainly 35 guns and a great many prisoners.

General Ned Johnson* was at our camp all this morning. It was he who nearly turned our right at Germania Ford.

General Stuart [Johnson's associate] refused to shake hands with General Hancock and was made to walk to the rear with his men.

We shall probably be cut off from any communication with Washington in a day or two, but I will scratch a few lines whenever I can.

G. M. W. at Fredericksburg. It was an understood thing with the Sanitary Commission and myself (G.) that I was to be called on at any time for hospital service at the front ; and immediately after these late battles (May 12th) the summons came— a courier arriving at the Fairfax Seminary Hospital to summon me. I left at once via boat down the Potomac for Fredericksburg.

A. H. W. to H. Gilman.

NEW YORK, May 16.

Mrs. Gibbons called here Saturday afternoon to let us know that she was going to the front. But we couldn't tell what to send by her to Georgy, and the trunk with G.'s boots, gloves and thin clothing had already started by express. Mother gave Mrs. G. some money to do army

---

* The rebel general, taken prisoner with his entire force by bayonet charge under Hancock, in the fog, May 12.

shopping with on her way up town—some *good tea* for G. and herself for one thing—and then we collected a quantity of old linen, towels, mosquito-bar, etc., whatever we had in the house, and took them up to Mrs. Gibbons.

Some of us went to General Rice's funeral at Dr. Adams' church yesterday afternoon. Mr. Prentiss was to assist Dr. Adams. The church was jammed to suffocation.

General Rice was a very devout as well as a gallant man. Just as the army marched, he had written to Dr. A. and enclosed him a manuscript tract of his, a little story of his own soldiers— the "Dying Sergeant," which will be published by the Tract Society.

The General's aide—Lieutenant Bush, a young fellow of 17—brought the body on, packed in ice, for he said they found many Virginia mansions with *ice-houses* well stocked, near the field, and everything was seized of course for the hospitals. There was an abundance of it. Dr. Adams asked Lieutenant B. how they all felt— in the fight. "Feel," he said, "why we are *worn out*, we couldn't feel—we couldn't eat—we did what we were told to do, mechanically."

A. H. W. to H. G.

BREVOORT PLACE, May 17th.

We all had a very solemn week, last week; people felt that it was no time for shouting or flag waving, it was all too tremendous, too serious for that. They count up now our loss and our advance—more than a thousand men to every mile, probably, and feel that it is going to cost us very dear yet to conquer Lee or reach Richmond. Our personal anxieties were soon relieved by daily letters, or rather pencilled scraps, from Charley, which were always confident and hopeful about our movements, reflecting the tone of Army Headquarters. . . .

Charley, in his last note, says that Fredericksburg is not their real base—was only used as convenient for shipping the wounded, and that they will soon cut loose again from communication with Washington. Where they are going to swing to we do not know. . . .

You will have seen from the Times or Tribune that Georgy is at Belle Plain. She went off very suddenly last Thursday, through the "open door," she always sees,—the Sanitary Commission sending a courier out to the Hospital for her ; and to-day we had a letter from her. On board the boat going down was " C. A. P.," Mr. Page, the Tribune reporter, a gentlemanly nice young fellow, the one who told the pretty little story of the wounded boy crawling about on the battlefield with his hands full of violets. So Georgy made friends with him, sent a note to Charley by him, and got him to promise he would sometimes say in his letters to the Tribune that the staff were all well.

He grants her request this morning, or *some* letter-writer does, by a publicity which neither she nor Charley will relish. . . .

Mother is well and weak by turns. She drives about the house faster than ever, to forget thought now. . . .

Mrs. Gibbons and Sally have gone from here, and Georgy will be with them when they reach Belle Plain; also with Mrs. John Barlow, who is active and first-rate, I believe. Her husband, General B., was carried about all summer at Brattleboro on a stretcher, after Gettysburg, but is now in the thick of the fight again. . . .

G. M. W. to J. S. W.

BELLE PLAIN ON THE POTOMAC,
May 13, '64.

Dear Jane: On the Sanitary Commission boat, pulling up to the shore the Government flat-boat of horses and cavalry recruits. There are no docks and the supplies are landed by pontoons—a constant stream of contrabands passing with bags of grain and barrels of pork on their shoulders. Drs. Agnew and Douglas and Cuyler are here. We have a feeding station on shore, and another two miles away, where ambulance-trains halt sometimes for hours. The mud is frightful and the rain coming on.

G. M. W. reports from the Front.

We are to take the returning ambulance-train
for Fredericksburg. . . .

Just as I finished, the train of ambulances
arrived *from* Fredericksburg. Nothing I have
ever seen equals the condition of these men;
they have been two or three days in the train,
and no food. We have been at work with them
from morning till night without ceasing, filling
one boat, feeding the men, filling another and
feeding them. There's no sort of use in trying
to tell you the story. I can scarcely bear to
think of it.

All the "Invalid Corps" from our Hospital,
who marched off that day, are down here guarding prisoners, Generals Stuart and Bradley
Johnson among them. The wounded arrive in
ambulances, one train a day, but the trains are
miles long, plunged in quagmires, jolted over
corduroys, without food, fainting, filthy, fright-
fully wounded; arms gone to the shoulder,
horrible wounds in face and head. I would
rather a thousand times have a friend killed on
the field than suffer in this way; it is worse than
White House, Harrison's, or Gettysburg. We
found thirty-five dead in the ambulances yesterday, and five more died on the stretchers while
being put on the boat. Mules, stretchers, army-
wagons, prisoners, dead men and officials all
tumbled and jumbled on the wretched dock,
which falls in every little while and keeps the

ambulances waiting for hours. We fed all the
five boats that got off yesterday. There is no
Government provision for this beyond bread : no
coffee, soup, cups, pails or vessels of any kind
for holding food. The men eat as if they were
starving. We are ordered to Fredericksburg,
where there is more misery than here. . . .

Mr. Andrew Cheesbro, of the Canandaigua
"delegation," who was with Mother and G.
at Gettysburg, and was now again at Belle
Plain, working hard, writes:

WASHINGTON, May 20, 1864.

Dear Miss Woolsey : Thinking you may have
received my spasm of a note, written in a moment of desperation and an exaggerated condition of mules, mule drivers, nigs and other
animals on that horrid pier on the Potomac—it
should be spelt with a b—and that you may
have answered the same, I take the liberty of
saying that I am in Washington and not there,
thank God ! I didn't leave until the last minute
(who ever did?), but I grew seasick and land-
sick till I would have thanked and absolved any
rebel who would have shot me. Then I came
away. The ladies didn't come. . . .

After you were gone on to Fredericksburg,
imagination suggested that a face lying far off
in the crowd was "Charley's;" I hurried to him

through mule heels and the "innumerable cara-
van," but found, when I reached the utmost
stretcher, the resemblance was gone—though the
Captain's name *did* begin with a W. I treated
him to punch for the suggestion. . . .

I hope that in no wounded man you will
find a nearer resemblance than I did. . . .

I hear of you as cooking in the rear of some
hospital. Let me serve you, if I can. . . .

There's no news here. General Wadsworth's
body went off yesterday A. M., under General
Auger's escort to the cars, and five Congressmen
to New York with it. . . .

Mr. Cheesbro's letter directed to Fredericksburg, was long in coming, but finally got
round to G., endorsed in pencil in Charley's
handwriting from the field: "Sent to the
front by mistake, unless, indeed, Miss Woolsey has established a feeding station at Bowling Green, Va."

G. M. W. to Mother.

FREDERICKBURG, SUNDAY, May 15.

Dear Mother : Charley all safe by to-day's
report as enclosed. Mrs. Barlow and I at Fredericksburg—town full of badly wounded, Commission feeding *all the houses*, for men are put
in anywhere, the regular hospitals being full,

and hundreds of poor fellows report to any one, or no one, as the case may be. The stores on both sides of the streets are full—filthy shops, old shoe stores, old blacksmiths' rooms, men lying on the floor without even straw under them, and with their heads on old bits of cast iron. I saw a boy sound asleep on a pile of old iron last night, as we made the rounds late after arriving. This A. M. we started a diet-kitchen, and have fed several hundred in the little rooms and houses about here. The Commission has a large corps of volunteer nurses, men, who go right in and work under the surgeons, and get all the supplies they want from the Commission. Lenox is here ; I saw him in the street while we were at the purveyors this morning, wriggling a great camp stove out of the depot. You will have more good news before this reaches you, of our successes. The wounded men are as happy as possible over it, *some* of them. The road from Belle Plain over here is more abominable than anything you can imagine ; corduroy, and filled with holes and bogs, and the wounded are sent in army wagons over them. We have our hands full here, and I am glad I came. The hospitals are delighted to have ladies come right in and feed the sick ; we can go in any where. From the extreme difficulty in getting supplies, there has been very little food in town. To-day ten great wagons full of stores came for the Sanitary Commission, and really I don't know what the sick would do but for this society. Their nurses and supplies are everywhere. Ammunition was needed for the army two days ago, and was of course sent before all other things, which stopped all other transportation. I have sent a note to Charley to-night by the Tribune reporter, who comes and goes, and brings us all the news. Good night.

G. to Mother.

FREDERICKSBURG, MONDAY, 16th.

Dear Mother : Charley's note was brought to me to-day by Charley Coit. How good it is to get a line the same day on which it is written ! Mr. Clark and all the gentlemen were interested in reading it. I have almost daily communication with Charley, and have sent a note and two messages to-day.

Just as I was going to write, a message came from one of the hospitals to say that my little boy on the floor in the corner wanted me. Such a dear handsome young fellow—*going*, like all the rest. " Where is my lady?" he demanded, " Will she come soon ?" And when I got to him he took hold of my hand tight, saying, " Is this my lady—that's all right then." No straw yet to put the men on. The transportation is dreadful ; all the ammunition, food, and forage for the army, and all the food, clothing and medicines depending upon a line of army-wagons, over a frightful road, after reaching a distant and most inconvenient point on the Potomac. There has been no bread or hard-tack even, for twelve hours in town. We have beef only, and make soup all day long, and farina gruel. The supplies are *expected* to-night; also Sanitary Commission wagons, but none have come, and it is now 11, and we shall have to turn our wits inside out for breakfast. Some hospitals have been provident and have drawn for several days in advance. I think, now that I *do* think of it, that some one said they saw hard-tack going up to the Sixth Corps hospital this evening, so that it may be here in time for to-morrow. The frightful wounds of these men need everything; everything is provided, and nothing, comparatively, *can be got here.* The Sanitary Commission have fifteen wagons going and coming daily, but that is a drop. The Post Quartermaster told me to-day that the supplies had been delayed by the absolute necessity for sending army stores to the front, and if the enemy could only succeed in cutting our wretched line, we should be lost, from starvation. I must go to bed. Please send this note to Jane, I shan't have time, perhaps, to write to-morrow to her. One from her just now, for which thanks. We are required to show reason for being here, or go to the guard house. I have a pass from the

Surgeon-General as "volunteer nurse." . . .
Lenox over at tent to-day ; he has a Baptist
Church for hospital, and the baptistry in the
floor of the pulpit gives him a constant supply
of fresh water.

Two stained and worn little leaves from
Charley's war note-book give the following :

"HEADQUARTERS ARMY OF THE POTOMAC, NEAR
BOWLING GREEN, VA."
May 19, '64.

At 2.05 took dispatch to Tyler to attack enemy
if advancing as reported on our left.

Hancock to move his command at 2 A. M. to-
morrow to Bowling Green.—About 5.30 P. M.
enemy came round on our right, attacking
Tyler with intent to capture our trains. I was
sent to put Tyler's whole division in line of battle under fire. We drove them back, capturing
250."

[Charley adds : We used to say that the left
boot heels of the whole army were worn down,
there was such constant moving by "the left
flank," fighting by day, marching past Richmond
"by the left flank" at night.]

G.'s pencil notes from Fredericksburg were
scratched off when a spare moment came,

which was but seldom, and show by their disconnected sentences that they were written under great pressure.

G. M. W. to J. S. W.

FREDERICKSBURG, May 19.

All right. Hard work, dirt and death everywhere. Mrs. Gibbons arrived last night and she and her daughter are assigned to a fearful place and are working hard.

Men are brought in and stowed away in filthy places called distributing stations. I have good men as assistants, and can have more. We go about and feed them ; I have a room of special cases, besides the station ; three of these died last night. They had been several days on the field after being shot, in and out of the rebels' hands, taken and retaken. The townspeople refuse to sell or give, and we steal everything we can lay our hands on, for the patients ; more straw-stealing, plank-stealing, corn-shuck-stealing ; more grateful, suffering, patient men.

May 22.

No confusion was ever greater. Tent hospitals have been put up, and the surgeons ordered *not to fill them.* Orders came from Washington that the railroad should be repaired, then orders came withdrawing the guard from the road. Medical officers refuse to send wounded over an

unguarded road. Telegram from Washington
that wounded should go by boat. Telegram
back that wounded were already over the pontoons, ready to go by rail if *protected*. Telegram
again that they should go by boat. Trains came
back to boat, river falling. One boat got painfully off ; second boat off ; ambulance trains at
many hospital doors ; got on train and fed some
poor fellows with egg nogg ; moved on with the
slow moving procession ; at every moment a
jolt and a " God have mercy on me," through
the darkness over the pontoons to the *railroad*,
again ! I cooked and served to-day 926 rations
of farina, tea, coffee, and good rich soup, chicken,
turkey, and beef, out of those blessed cans.

The government rations are drawn *this* way :
The contract surgeon in charge of a little shop
or room full of wounded, reports to the surgeon
in charge of a *group* of such ; this officer reports
to the surgeon of division, the surgeon of division to the corps surgeon ; the corps surgeon
draws on the commissary for the number of
rations he needs for the day. It has often been
10 o'clock at night before dinner was ready.

You may easily see how important the *irregu-
lar* supplies of the Sanitary Commission and
other organizations have been.

We are lodged with a fine old lady, mild and
good, in a garden full of roses. We board ourselves. We have crackers, sometimes soft bread,

sometimes beef. Last night we had a slice of ham all round. The town will be deserted in a few days. We are sweeping and cleaning Mrs. ——'s rooms to leave the old lady as well off as we can, for all her slaves have packed their feather-beds and frying-pans, and declare they will go with us.

One bright spot there was in the midst of all this horror.

G. to Mother.

FREDERICKSBURG.

"Augur's reinforcements have passed through ; as the troops went forward they were met by the ambulances from the front full of wounded men, who thrust out their poor hands and waved, and weakly cheered them.

Mrs. ——'s house has a large old-time garden full of roses ; indeed, the whole town is brimming with early flowers. We begged. and received permission to take all we could gather, and filled the baskets and trays and skirts of our gowns with snowballs, lemon-blossoms, and roses, yellow, white and red. The 8th New York Heavy Artillery was in the advancing column. In the headstall of Colonel Porter's horse I fastened a knot of roses, and tossed roses and snowballs over the men. They were delighted. "In *Fredericksburg!*" they said ; "O! give me

Roses at Fredericksburg.

one," " Pray give me one," "I will carry it into the fight for you," and another cheerily, "and I will bring it back again."

Three days afterwards the ambulances came, and in them came some of the same men, shattered, dying, and dead. We went out, but this time it was with pails of soup and milk punch ; one and another recognized us—all were cheery enough. " A different coming back, ma'am," " no roses to-day " ; and one said, pointing over his shoulder, " The Lieutenant is there on the stretcher, and he's brought the flowers back, as he promised." I went to his side, hoping to help a wounded man. The Lieutenant lay dead, with a bunch of roses in the breast of his coat.

Our friend and fellow-worker at Beverly Hospital later, Miss Sever, sent me, a year after, this little allusion to Fredericksburg :

"Levi Thaxter (Celia Thaxter's husband) sat with me a long while the other day, and we talked of you, dear Miss Georgy. He says the most beautiful moment he has ever seen in life was at Fredericksburg, last summer, when you were giving roses to the regiment who were marching to almost certain death, and a soldier stepped from the ranks and seized your hands." . . .

C. C. W. to G. M. W.

Dear G.: If you were not frightened away by the teamsters' reports on Friday, I suppose you are still pursuing your " labors of love " in Fredericksburg. Your old tow-headed friend of the Peninsula is a co-worker; perhaps not equally efficient with yourself, but willing to be obnoxious in any way. . . .

Door-bell—Miss E. M. wants to know if I wrote those everlasting Three Weeks at Gettysburg. Having read them, she cannot stay at home, and would like a little information as to what was needed for a nurse. We have just finished breakfast, and she is the second anxious inquirer this morning. We think of opening a branch office of information and drawing a salary from the Sanitary Commission. This elderly spinster wants to know if she can have a bath daily, and if her night's rest will be interrupted, as her health depends upon those two things. I haven't heard of any bath-tubs, and I believe day and night are all one in Fredericksburg. What it is to be the sister of an authoress! especially one who " has a brother on General Williams' staff ! " I wish we could send both of you something to eat and to wear. . . .

Yesterday (Sunday) we got into our new chapel for the first time—a long, narrow room, lighted from one end, aired in the same way.

Mr. Prentiss could scarcely conceal his delight at being there, and tried to convince us all that it was " built by God, stone on stone," though we saw evident signs of James Renwick, and thought the ventilation was not altogether providential. . . .

Later, A. H. W. writes :

Miss P. has called to get Mother to go on a Literature Committee and collect matter for a book she wants to publish—advertising first the names and residences of the committee, and appealing to mothers and families to forward the dying speeches, messages, battlefield-incidents, etc., of their sons and brothers ! Mother sent her down word that she had a son in the army herself, and that all such matters as " dying words " were too sacred for intrusion. She declined going upon any committee, or appealing to *any* mother for such a purpose. Whereupon Miss P. said she would scratch out those words and modify her purpose, which didn't modify Mother, however.

Now that we are receivers for the North Carolina refugees, every time the door-bell rings Carry says, " Cooking stoves !" or Hatty cries " Bed-ticks ! " but nothing has come, except five dollars through the city post from some gentleman signing himself " Pity." . . .

Mother to Mary and Eliza.

BEFORE "TAPS,"
MONDAY P. M., May 23d.

I have made several attempts to write a line
to you to-day, my dear girls, for I hope Mary is
still at Fishkill, but this has been a day of unusual interruptions, and I have now only a few
minutes and half a sheet, but shall make the
most of it. . . .

Home is our best place, "until these calamities
be overpast," which are now keeping us in a
state of anxiety and uncertainty as to what is
best for us to do.

We have thought perhaps G. may like to
run on for a little rest and refreshment after
Fredericksburg. I wish it may be so that she
and Jane will both come. I send you their letters received to-day. Jane writes "chirkly,"
and seems to require no sympathy or aid; in
fact, she scorns them both. Amongst a host of
others, Lizzie Thompson called to-day. Her
husband is at Dalton as Christian Commission
delegate, aiding the poor men there in every
way; was in the front of the battle there and
saw the whole thing; is very busy and deeply
interested in his work. His letters are charming. Mrs. McKeever was here too, and asked
for you all; asked me to "let her know some
day when I go to see Mary, that she might join
me." . . .

We think of adding " Army Gen'l Directory "
to our door-plate, so many people of all sorts
come to us for information, and for aid in various enterprises. . . .

From C. W. W. at the Front.

May 24th, 1864, 7 A. M.

Dear Mother : All day yesterday we were
marching South by many roads, to the North
Anna ; and towards night Warren, who had
reached an excellent position, was attacked by
the enemy, and for an hour before dark and half
an hour after, there was a heavy artillery fire
and some musketry, which resulted in his favor.
It was a fair stand-up fight, neither side having
any other defence than the lay of the land.
Wright was in Warren's rear, on the same roads,
and is up this A. M., and Hancock farther to the
south and left. Burnside is on the right in het
rear of marching column. The Ninth Corps
marches badly and there has been difficulty
about their trains each day. Headquarters saw
nothing of the fight yesterday, but we are to go
nearer the front to-day. We are over the North
Anna, and shall probably come up with the
enemy in force to-day or to-morrow. The fight
yesterday was by advanced guards of either
army—the enemy hoping to find us in column,
before line of battle could be formed. We are
more than half way to Richmond—last night

camping *just* half way—30 miles, at the house
of a proud old F. F. V., whose sheep and chick-
ens, I regret to say, were paid for.

We have heard from Sheridan to-day : the
staff officer who came through brought word
that he was 35 miles from here, and he will join
us to-night or to-morrow. His command is all
right except for fatigue and hunger, and he will
return from his raid in better condition than
ever before after so long a march. The North
Anna divides our army, but it is an easy stream
to cross, and the rest of the troops can easily be
thrown over, if that is the intention.

The wounded from Warren's fight last night
will be sent to Port Royal, I suppose.

Getting Sheridan back will be a great gain to
us ; two days' rest and recuperation will fit them
for duty and they will be invaluable on our
flanks. They can easily avoid the rebel infantry,
—the confederate cavalry, the prisoners acknowledge, " is about gone up."

12 M.

We have our Headquarters in a roadside
church, Mt. Carmel Church, and General Grant
is in a pew near me, whittling and talking to
General Meade. We are making up a mail, and
I am just in from Burnside in time to put my
letter in.

The weather is very pleasant and the country
beautiful, so different from our winter camps.

I have found the negroes very friendly and useful as guides. Their masters and missuses have, as a general thing, "done gone clar out."

Aff'ly,   C. W. W.

A. H. W. to E.

THURSDAY, May 26th.

Dear Eliza : It is raining so hard that there is little chance of sending to the Post Office, and you will lose the pleasure of getting Charley's letter, in *two days*, from beyond the North Anna. You see it was written at noon on Tuesday, and we had it at 8 this Thursday morning. Carry and Hatty came home late last night from Newark, N. J. A young officer was in the Fourth Avenue car with them who said that he was "just up from the Army of the Potomac by way of Port Royal. Grant was swinging round onto the Peninsula, and White House was again to be the base !"

We have nothing more from Georgy at Fredericksburg. Dr. Buck has got home ; said he couldn't stand the work any longer, he *had* to come away. He was here night before last— it was he who brought G's letter that was left at our door. When he left Fredericksburg things were more comfortable ; straw was beginning to arrive, or hay. He left from 7,000 to 8,000 wounded there, so I don't believe the Times despatch, that "all the wounded had been removed to Washington." If they have been, the Medical Department has murdered a good many in doing it.

By May the 28th, Charley found himself on the old ground again. Gaines Mill, where Joe was wounded two years before, was close by, and each army occupied the position its opponent held during the fight of those seven days in 1862 ;—Lee's men taking their turn in the Chickahominy Swamps now.

Mother to G.

MONDAY EVENING.

My dear Georgy: You don't know how we grab at your letters and how eagerly we read them ; nor do you know how much I long to be down *there* with you. I would give anything to start off to-morrow morning, and take the "new Tent Hospital Kitchen !" or even an "umbler" station. What scenes you are surrounded with, and what an experience you are having ! . . . It is a great pleasure and comfort to me to have you and Charley so near as to keep up almost daily communication. Yours of day before yesterday ! enclosing his little note of same date, reached us this afternoon—only think how quickly they came. I am glad, too, good old Dr. Buck has been with you ; it seems to bring you nearer home. Oh! Georgy, what heart-sickening sufferings our men are subjected too. . . . It is, I suppose, miserable management somewhere. . . .

It was a great day for the Church of the Covenant—the day we assembled in our new room. . . . Mr. Prentiss seemed inspired, and good old Dr. Skinner looked as if he could scarcely refrain from an outburst of applause while Mr. Prentiss was preaching. . . . When you all come home we will have our nice seats there all ready for you. Oh, the happy day when we shall *all* as a family assemble there together once more! . . .

Impress it upon Charley not to expose himself *unnecessarily* to the enemy. Of course he must do as he is ordered, but I know he is anxious to be in the very front. I wonder if he realizes what it would be to be maimed for life with the loss of a leg or an arm, perhaps both! I do not think young men think soberly enough about it. Surely, Charley has seen suffering that might put him on his guard. I tremble for him, and a dread comes over me when I take up a newspaper. We are all well, and shall not go out of town till the army is at rest. A loving kiss to you, my dear child. Take care of yourself for the sake of your loving

MOTHER.

Mother's longing for our meeting as a family once more, was never satisfied. Our dear, beautiful Mary died, May the 31st, in her Astoria home. Rose Terry, who had been with her there a year before, wrote: "I used to sit and look at your sister like a person in a dream. I did not think any mortal woman could be so exquisite, so like a *flower* with a soul in it. She was not less human, but more spiritual, than any other mortal I ever saw; and now she is immortal."

These are, we think, the last verses Mary wrote, "Taps,"—the army bugle-call to sleep, to put out the light. "The notes rising and falling, say as plainly as music can say anything: "Put it out; put it—out; put—it——out!"

"It is a clear, golden call, almost a human voice, falling softer and slower to the end, and, when well played, lingering a little at the last, like some one very cautiously hushing a baby to sleep":—

Mary.

"Taps.

"TAPS."

Put it out ! Put it out ! Put it out !
    The clear notes rising, climb
    A ladder of sweet sound,
    And from each golden round
The ascending angels, nearing heaven, do chime,
" God's watch begins, put your dim lanterns out !"

    Put out each earthly light ;
    It is God's shadow falls
    Along the darkening walls,
Closing us round, when men say " it is night ;"
He draws so near it shuts the daylight out.

Put it out ! Put it out ! Put it out !
    Forbear each scheme of ill ;
    Good angels walk the ward,
    And heaven is all abroad
When twilight falls, and earth lies hushed and still ;
Room for the angels ! Put the dark deeds out.

    Put out all thoughts of care :
    Rest gently, aching head ;
    He stands beside the bed
Who brings in peace and healing, unaware,
And sends soft-footed sleep to shut pain out.

Put it out ! Put it out ! Put it out !
    Put out—quite out—the light.
    Hark ! as the notes grow faint,
    Was that a new-voiced saint
Who climbed with them, and scaled the starry height ?
Has from among us any soul gone out ?

God's love falls as a screen.
Where lights burn dim and pale
No flickering flame shall fail,
For with His hand held steadfastly between,
No wind can blow to put these life-lamps out.

Through earth's long night He waits,
Till, to the soul's glad eyes
Filled with divine surprise,
Heaven opens wide her golden morning gates :
Then, day being come, He breathes the candle out.

We had hurried home, too late—from hospital work. Jane went back to her duties at Fairfax. Two of us were not needed there longer, and I (G.) felt that I had wounded in our own home to care for, a while. Charley was still at the front.

C. W. W. to E. J. W.

HEADQUARTERS A. OF P.
July 13th, 1864.

This is but a line to acknowledge the receipt of the package and to say how much I should like to take a breath of Lenox air with you. Things don't look to me over-promising just *now*, but I shall not give way to any feeling of discouragement.

I wish I could be at home for a while with Mother, but this is impossible.

Always aff'ly yours.

CHAPTER XIV.

The
Army of
the Po-
tomac
before
Peters-
burg.
The effort to out-flank Lee and push on to
Richmond by the old line was unsuccessful.
Great battles with enormous losses had
occurred—though, as Grant reported to the
Secretary of War, with general results "in
our favor"; adding, "I propose to fight it
out on this line if it takes all summer."
There was no retreating under Grant, but a
concerted plan to close in on the enemy,
which included a settling down before
Petersburg, on the line of railroad by which
the rebels received their principal supplies.

Here occurred the explosion of the mine
and its utter failure through the blunder of
some commanding officer, to which Charley's
letter, copied and sent to a friend abroad,
refers. Grant had established his headquarters at City Point on the James.

C. W. W. to Mother.

HEADQUARTERS ARMY OF THE POTOMAC.
July 27, 1864.

The movement of troops yesterday, which
we have tried to keep very quiet, is part of a

programme which, if successfully carried out, will change the look of things in our front. A very important move is to be made to-morrow. I try, on principle, to expect success, but the chances for it to-morrow seem small to me. Complete defeat is, I think, impossible, for no matter how severely we may be repulsed in the offensive, our line of *defence* is a very strong one. I shall feel more at liberty to write to-morrow.

July 31st.

Got back to camp at 2 P. M. yesterday, but went off to sleep after much hard riding. We had been expecting the explosion of Burnside's mine for weeks, and though *I* have not felt at liberty to speak of it, I dare say it has been kept so little secret, that you, and no doubt the enemy, have been expecting it too. Here, scarcely any one expected complete success, and it had been so delayed from day to day that we expected a counter-mine to blow *us* up. The movement of Foster and Hancock to the north of the James was a successful diversion. The secret service proved that the enemy detached large bodies of troops and maintained but a thin line in our front. But for the invariable delay of the 9th Corps we might have had Petersburg at noon yesterday. The 18th Corps held the trenches on the right of our line and had orders to form, with the 9th, the assaulting

C. W. W.'s Account of Burnside's Mine.

column. The 5th Corps, holding our left, had orders to reduce its front line to a minimum and mass in the rear of its trenches to follow up the 9th. The cavalry had orders to demonstrate on the extreme left and threaten from the south. The mine was to explode at 3.30 A. M., when our artillery on either flank of the crater was to open, leaving the space of the breach through which the assaulting column was to pass. The mine did not explode until 4.45, but even then the attack would have succeeded if the troops had been promptly advanced. An hour passed, and no advance. Daylight came, the enemy recovered from their scare and concentrated what troops they had at the breach, and got an enfilading fire on our column as it was forming, a thing which couldn't have happened in the dark. The column was heavily shelled and somewhat broken, and the men were advanced down the covered way, artificial approach, two abreast (instead of regimental front, as might have been in the dark), and over the open. The wounded began to come back, blocking the way and halting the column. Our men were hit before they got out of the approach. Finally the column advanced to the crater, with its tail end still in the narrow approach, found that the enemy had had time to make the best dispositions, and received a tremendous fire, front and both flanks, lost very heavily, and

were withdrawn. Many lay the blame on a
regiment of negroes that broke. This may be
part cause of the failure, but I will not make
them responsible for it because they are "niggers," as do many of the officers here. I think,
if the assault had been made immediately after
the explosion, that any troops, even the green-
est and blackest, would have gone through.
The Brigade that led our column was chosen by
lot. It fell upon Bartlett, but he has a wooden
leg, and they drew again. It fell upon a brigade of dismounted cavalry, some artillery-men,
and a mixed-up lot not fit to lead a forlorn hope.
When it was found they wouldn't and couldn't
advance, General Grant, who, with General
Meade, was at Burnside's headquarters (General
B. being at the front), said : "Well, we've made
the attempt and it has failed ; that's the amount
of it. The troops had better be withdrawn."
General Burnside's failure and a more personal
matter will, I am afraid, bring him to grief. I
am sorry. I'm afraid he'll go under. It is but
a hundred yards between the lines, *called* fifty,—
and the wounded are lying in the sun. The
rebels have refused General Meade's flag of
truce ; why on earth I see no reason. We took
one gun and left three in the ruins. The mines
are occupied by the rebel sharpshooters, who
fire incessantly at us over the wounded on the
field. We shall have a quiet spell I suppose

before trying again. It was a golden chance and a disgraceful failure.

August 2nd.

The failure of the assault has given us a bluish tinge here. General Grant and General Meade are a good deal cut up by it. Our loss is heavy. I went with the flag of truce *yesterday*. At the point of the explosion the rebels and our officers and men mingled freely. The rebels and the nationals, in their shirtsleeves, are not to be told apart, for very many of the rebels had on United States regulation blue trousers. The hot sun had done dreadful work. Nine-tenths of the men I saw were negroes. They had apparently been killed in running to the rear, but beyond the crater they (the blacks) had held their ground well, some of them to the last. The officers and men were friendly with us. To-day there is a court holding in our mess-tent. Burnside's telegraph men are accused of intercepting messages between Generals Meade and Grant. Their defence is that they did it under General B.'s orders. All this will "lead to complications." The explosion, I fear, has made a wider breach than the one in the enemy's lines. Some changes in command and move-ments of troops are taking place. I will tell you when the right time comes. Private letters from this army are opened by the secret service men. I congratulate H. J. on his 30-day bullet. No chance for me.

We have no more of Charley's army letters this summer, but Rev. H. Hopkins, who
had at last accomplished his desire and was
a chaplain *in the field*, tells of some of the
experiences of the A. P.

CAMP 120TH N. Y. VOLS., A. P.,
August 11th, 1864.

Dear Georgy: Since our expedition to Deep
Bottom, and short sojourn in the trenches at the
time of the explosion of the mine and assault
on the enemy's lines, we have been enjoying
regular camp life. . . .

The industry of the men has provided deep
wells abounding in cool, clear water; so that for
all, the heat is endurable.

Here at Headquarters we luxuriate. We no
longer creep on hands and knees into our sleeping places, but *live* in ample wall-tents. . . .

All the routine of the camp, even to the school
in tactics, has been re-established and the calls
from reveille to tattoo are regularly sounded.
Our regimental band, an unusually fine one,
plays for us after dress parade, while we take
our tea, and all goes pleasantly on.

IN A BOMB-PROOF,
August 20th, '64.

My experience since the above was written is
a good commentary on the uncertainty of human
affairs, and a good illustration of a soldier's life.

I was going on to tell you of the rural chapel
we had built, and the services we were daily
holding, etc., when I was interrupted. I went
over and dined with your brother and returned
to finish my letter, when lo! my home, the
camp, my flock, my property, had vanished like
the baseless fabric of a dream. The whole
Corps had gone towards City Point. It was a
week of excitement and danger. Several lay
dead by the roadside before we reached City
Point, though the troops were marched more
reasonably than usual . . .

A profound mystery shrouded the whole
movement and was a delightful feature of it.
Division generals were as much in the dark as
any of us; and as the fleet dropped down the
river, every place from Mobile to Atlanta was
looked forward to as our destination, by the
sagacious prophets on board. It was generally
supposed that we were going to Washington.

It was a beautiful sight at sunset on the James,
that night, as our thirty-two transports turned
their heads up stream and cast anchor just above
Harrison's bar. . . .

The army was back again at the same spot
from which it and the Sanitary Commission
—ourselves part of it—had retreated two
years before; but the Chaplain's regiment,
far from falling back on Washington, as we

did, was to engage later in heavy fighting for the capture of Petersburg.

G. to Mother at Fishkill.

NEW YORK, August 6, '64.

I have been in to see Mrs. Gibbons, who has Beverly written to know whether Carry and I would go Hospital with her to Beverly, fifteen miles from Philadelphia, and help put in running order Dr. Wagner's new hospital, to open on Tuesday, for 2,000 men. He implores Mrs. Gibbons to come and help him. She is to appoint all his nurses, and do as she pleases. *She* is to go at once, so as to be there for the first arrival of sick, which will be early in the week, and is to let us know all about the place—diet-kitchens, accommodations, etc., etc.—after she gets there, and then we are to decide and join her if we like the look of it. If she won't go, Dr. Wagner says he will not have any women nurses, and that is such a loss to a hospital, that she feels obliged on that account, if on no other, to help him. . . .

Scrap in Mother's handwriting :

About Mrs. G.'s plan you must let me know. It seems much more desirable *to me* than going to the front, but you must judge for yourselves, of course. Pennsylvania is a more healthy region by far, than the South at present. My love to you all. . . .

A. H. W. to H. Gilman.

August, '64.

The girls' new summons to hospital work came a few days ago, and yesterday Georgy and Carry started for Beverly, N. J., where Mrs. Gibbons and others have been hard at work for a month organizing a new military hospital to accommodate 3500. She says they are very short of help, and there is a village full of malignant people who are ready to make trouble if they are not allowed to sail through the wards with *their* help. It will be new life for Carry, but she is quick-witted and "handy," and was very anxious to go, and we couldn't refuse when there were hundreds of badly wounded, and few nurses to be had. . . . I don't believe you will be long without finding what you wanted—"something to do"—in Norwich. Trust you for not being "lazy" long! or blue either.

Abby herself was still hard at work cutting out shirts, and packing boxes, wherever she happened to be.

A. H. W. to H. G.

CORNWALL, N. Y., Sept. 23, 1864.

The Family take a rest at Cornwall.

The bale of "California flannel" came, and no doubt the Ladies' Army Sewing Circle will need it all, and justify my purchase. A few of them who had heard of it have sent me money enough already to pay for one-third the expense, so we shall begin swimmingly. We came to this place last Saturday, and at first felt forlorn enough, but we secured an extra little room which Mother has taken pleasure in fitting up as our so-called private parlor. . . .

I cannot help wishing that we could have maintained a longer seclusion, just among our own family. This coming among outsiders seems to bury our sorrow deep from sight, to put it far back in the past. . . .

We can see Eliza's house plainly across the bay, and with a spyglass make out some signal, which, hung from an attic window, means, " We shall drive over this morning to see you," or, a story lower down, " Expect us this afternoon." It takes three days for a letter to come or go, all mail communication between this township and the universe being by stage to Newburgh, so we drive over when we want to say anything to Eliza ! . . .

We have nothing very recently from Georgy and Carry. Their experience has been new and very trying—more wearing, Georgy says, than anything she has gone through before, because of the mental anxiety to provide for so many wounded men without means to do it with, and without authority to *compel* the means from the hands of dishonest stewards and indifferent doctors. She and Carry have been buying *all* the food that *all* their worst patients needed—forty in number, at the Beverly grocery. The cooks and stewards make a clean steal of at least one meal a day from these two surgical wards—and the meals, when they *are* served from the hospital, are just the usual pork fat, and greasy slops. The men cry like babies, and *Carry* cries with them, and then laughs with them, and then does better than that, by taking the eggs she has sent to the grocer's for, and scrambling them on a spirit-lamp—to feed and keep life in some dying man. They are common ward nurses—Mrs. Gibbons having the position at the head of the women. . . .

The girls say they ask each other, every day, "*How* can we stay? and yet how *can* we go home?" They will wait and see this set of men on the road to recovery, if possible.

John Packard goes up from Philadelphia every day as a sort of Inspector—to show the contract men what to do—with the wounds, etc. ! Of course the girls' own accommodations are miserable, but that is nothing. Georgy says she has really "at last an opportunity of exercising some of that self-sacrifice which her misguided friends have sometimes given her credit for." They say, however, we must not think it is all gloom and forlornness. They have rare fun between themselves about what goes on, and the airs and ignorance of the young doctors, etc., etc.

As a sample of this G. writes from Beverly to Mother :—

September, '64.

This set of regulations was promulgated this morning regarding "female nurses : " "All deliberations, discussions and remarks having the object of expressing comparative praise, or censure, of the medical officers of this hospital, or their individual course or conduct, are positively prohibited ! " The provision against our "*praise* " is truly judicious. C. and I have 100 men in our wards, all in bed. It is grimly amusing to hear the ward-surgeon say day after day, "Milk and eggs for 38." For two days there have been no eggs at all, and the milk rations are always short. The ladies are not allowed in the kitchen, or to have anything to do with the food for the patients. No steak or potatoes or milk punch come into this ward. We have opened a private account for bread, and milk, and butter and eggs, enough for this ward, with the village store. Our ward-surgeon has gone to a horse race, which seems a pretty long one ! The surgeon-in-charge is kind in manner, and draws rations strictly according to army regulations ; and seems to think that the stewards are the best persons to manage the food business. The object of the minor officers seems to be to subsist the men on nothing, and avoid making a row. We cannot keep our men alive; eleven of them have died in three days.

Rocking-chairs were still our craze. The Government furnished absolutely nothing for a sick man to sit on. These were for our Beverly ward:

H. L. H. to G.
PHILADELPHIA, Sept., '64.

Dear Georgy :—I hope that Pomegranate rind has already reached you in packages as desired. As you suggested, I have ordered 10 Boston Rockers. . . . I have on hand twenty-six dollars and forty-five cents, . . . subject to your order. Do let me know whenever I can be of service in any way. . . . I am glad to hear that Dr. Packard is on duty at Beverly, as he may be of service to you and your patients, if you will only give him a hint.

We had a good-natured laugh over a visit from Miss Dix, who, poor old lady, kept up the fiction of appointing all the army nurses. She descended upon Beverly for this purpose, when, finding us already established without consultation with her, she served this printed assignment to duty—not on me only, but on Carry, whom she had never spoken to and knew nothing about!

" OFFICE OF SUPERINTENDENT OF WOMEN NURSES,
WASHINGTON, D. C., August 30, 1864.

Miss Woolsey having furnished satisfactory evidence of her qualifications for the position of a " Nurse" in the employment of the Medical Department U. S. A., is approved.

D. L. DIX, Superintendent.

Assigned to duty at U. S. General Hospital, Beverly, New Jersey, 1864, upon application of Surgeon in charge."

A. H. W. to H. G.

Carry writes us about the visit of a Christian commission delegate to their hospital and the gloomy sermons on death he preaches to the convalescents, till her hair stands on end. He also haunts the wards early and late when no one is on the lookout for visitors, loaded with pocket-handkerchiefs and *pickled quinces*, demanding all round who has the diarrhœa, and quite pleased to find that *no one* has and all glad to get the sour fruit, though in truth eleven of the men had died in three days of that chronic complaint.

Carry writes: "If *I* owned a hospital no philanthropist should ever enter. I could have pounded two benevolent old ladies yesterday on

a tour of "inspection" through my ward. One
of my poor little boys, feverish and restless,
tired of lying in bed for days and days, had
crawled to the stove and been tucked up in one
of our rocking-chairs in his blanket. I had
given him a hot drink and he had fallen into a
doze, when these elderly philanthropists arrived,
shook him by the arm, yelling, "Poor fellow,
what's the matter, fever? O! my! you're too
near the stove; get right back to bed. There
now, that's it, you're too weak to sit up;" and
so having saved one life as they thought, they
passed on to the next."

You see Carry has *her* trials like all hospital
nurses.

Jane writes at this date from her hospital:

I should think Beverly must be one of the
worst conducted places in the service except
Willett's Point Government Hospital, Long
Island, where in August I saw them handing
about pieces of fat pork on newspapers, to
wounded men, for their dinners.

The Beverly Hospital was perhaps the
worst one claiming to be a Regular Army
establishment that I (G.) ever went into,
and the conditions exasperating, because it
was in the midst of a land of plenty. But

it was dominated by the same Regular Army spirit which we had encountered all along, from the very first day of our army experience.

As in our late Spanish war, the system adapted to the case of a frontier regiment in time of peace was expected to cover all the emergencies of a large army in time of war. At Beverly the surgeon in charge was kind, but strangled in red tape. Mrs. Gibbons made the effort to keep us comfortable, and her daughter herself prepared in one corner of the kitchen articles for our table, to mitigate the army ration. Our own discomforts on the top floor of the board shanty are not worth speaking of, but one incident will illustrate the general conduct of affairs. I was pursued up-stairs one day by the man detailed to wait on the nurses' table, (a huge private in shirt-sleeves and *bare feet*), and violently berated for taking a piece of dry bread from the table to eat in peace in my own room, "contrary to regulations," I suppose.

Cousin Margaret Hodge and home friends helped us constantly to feed our poor men, and Robert sent weekly boxes of fruit and flowers. At last a tent hospital took the

place of this wretched old tooth-brush factory building (where, through the wide cracks
in the single plank floor of my ward, we
looked down into the dead-house), and, matters having improved, we came away.

The poor fellows' Christmas day was
happy. Miss Sever, our co-laborer, who remained, in acknowledging Christmas boxes
from us, writes: "The dinner was a great
success, and Mrs. Grant, the General's wife,
spent the day going about among the men,
which delighted them."

In the course of this summer of 1864,
Admiral Farragut's splendid taking of Mobile
came as a comfort, after the failure of the
mine explosion before Petersburg; and
Sherman and Sheridan were working out,
through victories elsewhere, their part of
Grant's plan for closing in round the rebel
Lee.

McClellan, the "lost leader," while his old
command still faced the enemy in the field,
was occupied in offering himself as a rival to
Mr. Lincoln's second presidency, and as the
regular nominee of the Democratic party
with its "peace at any price" morals. Chaplain Hopkins' letter fills a gap in the record.

Chaplain Hopkins to E. W. H.

In the Field.
Camp of 120th New York, Sept. 29th, 1864.

My dear Mrs. Howland: I have just returned to camp from City Point, whence I have just dispatched over eighteen thousand dollars out of their pay to the homes of our men. I find tents down, baggage sent to the rear, and everything ready for a move at a moment's notice. . . . Thank you for your kind, good letter. . . . It is pleasant to know that one has the hearty approval of his friends in a step like that which I took in leaving the hospital. To be congratulated therefore by you, through whom I was first introduced to hospital life, on my escape from it, is peculiarly gratifying. . . . It was three years ago last Saturday, I think, that I waited in the parlor of the Ebbitt House, filled with misgivings at the thought of my temerity, to see the two elderly ladies to whom Prof. Smith had bidden me to report! I trembled lest, like a gentleman in New York whose son I offered to teach, they should look at me through their spectacles and think me too young for such a work. . . .

While I write Fort Morton, a hundred yards from me, is thundering with its heavy guns and mortars, to try the enemy, but they scarcely deign to reply. . . .

These soldiers, so apparently remorseless at times, were yesterday stealing out between the lines to talk and trade, together, exchanging papers, and comparing news or politics. They wrote each other notes as "My dear Johnny Reb," "My dear Yank." They had a little dog for a mail carrier, and enclosed the orders of opposing generals, inviting desertions. The Johnnies were coming over to us a dozen or more a day. This afternoon in the hottest firing a rebel jumped up, swung a towel and called out, "Stop firing, and we will!" and in a moment it was as quiet as a New England Sunday. Their officers did not agree to this, and ordered firing to begin; so they shouted, "Get down, Yanks, we are going to open." I long for victory not less that the enemy may be defeated, than that the peace party of the North may be utterly confounded. Not an officer in our regiment will support McClellan. . . . To-day I hear that Col. —— and Lieut.-Col. ——, both New York city democrats of the baser sort, who were never known to swerve from any nomination of the party, have declared themselves against little Mac. They can't, they say, as soldiers vote for him. Poor man! the loyal thousands of the army used to greet the mention of his name with a perfect enthusiasm. Now he is cheered for by traitors and their friends, and

builds his fortunes on the disgrace of his government. . . .

Your letter, which said in every line from beginning to end, " Let the war go on !" came to
me just as I had come in from gazing on the
noble, manly face of one of our Lieutenants,
who half an hour before had been killed by a
rebel bullet. There was not a more promising
young officer in the regiment. We all expected
much of him, and at home he was the idol of
his mother and sisters. I was pondering on
how best to tell them the heart-rending news
when your letter came ; and I confess, that even
then, with those pale features before my eyes
and that desolate home in my thoughts, I could
say too, " Let the war go on !"

A. H. W. to H. G.
Cornwall, Oct. 13th.

Charley writes us with great pleasure of
the gradual change that seems to be coming in
the opinions of army officers. Those who have
always had *personal* friendship for McClellan
begin to see that they cannot vote for anybody
on the Chicago platform, and are coming over
to the right side. Colonel McMahon of Dix's
staff had been down to Headquarters on a visit,
and carried them the assurance that " McClellan
was sure to be the next President ; bets in
New York ran four to one in his favor." He

came away from camp rather cast down at the growing confidence of the army in the administration.*

Charley has not been at home since March, and is not likely to come until the election is over ; when, if Lincoln is successful, there may be a " let up " in military movements. That is *my* idea you know, at least. . . .

This afternoon we shall take an early start after dinner and drive up to Newburg and over the river to Eliza's at Fishkill, where Robert Howland and our four dear little girls are staying on a little visit. This is to fill up the time for them, till we go back to New York, when they are all coming to live with us for the winter, a long, long visit. Mother is going to give them the third story, and we shall find them the life of the house ; I think, though, it will bring some responsibility. *That* we should feel, however, wherever they lived. May tells us, she " saw that there was a bill on their house in 23rd street, and asked papa what it meant, and where she and little sisters were going to live ;" and then he told her Moremamma's and his secret.

---

* It is satisfactory to record even at this late date Mc-Clellan's overwhelming defeat ; he received 21 votes of the Electoral College, in a total of 212.

The wretched men who had lived through Re-
the brutalities attending their imprisonment Prison-
in Southern pens, were now being exchanged ers.
for the hearty, healthy rebels we had so frequently seen during our service, Government established a large receiving hospital
at Annapolis; good women were put in
charge, and steamers brought their appalling
loads to that port. Our old commanding
officer, Dr. Smith, was called to superintend
the transportation, and sent Jane, just then
at home from the Hospital on leave, an account of this service.

J. S. W. to a friend abroad.

NEW YORK, Nov. 29th, 1864.

We are painfully interested just now in the
coming home of our long-captive soldiers from
the South. Our friend, Surgeon Smith, went
down with the truce fleet. Perhaps you will let
me quote a sentence or two from his letter dated
at Savannah, Nov. 20th. "I have just received
560 poor, wretched, miserable sufferers. All
their being, all mind, seems to be absorbed in
the one idea of living. They are too low, too
utterly wrecked to have hope. They can't even
conceive the idea that they are going home.
Hope and remembrance are lost. They are sunk
almost to the level of beasts   God help and

pity them and take home the wretches that will die to-night. These living skeletons and puling idiots are worse to see than any sight on battle-fields. In helping them on board it is frightful. You see a head, then a double handful of something in a bit of blanket or heap of rags! It weighs what the bones would weigh. Whiskey and hot strong broth are being served out rapidly."

Same day, later : "The whiskey and broth, sweet soft bread and onions are working wonders. One poor skeleton said to me just now, 'Why, Major, I could but just crawl on board, and now I'm bully.' 'How is that?' said I. 'Oh, its the grub; I was starving to death.' Another skeleton head near by, speaks; ' This is Heaven; I have often envied my father's pigs their food and shelter.' O my God ! it is dreadful to see these things." This surgeon is no weakling. He is called a hard man. He tells me later that our men are ill only with hunger and abuse, and the *incident diseases.* He says they have been subjected to every cruelty, every infamy of cruelty, we can conceive of. I have seen the prison camp and hospitals at Point Lookout, have lived in them for a month, and I *know* what the contrast is. How can I help bitter indignation when I read the over-seas talk of how the war is degenerating on the part of the North into a system of violence and cruelty, etc., etc. !

From the Army of the Potomac we get no important news. The "Turkey fleet" for Thanksgiving day arrived on time, and there was great merry-making in the camps. It looks like winter quarters, and then again it doesn't look like winter quarters, and they are holding their breaths for Sherman, and wondering when General Butler is going to give another "on to Richmond." That is the substance of our advices. Headquarters A. P. have a standing feud with Headquarters A. J. Butler is a thorn in the flesh of Meade. Charley is copying and *punctuating* Meade's report of the unsuccesses of the A. P. since May 1st, with the reasons therefor; he feels the responsibility of his semi-colons, and thinks that if the American people would only mind their stops, all might yet be well. He sighs for promotion (there is no promotion in the General Staff) and wants to be a Captain in a colored regiment; but when I think of the dreadful anxiety it would cause Mother, I hope, unless it is a very clear case of duty, he will not join the black brigade. He was a prisoner for an hour or two in the late advance of the left, but after some hard and unequal fighting got away with his orderly and his dispatches, safe to our lines again. It would have been a terrible thing for us to have known him a prisoner in Richmond or Andersonville.

Colonel and Mrs. Howland are well. Georgy is with them, recruiting after her rather hard campaign at Beverly. . . .

We are all lighter-hearted since the election, although we never allowed ourselves to doubt seriously of the result. As far as I know there are no McClellan men left anywhere. They are gone, no one knows where, and the "era of good feeling" appears to have set in. . . .

The newest sensation is the incendiary fires and the registration of secessionists. It is astonishing how many of these people are here "eating of our bread and lifting the heel against us." I hear stories every day of the impertinence of Southern women who are in sanctuary, so to speak, here, while their husbands are fighting against us. But we can afford magnanimity, even though our magnanimity be called weakness by the over-seas people, whom we *cannot* please.

All that could be done for the saving of the wretched exchanged prisoners was at last done. Supplies were sent from the Sanitary Commission and many homes—from Eliza's and ours among them, to the lady in charge, an old friend of ours since the first days of the war, who writes :

ANNAPOLIS, Dec. 15th, '64.

Dear Mrs. Howland :—The boxes of lemons, wine and brandy came in perfect order, and in good season. Many thanks for the kind and generous response to my suggestions for the benefit of our boys. The condition of them is very sad. I am afraid to say how many have died in the hospital. . . .

A most touching letter was written a little while ago, dictated by a man to his wife. If I can get a copy of it I will send it to you—expressing simply the feeling of contentment to die, since he had once more come under the "starry folds of the dear old flag"; and, commending her and their one child to God, he bade her good-bye in the full consciousness of the nearness of death.

The flannel shirts will be most acceptable to us. The Sanitary Commission have so far furnished us large quantities of them, but as fast as the boys get their furloughs they go off, wearing in many instances the shirts that we have given them. The Government shirts are so rough and harsh that, if they can get others, the boys do not feel willing to wear them, and for my own part I have hardly the mind to put the poor skeletons into nutmeg graters, to lose what little flesh they have clinging to their bones. . . .

Another boat is being unloaded.

From the Same.

ANNAPOLIS, Dec. 27th, 1864.

Dear Mrs. Howland:—The barrel containing the shirts from your Ladies' society was delivered promptly at my store-room on Saturday. . . .

I was very negligent not to tell you particularly of the condition of your pickles. They were in most excellent order. Nothing could have been more *àpropos* than that very barrel. In some of the wards I sent them every day, and actually believe that nothing else but pickles saved the life of one man who would eat nothing till he tasted them. After the first one, he could not live without a jar of them in his room, and said they seemed to "rouse up the vitals pretty sharp," and gave him an appetite that nothing else could do.

You may indeed consider the experiment a perfect success.*

Our Christmas passed off very well. I hesitate for a word to express *how* it went. "Happily" could hardly express the manner of it if I mention at the same time that *ten deaths* were reported to me the same day. But we had a very nice dinner of proper Christmas eatables, such as turkey, cranberry, celery, pies, plum pudding,

---

* E. had them made by the barrel—sometimes by the hogshead—for this very purpose, as anti-scorbutics.

with vegetables, for all full diets, and all sorts of goodies for the sick ones. Our decorations were not extensive, and confined mostly to the chapel, for all the ladies were too busy to trim the wards. The general condition of the patients is improving, I think, but the mortality has been fearful. Large numbers of the returned men were able to get off for home before Christmas and others are still going.

Very truly yours,
MARIA M. C. HALL.

Work for the Union Refugees was meantime going on all over the North. As an indication of the general interest in them, the " Highland Serenaders," a village band of Matteawan, N. Y., sent E. W. H. a check for $100, asking her to " accept this small sum, the profits of their first concert," and to use it for the benefit of the Union Refugees. They add, " We hold ourselves in readiness to do our part in anything for our Free Country."

Mrs. Joseph P. Thompson to E. W. H.

32 WEST 36TH ST., N. Y., December.

My dear Eliza :—Abby tells me that your Fishkill ladies are busily at work for the refugees, and she says you want to know what organization there is at the Southwest, for receiving and distributing the supplies. . . . The Union Commission are exploring through all those states, and reporting constantly. The most urgent calls at present are from Memphis, Nashville, from Helena, and from Cedar Keys, Florida, all reconquered from the rebels, where the destitution has been most appalling. Twenty barrels of clothing, potatoes, &c., have been shipped to Cedar Keys, to the care of Captain Pease, of the 2nd U. S. Infantry. There will be shipped for Memphis to-morrow seven barrels and boxes of the largest kind, of second-hand clothing, and there are probably at the rooms 40 barrels and boxes that will be forwarded as soon as possible.

A. H. W. to H. G.
NEW YORK, Dec. 21, '64.

Our household moves on with the usual ups and downs. We see and hear nothing from the outside world except what the newspapers bring, but that is stirring enough. Sherman's march proves, at last, our numerical superiority. We have *one* army free to move where it likes and have an "agreeable time" in the enemy's country. We may soon have *two* surplus armies, for Thomas' victory over Hood seems to have been a crushing one. Hood had forty thousand men engaged in that fight, but, a

very large number of them Tennesseans, who
are evidently "demoralized"—if that slang
word has not lost all its force, and he has three
swollen rivers to cross in his retreat. . . .

I must see Lizzie Thompson soon, and hear
how the refugees fare. Carry went round one
morning to the office, but her zeal only held
out for that one day over the rags and vermin
which some people find it convenient to dump
on benevolent societies. We have packed one
barrel, and hope to get off another before the
close of the year, while Fishkill seems all agog
on the subject. Poor creatures, homeless and
hungry; these winter days must go hard with
them in those border towns where the tide of
war has stranded them. Our Thanksgiving box
to Charley, which you were witness to, was so
long delayed that the game in it must have been
very gamy, so it has had to be followed by a
Christmas box, which we sent off yesterday, and
as another must go to the little Jerome children,
(the Chaplain's family), at Fairfax Hospital, and
another to the soldiers at Beverly, etc., we have,
in that particular line, a rather busy time. . . .
Carry is filling the month with weekly visits at
Bloomingdale Orphan Asylum. She always
comes back full of experience and pleasure, and
has much to tell of her pow-wows with Mrs.
Anthon and Mrs. Satterlee and the other elderly
and revered ladies of the board. . . . They have

been engaging two teachers, for the boys and
girls' departments, the two young people who
have had charge so far having romantically
fallen in love. . . .

The girls' teacher, it seems, was herself
raised in the asylum, and great interest has
been felt in her approaching marriage. . . .
A sad and romantic turn has been given to
the affair, however, by the appearance on the
scene of a first-love whom she had secretly
jilted for the sake of the new teacher.
This first-love, a gallant, noble young Captain in the army, obtained a short leave and
came dashing into Mrs. Pell's room the other
night, to know what it all meant ; why his engagement ring had been returned ? So then, it
all had to come out. The young Captain was,
himself, an asylum boy once, and a match with
him would have been the wisest thing. . . .
Poor young soldier, he is heartbroken, and has
gone into the *regular* army, now, as a career. . . .

Surgeon Smith has been ordered back to Fairfax Hospital, the transfer of prisoners from
Savannah and Charleston being nearly at an
end. . . . I don't wonder that the girls are enthusiastic in their praise of him ; he looks so
carefully and personally into the condition of
his patients, instead of being satisfied with giving orders to subordinates and sitting at his
ease, as the surgeon who took his place for a

time did. He has sent the girls *his* first two
general orders issued on his return, and they
are an indication of what sort of a man he is
and of how shamefully his predecessor has
acted, shutting up the chapel and snubbing the
Chaplain. By "No. 1, Dec. 14, Surgeon David
P. Smith hereby assumes command of this hospital." In No. 2, dated next day, he orders the
chapel opened, divine service held on Christmas
Day and every Sunday thereafter at 10.15 o'clock.
Also afternoon and evening weekly services at
such hours as the Chaplain may appoint; and
officers and soldiers are referred to certain articles of war and advised to be reverent and dili-
gent in their attendance upon divine things. . . .
Charley has been brevetted Captain, for "gallantry on the field," and all the rest of the "clap-
trap" (as *he* says) that his complimentary letter
was filled with.

C. C. W.
Brevet-
ted
Captain.

"The complimentary letter" unfortunate-
ly is destroyed, and as we were all at home
and no family letters were exchanged, there
is nothing further to add to the simple fact
that for "gallantry on the field" Charley
could always be relied on. He came home
for a while apparently, as this extract from a
note from our co-worker at Beverly shows.

Miss Annie Sever to "Dear little Miss Carry."

BEVERLY HOSPITAL.

I was very glad to have the little note from you to-night and to think of your enjoyment in having your brother at home with you. You must let me give you my congratulations on his promotion.

And so the fourth year of the war closed with a united family—save one.

THE WAR ENDED
1865

CHAPTER XV.

January, 1865, found Sherman master of Savannah. The victory at Fort Fisher un-der General Terry followed. Columbia and Charleston within a month were occupied by Sherman, and he was marching north. Sheridan was making harassing raids, cut-ting off supplies, and breaking up railroads, and the rebels under Lee, held to their posi-tion at Petersburg by Grant, were gradually being surrounded and shut in on every side.

In the absence of Charley's letters Chap-lain Hopkins again helps to make the story continuous:—

CAMP 120TH N. Y. VOLS., A. P.
BEFORE PETERSBURG, Jan. 8th, 1865.

Dear Georgy: That prince of Christmas boxes! . . . Fresh from the perusal of one of Dr. Bushnell's masterly sermons, with the linen pockets hanging "from the ridge-pole," paper-cutter, etc. enriching the pigeon holes before me, new books adorning my table, and a fabulous array of goodies close at hand, while the match-box lies lovingly beside a little copy of the Psalms in a safe pocket, and a sugar-plum is rolled even now as a sweet morsel under my tongue—what wonder that my heart is too full for utterance. . . .

I had heen hard at work for many days with the axe, helping the men build the log chapel another Chaplain and myself are building for three regiments. We had had such trials and disappointments. . . . I had found coldness where I had expected sympathy, and even selfishness and meanness where I thought to be met with generous co-operation. My heart was as sombre as the winter sky when I came to my tent. *There was the box!* . . .

Since then all has gone well; the afternoon was a happy one. The next day, teams, tools and willing men came with a pleasant day for the chapel, and to-day I have found in the huts of the men some such bright good souls that I feel strengthened and blessed by seeing them. See how much a box of sugar-plums can do! I beg you to distribute my thanks where they belong, not forgetting Bertha and Una. . . .

I have thought that part of your Mother's money could not be expended more satisfactorily than in supplying this brigade regularly with a number of copies of the Messenger and Sunday School Times. It would be a pleasant thing for your Mother to know that she was putting a copy of each one of these good sound preachers into every hut in a whole brigade, regularly, through the winter months. We mean to make a reading-room of the chapel, and I have already made arrangements for the secular papers. . . .

I should like to give every soldier in the regiment a copy of " The Rainy Day in Camp." I never knew of a copy of it being destroyed; it is usually sent home in the first letter. Four hundred and fifty would be enough. Has Jane gone back to Fairfax Hospital ? . . .

Both of my brothers are near me, one, Archy, in 37th Mass., 6th Corps, and the other, Lawrence, in the 1st Mass. Cavalry. I expect them to spend Thursday evening. I am about moving into a new and elegant shanty, and shall have a house-warming. I am saving cake, figs, prunes, nuts, etc. from the box, to garnish the feast. . . .

CAMP 120TH N. Y. VOLS.,
NEAR HATCHER'S RUN,
Feb. 12th, 1865.

Dear Georgy : For the first time in a week I have a tent and table. Outside, the winds howl and shake the canvas like mad, but my little fury of a stove makes it summer within. . . .

The Fortunes of War. " By the left flank."

I am unable to understand what we have accomplished by this week of fighting and exposure, unless it be a diversion in favor of Sherman. . . .

When we came away from our old camp, there was a manifest improvement going on in the brigade, in the health, discipline and morals of the men. Our two chapels were none too large, and the attendance was increasing from night to night. The Dinwiddie Literary Association, carried on by officers of the brigade, was a capital institution. . . . Then we had, every Thursday evening, a general singing exercise under a first-rate leader. Besides I had an interested and interesting Bible class. . . .

To-day the chapel and the camp are desolate, and not one man in ten of the brigade knows that it is the Sabbath. By the end of the week we hope to have a new chapel up, though by the end of the week we may have made *another* move "by the left flank." . . .

J. S. W. had gone back to the Fairfax Seminary Hospital, which was filling up with sick men from the camps abandoned as the army had advanced. Her hands were full of work again.

J. S. W. to J. H.

FAIRFAX HOSPITAL, February 16, 1865.

Dear Colonel: Many thanks for your neat and appropriate gift. The thin disguise of writing backwards—not to mention the postmark—shall not prevent me from claiming "thee as my valentine." . . . The last camelia G. sent me remained "quite fresh yet," till yesterday, when I turned it upside down, and it lasted some hours longer. . . .

See how it is: you sit at home at ease, waxing fat on petroleum stock and *purée aux quatre saisons*, while we, whose bosoms are the bulwark (you may have heard something like this before) between you and your country's foes, are obliged to turn our camelias wrong side out to economise them. But you also have been in "Arcadia." . . .

Here there is nothing but shop to tell, and nothing of shop, but that we are continually expecting to be reinforced with every species of the genus Bummer from the breaking up of Alexandria hospitals. *Some* among the men will be bad cases; they shall have the shirts of "the benevolent."

The individual who has ten small children to feed on four months' arrears of pay—*il y en a*—he shall have a shirt too; while "Mr." B., an inmate of ours, who boasts of having "jumped" a thousand dollars or two, has been six months

in the service, in hospitals, and has just procured his discharge on the ground of epileptic
fits of fifteen years standing, will be requested
to clothe himself out of his last bounty. The
doctor sends me up now, the names of all discharged men with a mark against those he considers "unworthy of my charity"; so I have
only to refer to my list, on the application.

Ask Eliza how she gets the wine out of the
"kag." Do you take off the hoops? or gimlet-
hole it in the side? I was rather afraid of a
jet de vin if I meddled with the little square
piece of tin on the side of it.

My love to the orchid-house and incidentally
to the members of the family.

A. H. W. to H. G.

NEW YORK, March 9th, 1865.

C. W.W.
on In-
specting
tour
with
General
Wil-
liams

We plod along here, one day very much
like the rest, and a large proportion of them
rainy ones, when we stay indoors, and sort over
closets, or get a good pile of mending, and some
lively story for one to read aloud.

Jane writes rarely, and always hurriedly; so
many hospitals have been broken up in Alexandria that she has had a large accession of
"lame backs" and despondent "chronics." It
seems to be felt that the Department of Washington will not be the depot for the wounded

from our next battle ; but that they will either be kept in North Carolina or sent up North, here. We hear nothing from Headquarters, now that Charley has left temporarily, but are looking with interest for a letter from him from *Charleston*, where he was going with all speed when he last wrote. General Williams and himself went to Hilton Head a month ago on "inspecting" duty, and Charley has written us about his Savannah and Florida trips, which were all novel and charming to him. General Gilmore had given them the use of a little steamboat, the Delaware, and on that they live, and shoot in and out along the coast. He tells us of the excellent order, appearance, and "snap" of the colored troops—the Third United States particularly—and mentions one company of artillery garrisoning a battery, where the Sergeant was a field hand five months ago, but now "keeps the company books, and in excellent order"—no small mark of intelligence, in an officer of *any* standing, I am told. . . .

We have gone into a new business, Georgy and I, collecting fancy articles for a *colored fair* in Alexandria. We have made a few gay silk neckties, some fancy aprons for colored babies, highly-colored pincushions, &c. It seems that articles for a fair will fill a place that mere money won't. Mrs. Jacobs (perhaps you have heard of her), a mulatto, formerly a slave, long

living in Nat Willis' family, and a "big, noble,
Christian lady" as described to me, has gone
back to Alexandria to help educate her race.
She found so much coldness and reserve among
the well to do—those who were free before the
war, and live comfortably—so much fear on their
part that this great influx of degraded contrabands would drag them all down to the same
level in social estimation, that she has done her
best to bring out their sympathies and break up
this selfish, aristocratic notion. A fancy fair last
spring, where the young colored "ladies" held
tables, was most successful in more than mere
money, and now Mrs. Jacobs wants to repeat it.
The proceeds are to supply delicacies, &c., for
the colored soldiers in the great dreary hospital
at Alexandria appropriated to them.

Charley and General Williams completed
their inspection of the troops at Southern
stations, and were back again at Headquarters of the Army of the Potomac in time for
the final act of the campaign.

Capture
of Rich-
mond.

On April 2d, Grant's whole line advanced
against the rebel works at Petersburg, cutting Lee's army in two. The rebel General
telegraphed to Jeff Davis that, his line being
broken, he was compelled to abandon his
position.

He evacuated Richmond and Petersburg, closely pursued by Grant, while loyal forces occupied both cities; Weitzel's black troops being first to march into Richmond. The rebel president fled before them towards North Carolina.

C. C. W. to E. W. H.

NEW YORK, Monday Night, April 3d, 1865.

Dear Eliza: Isn't it Glorious? New York has stood on its head, and the bulls and bears of Wall street for once left their wrangling, and sang Old Hundred.

"Bless the Lord, oh, my soul," and don't you hope Lee will not escape? We have felt very sorry you were not here to see it all; can't you come down?... Suppose you and Joe go to Charleston and take Hatty and me to see the flag-raising at Sumter? Com. Draper can give passes to *any one;* and the opportunity will never occur again. Go! do go! It is hard to sit still with the excitement and commotion which you know can never be repeated, and you not there. "Plenty of good times, only I ain't in 'em."

The lion has not yet lain down with the lamb, but one evidence of peace we just had. G. was sitting by the little table with her cup of tea on it, when, looking up suddenly, we saw a small mouse quietly drinking the tea, his nose in the cup and his tail in the air! Glory, Hallelujah!

Good-bye.

The following was the glorious sight that Carry longed to see :—

GENERAL ORDERS, No. 50.
WAR DEPARTMENT,
ADJUTANT-GENERAL'S OFFICE,
WASHINGTON, March 27, 1865.
ORDERED—

First. That at the hour of noon, on the 14th day of April, 1865, Brevet Major General Anderson will raise and plant upon the ruins of Fort Sumter, in Charleston harbor, the same United States flag which floated over the battlements of that Fort during the rebel assault, and which was lowered and saluted by him and the small force of his command when the works were evacuated on the 14th day of April, 1861.

Second. That the flag, when raised, be saluted by one hundred guns from Fort Sumter, and by a National salute from every fort and rebel battery that fired upon Fort Sumter. . . .

BY ORDER OF THE PRESIDENT OF THE UNITED STATES :

EDWIN M. STANTON,
Secretary of War.

Lee Surrenders at Appomattox.
On April the 9th, held in a vise, cut off from all supplies, utterly and hopelessly beaten,—Lee surrendered. His starving troops were eating the buds from the trees

to keep life in themselves, that pleasant spring day.

Grant's first act after the formal surrender, was to issue rations to the famished rebels. "If thine enemy hunger, feed him." Riding to his camp after a three hours' interview with Lee at Appomattox Court House, Grant heard the firing of salutes, and sent at once to stop them, saying: "The war is over, the rebels are again our countrymen; the best sign of rejoicing after this victory will be to abstain from all demonstration in the field."

Charley's letters at this time, it is remembered, gave us striking accounts of these last days. He wrote out one of the five copies of the terms of surrender from Grant's notes, which for a time he had in his hands; and he saw what has not been mentioned in any account of the closing scene.

The very small room in which Grant and Lee met was crowded with officers, and it was an easy thing to miss seeing an action which passed in an instant. At a certain moment, Charley is positive that he saw Lee make a motion as if to offer his side arms, and saw Grant also silently, and immediately, with a gesture, refuse to accept the humiliation.

At last! And so the great Rebellion came to an end. The armies immediately under Grant had captured in Virginia 75,000 men and 689 cannon; and the forces under his general command had, in addition, taken 147,000 prisoners and 997 cannon in the final campaign of April and May. So that it was not altogether the giving in of a remnant of dis-spirited men to superior numbers, but the out-generaling by Grant of the traitor Lee, false to the Government which had educated him, and to the flag which, as an officer of that Government, he had solemnly sworn to protect.

It was just and comforting that what was virtually the final surrender of the rebel cause, should have been made to the General in personal command of the Army of the Potomac,—that courageous, long-suffering army, whose fortunes we have followed, and with which it seemed to the members of this special family they themselves had been marching, for four weary years.

On the day that the news of the surrender of Lee's Army came to New York, it was impossible for this family to accept it as a matter of course. The silence and lack of enthusiasm up town, and the sight of the women going in and out of the dry goods shops as usual, was unbearable. Mother and I (G.) said to each other, " Come, let us see what Wall Street is doing." We took a Fulton Street omnibus, which was entirely empty but for ourselves, and drove down to the neighborhood of the Custom House. As we came near, the streets were more and more blocked, thousands and thousands of men standing, crowding upon each other, not a woman's face among them,—all the narrow streets which converge to that point black with men, thousands more, solidly packed. As the omnibus came to a stand, not able to move a step further, they were singing as if their hearts would burst :

> " Praise God from whom all blessings flow,
> Praise Him all creatures here below ;
> Praise Him above ye heavenly host,
> Praise Father, Son and Holy Ghost."

A young man, half fainting with fatigue, threw himself into the omnibus, saying, " They have been at it for hours."

At Joe's and Eliza's home at Fishkill peace was celebrated by the building, in the spring and summer of 1865, of the Tioronda School House. Two little framed photographs—one of the tattered battle-flags of the 16th N. Y. as *War*, and the other of the School House as *Peace*,—always hung side by side in J. H.'s dressing room, and travelled with him whenever he and E. went abroad.

Mother to E.

NEW YORK, April 13th.

My dear Eliza :—Your very jolly, hallelujah letter came yesterday, while Mrs. Joseph Thompson was sitting with us, and I could not keep it to myself, but read it aloud, and we all enjoyed it together. Your patriotism is grand, and I have no doubt you have done your part in firing the hearts of the Fishkill people, and working them up to their unusual and commendable ardor in the cause, especially the women and "their sewing-machines." I really think your neighborhood has accomplished wonders, and the people of Fishkill deserve great praise for their energy and industry. I want you to come down for the grand illumination on the 20th to celebrate the surrender, which will be next Thursday, that you may see the city in its glory of thanksgiving display.

We have Abby's pretty silk flag in one of our windows pinned across the curtains, and Willy G.'s little one in the other, with our larger one over the front door outside, which has hung through the rains and sun, day and night, since Richmond was taken, and begins to lose its bright color. You can bring your little silk one with you. The girls have been getting some colored lanterns to decorate the balcony and street door ; and this, with the gas all lighted and the windows open, will be the extent of our illumination, but we can drive round and see the city. I hope you will come certainly.

Calvin Goddard and his wife made us a long call last night, and this evening Calvin came in again . . .

I enclose our last from Charley ; he is undoubtedly in Richmond before this—probably one of Lee's escort into the city, as the papers mention General Grant and his staff accompanying him. Isn't it grand to have all these victories coming so fast, and the rebels giving up, in a forlorn hope, their boasted Confedracy. . . .

Robert told me last night he meant to spend August at Sharon Springs—taking the children with him, to be with Mary G——. Poor little darlings, they are very precious to me. My love to Joe and your dear self.   MOTHER.

P. S.—Charley is in Washington with General Williams. . . . Drafting stopped ! !—all over the country ! ! !

From a letter of E. W. H.'s.

April, '65.

"Charley is still in Washington. He had just had an interview with an old friend, Captain Carpenter, who is now a miserable cripple, all doubled up with wounds from the *blood-hounds* which chased and seized him when he tried to escape from the rebel prison at Columbia."

The great President's second term of office began with such lofty words as these:

" The judgments of the Lord are true and righteous altogether. With malice towards none; with charity for all; with firmness in the right, as God gives us to see the right, let us strive to finish the work we are in; to bind up the Nation's wounds; to do all which may achieve and cherish a just and lasting peace."

Mr. Lincoln was personally with the army for the last few days of the campaign, entering Richmond immediately after its surrender, riding through the city in a common U. S. ambulance, greeted with the benedictions of the negroes whom he had set free.

On April 14th the civilized world was startled with the news of his assassination. He was shot in his box at Ford's Theatre in Washington by a rebel bullet, and died in a small house on the opposite side of the street, without regaining consciousness, at about 7 A. M. on April 15. The joy over the return of peace was eclipsed by the grief of the whole nation.

All that I can remember about the first moments of that awful morning at home, is that I rushed to Hatty's and Carry's bedroom door, pounding it, and crying, " Let me in, let me in ! Mr. Lincoln is murdered."

C. C. W. to E. W. H.

SATURDAY MORNING, April 15th, 1865.

Dear Eliza : What can one do ? We are all dumb with grief. The extra has just been cried giving the awful moment of his death. What a moment for America ! When you think of his unvarying kindness toward those very men who now rejoice,—how his whole career has been one of goodness and mercy, and now at the very first beginning of reward, it is too hard to bear. The papers were brought up while we were in bed this morning. You have hardly heard it now. I suppose you will not come down today, but you must on Monday. Charley is in

[margin note] Assassination of President Lincoln.

Washington, in rooms with General Williams, on 15th Street. New York seems dead, the streets are quiet and the flags all covered with black crape—even the 'extra' boys subdue their voices. Work is suspended, and Wall Street is thronged with silent men.

Do come down; we ought to be together in these awful times.

Men, women and children went about the streets of New York, crying, and hardly a single poor tenement in the most impoverished quarters of the city was without its little black streamer. Clocks were stopped at the hour of his death; and on the anniversary of it, for years, on some of the principal buildings of New York.

———————

GENERAL ORDERS, No. 66.
WAR DEPARTMENT,
ADJUTANT GENERAL'S OFFICE.
WASHINGTON, April 16, 1865.

The following order of the Secretary of War announces to the Armies of the United States the untimely and lamentable death of the illustrious ABRAHAM LINCOLN, late President of the United States :

War Department,
Washington City, April 16, 1865.

The distressing duty has devolved upon the Secretary of War to announce to the Armies of the United States, that at twenty-two minutes after seven o'clock, on the morning of Saturday, the fifteenth day of April, 1865, Abraham Lincoln, President of the United States, died of a mortal wound inflicted upon him by an assassin.

The Armies of the United States will share with their fellow-citizens the feelings of grief and horror inspired by this most atrocious murder of their great and beloved President and Commander-in-Chief, and with profound sorrow will mourn his death as a national calamity.

The Headquarters of every Department, Post, Station, Fort, and Arsenal will be draped in mourning for thirty days, and appropriate funeral honors will be paid by every Army, and in every Department, and at every Military Post, and at the Military Academy at West Point, to the memory of the late illustrious Chief Magistrate of the Nation, and Commander-in-Chief of its Armies.

Lieutenant General Grant will give the necessary instructions for carrying this order into effect. Edwin M. Stanton,
Secretary of War.

On the day after the receipt of this order at the Headquarters of each Military Division,

Department, Army, Post, Station, Fort, and Arsenal, and at the Military Academy at West Point, the troops and cadets will be paraded at 10 o'clock A. M., and the order read to them ; after which all labors and operations for the day will cease and be suspended, as far as practicable in a state of war.

The national flag will be displayed at half-staff.

At dawn of day thirteen guns will be fired, and afterwards, at intervals of thirty minutes, between the rising and setting sun, a single gun, and at the close of the day a national salute of thirty-six guns.

The officers of the Armies of the United States will wear the badge of mourning on the left arm and on their swords, and the colors of their commands and regiments will be put in mourning for the period of six months.

By command of

LIEUTENANT GENERAL GRANT.

W. A. NICHOLS,

Assistant Adjutant General.

Mother to E. W. H.

NEW YORK, April 25, '65.

My dear Eliza : I was very glad to get your letter this morning, which was handed in with the enclosed from Charley. . . .

I am sorry you postpone your visit, as you would have seen something of the funeral pageant. It will be weeks before the country recovers from the first great shock of this terrible event, and as long, before the people of New York are quieted down again to their every-day occupations. We all feel unsettled, and can really do little else than read the newspapers. Robert left home on Thursday P. M. for Washington. . . .

Georgy means to deluge Lee with Northern newspapers. Commenced this morning by sending him the Post of last evening, with an editorial marked very strikingly, headed " General Lee."

It must have been about this time that Charley was brevetted Major, and then Lieutenant Colonel; we have no date, the record is destroyed.

The following letter contains the first intimation that earth was pleasant to Abby, since the war began nearly five years before : Abby takes a Rest.

A. H. W. to H. Gilman.
FISHKILL, May, '65.
When I came up here last Tuesday, I did not think that I should let a week of this easy, idle life pass without writing a letter or two that were due. But it is *so* easy to do nothing

but read the newspapers and stroll in the garden, if you only tried ! . .

This is the fifth season that I have failed to watch the gradual development of nature, as it used to be such an occupation and pleasure to do, even in city back yards and corner grass plats. For five years there has been something else, so overwhelming, so pre-occupying that Spring has burst upon us unknown, or rather, come quietly, unnoticed, till some day when we have looked up into the trees or out of the window, and found that it was Summer !

And *peace* has come, like the Spring this year, unheralded, unobserved, like the changes of the season. And, strangely enough, there is a dash of sadness in the thought of peace,—the scattering of the troops and the breaking up of brotherhoods and sisterhoods of patriotic efforts and hopes.

Jane thinks her duties will hold out, however, for awhile, and says she "shall stand by Mr. Micawber"—Fairfax Hospital. They have the great armies camped all about them now, the glimmer of the white tents by day and the fires by night being pretty to see, and the sick, who have borne up bravely through the march, or have been wearily dragged hither or thither after their regiments, are all brought into Fairfax,—it is so handy, and dumped, as if it were a matter of course. So *she* has plenty to do.

The following list found among Abby's papers gives an inadequate idea of the labors she needed to rest from. She cut out and had made a very large number of the gar- ments mentioned, knitted an untold number of the socks, and saw that all the articles in this list, and many more not mentioned, were safely forwarded to us at the front.

PARTIAL LIST OF SUPPLIES SENT FROM NO. 8 BREVOORT PLACE TO THE ARMY HOSPITALS; MOST OF THEM THROUGH G. AND E. AND JANE:

667 flannel and cotton shirts.
134 pairs of drawers.
165 men's wrappers.
628 pairs of socks.
107 pairs of slippers.
104 woolen mufflers.
1144 pocket handkerchiefs.
1036 towels and napkins.
203 pillow-cases.
121 pillow-sacks and twenty-five pounds of curled hair towards filling them.
26 sheets and several pieces of unmade sheet- ing and ticking.
36 woolen caps and 24 pairs wristlets.
58 pieces of mosquito netting.
Several dozen rocking chairs.

Blankets, air-pillows, india-rubber cloth, no end of lint, bandages, old linen, oil-silk, &c.

18 or 20 cases of brandy, wine, &c., of which ten cases were old port wine from Uncle Edward.

Cologne by the dozen boxes at a time.

Tobacco in large quantity.

Tobacco boxes; jack knives.

300 boxes of games, checkers, dominoes, &c., &c.

Lead pencils by the gross.

Tooth brushes, pocket-combs and pocket mirrors by the hundred.

Quantities of prepared beef and chicken.

Beef-tea, cocoa.

Canned tomatoes, &c.

Arrow-root, barley, farina.

Condensed milk.

Lemons, tea, crackers.

Pickles, oatmeal.

Currant jelly, &c., &c., &c.

Large quantities of clothing and other supplies were also sent South for the Freedmen and the poor white refugees.

A. H. W. to H. G.

FISHKILL, May, 1865.

Charley, frightened partly into resignation by the hint of the War Department that "resignations would be accepted until the 15th," and considering himself wholly superfluous now that General Williams is camped in E street, Washington, is out of the service.

Charley's own sketch of his army experiences, written out very reluctantly, and only after repeated entreaties on the part of his sisters, helps to fill the gap caused by the destruction of his letters from the front.
He writes:

WOOLSEY (near Asheville, Buncombe Co.) N. C.

Dear E. W. H.: I have a terrible letter from Georgy about my army "career,"—scarcely one of her terrific questions can I answer! It seems like a sort of impertinence to do it, but, by mail to-day, Jan. 13, 1897 (*33 years* after the event), a too long and stupid mass of scribbling is sent, but *only* "by command of"— G. W. Bacon!

REMINISCENCES OF C. W. W.

Lieut.; Brevet Captain; Major; Lieut.-Colonel—

A. D. C. AT HEADQUARTERS

ARMY OF THE POTOMAC

From Oct., 1862 to Lee's Surrender, April 9, 1865

———

Woolsey, near Asheville, N. C.,
January 13, 1897.

Dear G. W. B.: It so happens that other than
a battered and of course "blood-stained" en-
gine of war, a rusted regulation cavalry sword,
that now for a matter of *thirty years* has hung
over C. W. W.'s shaving table, peacefully pointing to the radiator, there is—extant—little or
no evidence of the existence of Lieutenant Woolsey, or that a lad of that name ever had any
hand in the suppression of the rebellion. . . .

If, by chance, he did "fit into" the war, it
was so long ago that no one now remembers
him or his exploits. Nearly all the fighting
Generals with whom, by a concatenation of
happy accidents, this young person was permitted to come so intimately in contact during
the field operations, have been brevetted to

higher rank than any conferred on earth. They
have surrendered to the All-Conqueror. . . .

It is a pity that there were not quite enough
graduates (outside of rebeldom) from West
Point to go round ! Such were the exigencies
of the hour, incidental to a *volunteer* army, that
everybody in the service, so to speak, had at the
outset to do a little of everything. It grew out
of this strange state of affairs, that the willing
but inexperienced lad who thirty years later is
the writer of these lines, really did have thrust
upon him and at the very outset, duties sometimes involving enormous responsibility. Not
once, but many a time did this youth of twenty-
two, absolutely without other military training
than a brief practice at the manual of arms in
a New York city militia regiment, have given
to him, verbally as a rule, but sometimes written, and rarely sealed, orders for the movement
of troops—"orders of march," or quickly-given
orders of manoeuvres under fire, orders for the
quick placing of batteries of artillery, for the
filling up of gaps in line of battle, for the sudden changes of position of tens of thousands of
men at a time, for the reversal of orders previ-
ously delivered, for night advances, for daybreak assaults, for retreats, for reinforcements ;
for the manifold operations of large bodies of
troops ; in fact, orders such as in the days of the
Napoleonic wars would have been confided alone

to the discretest, most skilled and grey-bearded veterans of Napoleonic campaigns. All young officers on the staff had just such duties as these to perform a hundred times over, until at last, as a matter of course, they learned their business pretty thoroughly. It happened that young C. W. W. being staff-officer (A. D. C.) to the Adj't.-General of the Army of the Potomac (and thus technically in one of the administrative departments of the service), was with his chief passed on to the military family of each of the three great commanders who succeeded McClellan, and was probably on duty at these Headquarters longer than any other young American officer not a graduate of West Point.

His rank and assignment to duty were as follows : In the second year of the war he was commissioned as First Lieutenant in Company A of the 164th Regiment of New York State Volunteers, a regiment belonging to the Irish Brigade, which was promptly placed in the field, and which did good service for the whole term of its existence in the Virginia campaigns. Desiring staff duty, he was, by means of the kind letters of friends (among them some from his cousin William H. Aspinwall to *his* warm personal friend General McClellan, to Generals Fitz John Porter and Burnside and others), presently given leave of absence from his regiment for the purpose of presenting his letters. The army was then in

motion southward after the battle of Antietam.
With one horse and no servant or proper equipment, he left Washington, and in a snowstorm
followed up the army via Harper's Ferry and
down through the valley, and finally, on the
third day, overhauled the Army Headquarters'
camp, tired and hungry and dirty ; completely
ignorant of the simplest and plainest rules
which regulate the duties of even enlisted
men, much less those which govern the actions
of officers of a general staff! He had the idea
of trying for a staff position in connection with
the signal service, a service which was to him
more abstruse than Chaldee! General Seth
Williams, in charge of the Adjutant-General's
department, introduced him to Major-General
Burnside, who that very day succeeded McClellan in command of the Army. "Too busy now.
Send Mr. Woolsey back to Washington to wait
orders. Will see, later," was the upshot of his
tremendous forced march in search of a job.

Williams fed him, and his horse which had
gone very lame, told him what he ought to have
by way of a small camp equipment in case he
should be directed to return, cheered him with
hope that " something might be done " for him
a little later, and had an order, with proper
passes, written directing him to return at once
to Washington and wait for orders. This he
did through another snowstorm. It was a week

or ten days before the summons came : " You
will proceed at once with two horses, a servant
and proper equipment to report to the Adj't.-
General of the Army of the Potomac in the
field." On his second arrival, he was invited to
become A. D. C. to General Seth Williams, and
the order thus fixing him at Headquarters was
issued at once. His only fear was that he was
destined to slave at a *desk* for the rest of the
war—a clerk in the Adjutant-General's office.
But the upshot was far different ; his actual
position, in his judgment, was *preferable to that
of any aide-de-camp he ever knew.* He preferred it,
and he prefers it in retrospect to any other staff
position in the whole army ! to that of Colonel
Lord Abinger of the Scotch Fusileer Guards,
of the French princes, of le Comte de Paris, of
the Swedish cavalry officer, Rozencranz ; of
the Russian nobleman who volunteered for
duty with McClellan ; of Dahlgren, and Mitchell,
and Russell, and Ludlow, and Dickerson, and
all the personal aides. Not one of them had the
freedom of action, the *opportunities* that came in
C. W. W.'s way ; not one of them, more responsible, active *field* duty than the tired and
dirty young officer who, a few weeks before his
assignment as A. D. C., was taken out of a
snowstorm and fed and warmed by Seth Williams, and then sent back to Washington to get
a tin basin, a small field desk, an extra horse, a

servant, some blankets, and a proper equipment
generally.

C. W. W. remained, technically, as A. D. C.
(once for a brief time as Acting Assistant
Adjutant-General) for the whole period of his
military experience. When General Grant was
given command of all the armies, Captain C.
W. W. accompanied his beloved chief and warm
friend, Seth Williams, to General Grant's headquarters. Williams was made Inspector-General of all the armies, and just previous to the
last campaign of the war, he, with his own staff-
officers, visited all the military posts on the
Atlantic coast, south of Yorktown. An ocean
steamer, the old "Daniel Webster," was placed
at his disposal, and every post, including St.
Augustine, Florida, was visited. Every able-
bodied U. S. soldier at all these posts was
ordered to inspection at dress-parade, and on
each and every occasion C. W. W. did the actual
work of counting, and, in writing, filed his share
of the trenchant criticism necessary, as to the
general condition of the troops. Thus, he be-
lieves it no exaggeration to state that he tapped
on the stomach—in the process of counting—
every single private and subaltern then "present
for duty," on the whole South Atlantic stretch
of military posts, many thousands in all — :—
"101! 2! 3! 4! . . . 199! 200; 201! 2! 3! 4!
5! 6! (*sotto voce*, two hundred and six! hold

your piece straight! where's your shoe ?) 7 ! 8 !
9 ! 209 ! (Hold your tongue or you're reported!)
(212, your cap's filthy! shame on you!) 215!
(your canteen is upside down!) 216! (this is no
time to spit tobacco juice!) 220! (excellent!)
222! (silence! not a word!) 224! (no excuse
for such filth!) 226! (*sotto voce :* "good for
you"!) 235! Ugh!"

At this point C. W. W. stops a moment in this
dry recounting to jot down a memorandum of
a purely personal kind—to record something
of the not-forgetable and most loveable traits
of personal character belonging to his late
chief and warm personal friend, General Seth
Williams.   To him, next to General George B.
McClellan, was distinctly due the credit of the
astonishing work accomplished in the actual
field organization of the Army of the Potomac, but
aside from these high public and historic func-
tions, back of any public expression of administrative talent, Adjutant-General Williams, the
organizer, was as nothing to Seth Williams, the
personal friend.   He had the modesty and gen-
tleness of a woman, coupled with the firmness
and courage of the trained veteran of a Mexican
campaign under General Winfield Scott.

He had under his pen at all times a power of
tremendous scope ; his work was far too great,
too exacting, for any one man.   His corps of
skilled adjutants and clerks, the complete print-

ing press which was part of his bureau, and the admirable telegraphic department, which all through the war did such efficient work, saved him something of the great burden of business. Even these aids, though, were powerless to avert the complete collapse which came suddenly to his once tireless brain. Just after the strain of the war was over he died of brain fever at Boston. No man of all the forces, whose names he kept upon his voluminous records, was more respected and beloved than himself throughout the whole vast area occupied by the Army of the Potomac. His gentle strength, his self-effacing courage in the presence of disaster, his indomitable power for ceaseless work, were an incentive and an example that is seldom set. To one especially, who knew him intimately and loved him well, his fragrant memory has been for many a year, and must be to the end of life, a perpetual stimulation and source of strength.

On the application of General Williams, C. W. W., while still in the field, was brevetted to the rank of Captain, and at the close of the war, two additional brevets—those of Major and Lieutenant-Colonel, were bestowed upon him. Under each of the three military administrations of this army—that of Burnside, of Hooker, and of Meade, General Seth Williams, knowing Woolsey's strong desire for active field service, had issued a special order, or conveyed to

C. W. W. the verbal command from the Com-
manding-General, directing the young officer
to report for temporary duty as A. D. C. to the
Commandant of the Army.   On the occasion of
all the great battles or movements of troops
he always served with the personal aides with
exactly their duties, including even the duty
periodically of "officer of the day," a post of
high importance at the Headquarters of the
Army.   It meant the receiving and passing upon
all despatches or messengers arriving at night,
the reception of all visitors and the general care
of the camp by day.   When Williams, accompanied by his aide, C. W. W., was promoted to
the office of Inspector-General and the two took
up their abode in the military family of General
Grant, Woolsey was again permitted to report
directly to General Grant, from whom he received frequent orders for very important work
involving movements of troops or material,
sometimes of great magnitude.   When Burnside
and Hooker were relieved of their commands,
their personal staffs were retired with them, but
in these changes of army commanders, the great
administrative departments, with the Adjutant
General's at their head, remained as a rule intact.   The heads of the Commandants might be
cut off, but the *machinery* of the army must continue.   Thus it was that C. W. W. was passed
on from one administration to another, . . . and

for years through a stroke of good fortune was retained at Headquarters through three success-ive administrations.

After awhile, having of necessity thoroughly learned the duties, he was more or less intimately associated with all of the important operations after M'Clellan's removal, and, incidentally, came to have an acquaintance with all the Gen-erals of higher rank and with a great many officers of all arms throughout the army. An undue number of lines in this account have been given to this unimportant particular, but they are to define, *by request*, C. W. W.'s peculiar-ly lucky situation. Among the pleasant details of his duty were more than one private inter-view—long ones—with the President of the United States, on the occasion of Mr. Lincoln's visits to the Army. He thus met the Secretary of State, all the great Generals of the Atlantic coast above Fortress Monroe, many Senators and other high functionaries and distinguished guests. His position took him on duty to every Corps and Division Commander in the field—many times over. It gave him active military duty that was often most exciting, often very hazardous, frequently entirely confidential and private in nature; it opened to him much of the romance of the Secret Service, the unwritten story of the Spy and Detective Bureaux; it sometimes put him in actual command of small

bodies of men; it often sent him to bring up reinforcements, and placed him in positions of
large responsibility, especially on those occasions when, as at Gettysburg, it became part of
his duty to use every effort to re-form lines of
infantry falling back in disorder from the front.
"To form on the colors," even when out of
reach of the musketry fire, was always a difficult
matter with a mass of demoralized, discouraged
men.   C. W. W. had this to do several times.
His lucky star brought to him, at the close of
the war, the good fortune of being one of the
twenty officers only, present at the surrender in
the little house at Appomattox.   Incidentally
it gave him the especial satisfaction of being
directed to make a "fair copy" from the original terms of the surrender as dictated by General Grant, for the information of the Army of
the Potomac.   This document, in C. W. W.'s
handwriting, *must* be on file somewhere in the
War Department.   It gave him sole charge,
with one clerk, of what was known as the
"Daily Memoranda" — a consolidated daily
statement of every occurrence of importance or
of great interest, made up from the reports of
all the Brigade, Division and Corps commanders
in the Army—sent in to Headquarters every
twenty-four hours.   These volumes—there must
have been ten or twelve thick ones—are also on
file in the War Bureau.   The practice was found

impracticable on the march, and after awhile
was abandoned. It gave him a privilege that
he recalls with keenest satisfaction, the chance
to go half way to the opposite lines under two
different flags of truce. In one case the flag
was a towel, which he now rather regrets not
having preserved. The use of these flags was,
on one occasion, to meet General Lee's messenger and arrange for the subsequent meeting at which the surrender occurred, on that
happy day when that great Southern soldier,
out-generaled and exhausted, was forced to seek
our lines and sue for terms. That WHITE rag!
—it was so refreshing to change from "red"
or "yellow" to *white!*—served as the signal
for the close of the war.

It was then, with this towel, that we washed
our hands of the whole business, and presently
went home to stay ; stopping only in Washington long enough for the "march past" on the
occasion of the final review. The other flag of
truce was used the year before, after the worst
fiasco before Petersburg—the explosion of the
mine in front of Burnside's command—and in
connection with the rescue of the few wretched
soldiers who, although exposed for more than
thirty hours to an enfilading fire from rebel
infantry massed behind breastworks, and from
rebel batteries on either flank, were found still
breathing on that shot-riddled, maggot-infested,

midsummer battlefield. This flag had also to do with the belated burial of the red-wet hillocks of humanity, mostly the trunks of human forms, with which the wide space was covered. C. W. W., at this distance, wonders how it could have happened that in an insane desire to "see service," he actually got permission to go out into those trenches with the storming party, in the advance, under fire, when the fight was hottest and deadliest ; and why it was that unslain, not a hair of his head touched, without a spatter of blood, he was able to creep and crawl back again to our breastworks over the heaped bodies of the colored *noblemen*, who obeyed their orders all that day, even if "someone *had* blundered," and who by hundreds were shot down like dogs in the trenches. The stupidities in the "order of march" on that day are matters of history, for they led to an abortive court-martial. It was one of the most abominable blunders of the whole war.

A now exacting, but attractive woman (whose "ambrotype"—to use an ante-bellum word to-day obsolete—was carried in the left vest pocket of the writer during nearly the whole period of the war, and which, in its blue-velvet case, no doubt served as a life-preserver), at this particular writing stands with her equally exacting and delightful daughter of nineteen, at the writer's elbow. They unreasonably insist that

he shall tell the story of how he was taken
prisoner in one of the operations before
Petersburg, late in the war. It was the occasion
of the reconnoissance-in-force known as the
advance on "Hatcher's Run." The Army of the
Potomac moved out in a manner represented by
two diverging spokes from the hub of a wheel.
From the head of one of the advancing columns,
(one of the "spokes"), General Meade directed
C. W. W. to take a sealed despatch to the officer
in command at the head of the other column.
Aides generally chose their own routes and had
much latitude in the matter of escort. They
soon learned that the fewer in the escort, the
better for all concerned. Instead of stemming
the advancing tide of infantry back to the hub,
so to speak, this aide, with a single orderly, at-
tempted to cross the unknown enemy's country,
or the space lying between the heads of the two
"spokes." After four or five miles of uninter-
rupted travel he came to signs of what he hoped
were the federal troops of the other "spoke."
Their *blue coats* convinced the orderly and his
superior officer that the posse of cavalry ahead
of them, ignorant of anyone coming behind
them, were our own people, and the order was
given to pass them as quickly as possible.
They were the rebel Fitz-Hugh Lee's cavalry
patrolling the roads in the vanguard of Wade
Hampton's command, and who, without Meade's

knowledge, had come in between the two columns, in heavy force. They were the mounted
outposts of the enemy who, earlier in the day,
had captured a lot of regulation Yankee blue
overcoats and were masquerading as Union
troops. "One was taken and the other left."
Woolsey, a rod or two in advance, was "gob-
bled"; completely surrounded with quite too
many carbines levelled at him to withdraw at
the moment. He was more or less gently led
in the direction of Richmond, and much cheerful, if profane, conversation followed. The
damned Yankee was fairly bagged. The orderly,
as he screamed : "No! they're *not* our men !"
wheeled about and escaped, reporting at home
that the Lieutenant would never come back.
But he did ! Our young friend watched his
chance, and in a moment of convivial glee over
his taking, by his captors, when one of them at
his left leaned over from his horse and embraced
him, in an affectionate, if profane, word of welcome to Dixey, he got out his revolver from an
inside pocket with his sealed despatch, tried to
discharge it into the breast of his companion,
and then (all in much less time than it takes to
write these two lines) striking the man a fearful blow in the face with his wet-capped pistol
which refused to go off, and which he is sorry
to have lost in the rumpus, turned his fortunately excellent horse, and galloped at top-speed

in the direction of Boston, the place of his birth.
In the meantime he had been robbed of all his
belongings except, strangely enough, one of his
pistols, and the despatches which were never
delivered. The talismanic "ambrotype" no
doubt saved his life, for in his rapid falling to
the rear, the ten or twelve gentlemen from Georgia shot at him again and again, following up
as fast and as far as they dared. They should
have made him walk! His capture had one
good outcome, for he was, on his return in the
course of the night, after having lost his way in
the woods for hours, able to inform the Commanding General of the presence in the gap of
Wade Hampton's command with infantry as well
as cavalry. This information changed the whole
course of the movement. A good pair of quartermaster's blankets replaced his stolen plunder,
and a good tin cup filled the aching gap made
by the theft of his silver one in the rifled saddle-
bags.

Among a multitude of highly important orders
and messages carried by C. W. W., he took to
the front the order for the storming of the
heights back of Fredericksburg, and the order
to Meade from Hooker for the retreat from
Chancellorsville. Meade was intensely indignant—even insubordinate in his comment.

C. W. W. was given more varied duties, on
verbal orders, from General Meade, at and after

the battle of Gettysburg, than from any other commander. . . .

But on the whole, one of the most pleasing orders he ever had given him was the one to place in line of battle, under fire, Tyler's whole command of heavy artillery at Bowling Green, Va., May 19th, 1864, to fill up a gap which, for a time, threatened fearful disaster to the whole army. The men, by hundreds, when word of what was to be done reached the company commanders, abandoned hats, knapsacks, coats, everything but their pieces with full complement of cartridges (and never saw their belongings again), and the whole immense line rushed in most forgiveable bad alignment, singing, screaming, bellowing, cheering, sweating, the line surging and bending like a snake, but the roar of their multitudinous voices never letting up for an instant until it was drowned in the rattle of musketry. There would come brief gaps in the rattle of the guns, when the men's voices would be heard again, only to be overborne by a louder roar from the stronger lungs of the rifled field batteries. All this time C.W.W. was with the troops, under fire, and by nighttime the losses among these same men were found to be very great. But the joyful thunder of that great cheer that went up, as a whole Division of fresh troops made good the dangerous gaps in the line of battle, was in itself a reinforcement, and we held our own that night and went at it again in the morning. To the young chap who took this order, there was the keenest possible satisfaction. He had often, on the march, set whole Corps, or even a Right or Left Grand Division, in motion, but he never "put in" so many troops in line, under fire, as on this occasion. To touch the spring that set them going and made them sing that song was *delightful!*

C. W. W. *could*, he supposes, dear G., spend a useless hour—far better devoted to the cultivation of "Symphoricarpus Racemosus"—in unfolding before you a musty and forbidding pile of photographic field-maps, yellowed to illegibility, such as were distributed for the private information of certain confidential staff officers at the Army Headquarters. Maps! Maps! Maps! They were a great part of an aide's existence in those far-away days now so vaguely mapped behind us all.

From a dusty upper shelf in the long-ago abandoned Witchwood "workshop," he thinks he could unearth a thick volume or two of faded files of "General" and "Special Orders," such as were *printed* daily, (but not by typewriters in those days), in the camps of Burnside, Hooker and Meade, and which formed part of the daily administration of the manifold affairs of their now historic commands; . . . but at these dry

statistics C. W. W. stops. He has no "incidents
of the war to relate," beyond the very unimportant personal details already given. The best
he could do would be to show you a camp-stool
from the officers' mess-room at Fort Sumter,
—for General Williams, as Inspector-General
of all the Armies, with his devoted subordinate,
went into Charleston with the troops—just in
time to sack Fort Sumter. He could exhibit a
grapeshot from Yorktown, a bit of a rebel flag
which floated and for a time *gloated* over Richmond. He could offer for your inspection a
sabre which he took from a battlefield, and that
has on it this engraved inscription : " Captured
by Daniel Driscoll from Stuart's cavalry at Tunstall's station." He could show a pathetic trifle
or two from this or from that battlefield. He
could frighten you with some barbaric knives
made by Southern village blacksmiths to cut
the Nation's throat with. These he picked up
on a smoking field from which the " Louisiana
Tigers " had just been driven, but the soil of
which these whelps of hell had left reeking with
the blood of Massachusetts. He could, if you
particularly wanted to give him a sleepless
night, tell you *all about* the ghastly horrors of
the first few hours (before the sound of human
voices stopped entirely) just after Chancellorsville, Fredericksburg, Gettysburg, The Wilderness, Cold Harbor, Petersburg, and many an-

other. He might (by word of mouth, but cannot commit these sickening things to paper) tell you of the fearful anguish of the semi-slain left on fields without water or food or even saws to make their own amputations—and this sometimes for *days*. He could tell you of men's lives that were sucked out by maggots, and of burials that consisted of spade-heaped mounds of human shreds and tatters of human forms,—of putrid heads alone, of mangled arms and legs and stomachs; of men who at Gettysburg cried to him as he passed (powerless to help), "Water! Water! for God's sake!" of disabled men who were dying of thirst with perhaps curable flesh-wounds, who actually refused to drink water brought to them from the stream near by, because it was too *red*. C. W. W. saw these things himself, and is too old and steady not to be a *credible* witness.

Beyond these tellings and these few relics of little value (and that will have *no* associations to those who may come after him), C. W. W. again regrets that he cannot aid and abet you in your dire proposal to encumber his tombstone. If you write anything about him, say only that he volunteered with the others to help *the Cause*, and worked faithfully according to his light.

To your unwilling but affectionate correspondent, those years of fearful yet splendid happenings,—those hateful yet beloved memories sometimes seem, in these closing years of a dying century, but a filmy cloud of vapor, scarcely visible on the vague horizon of a fast-fading sunset sky. A melting memory of long ago, a half-forgotten dream.

CHAPTER XVI.

When Peace had finally come we were all eager that Mother, who had seen so much of the dark side of the War and had known its anxieties so keenly, should see something also of the victorious army and of Washington with the smile of Peace upon it.

A. H. W. to H. G.

Charley has expressed a hope that Mother would go on to Washington before he leaves and let him show her about a little and take a peep at Jane, etc., etc. So quite suddenly at the last, after a good deal of that good-natured, kindly-intentioned goading with which people often press their attentions upon unwilling relatives, Mother was got off to Baltimore, with Georgy, Hatty and Carry. There Charley met them,—Robert Howland was also of the party— and to-day we hear for the first time of their further progress down the Bay and up the James to Richmond! the goal of so many of *Georgy's* desires. They reached there on Thursday night, and to our great pleasure were still in time for the passage of a portion of Sherman's army through Richmond next day. . . . I don't enjoy traveling at any time, least of all rebelward, and so came up here to be with Eliza and our little children, who are making their usual spring visit and revelling in the wealth of "daisy-lions" and blue violets on the lawn and in the ravine. There is soldier work here for Eliza to do too,—a returned prisoner, who is getting well on her good tea and brandy and fresh eggs, in a cottage up at Glenham, and another elsewhere who must die, and the family of a third who did die after two months of sickness, five miles from here, in a "copperhead" neighborhood, where folks said "rebel prisons served him just right, he oughtn't to have been such a fool as to go to the war." . . .

Mother to A. H. W.

BALTIMORE, TUESDAY EVENING, May 10, 1865.

My dear Abby: So far "on to Richmond" safe and well, without let or hindrance ; no mishap except the opening, in some miraculous way, of my inkstand in my handbag and spoiling a few articles—my paper, as you see, for one. We were scarcely in this city's precincts when Charley appeared in the car, taking us by surprise ; said he had walked out to meet us, and it was the third train he had met, not knowing by which we would come. He is looking very well, and seems greatly pleased to be a citizen again ; and as Carry says is "extremely civil." He had rooms all ready for us ; nice ones on the first floor ; we have had a hearty supper, waited upon by Gettysburg John, who was our cook there, and is head waiter here. We had a shaking of hands all round, and he got us up a very nice supper. . . . We are agitating the question of boats, whether to try the new line, which makes it first trip to-morrow from here, or to go to Washington, where, as Charley says, Mr. Dana, the Assistant Secretary of War, will be happy to give us passes in the Government boat. We think it will be pleasant to go on from here and return by the other way, and Charley says he can write to Mr. Dana to reserve our passes till then. . . . Robert is well, and glad to meet Charley. I hope you are safely housed with Eliza. Kiss the dear children for me and remember me to Ann.

Public conveyances had their discomforts just after the war ! as Hatty's letter shows :—

H. R. W. to A. H. W.
RICHMOND, May 14, 1865.

Dear Abby : Robert, I believe, gave you an account of our night on the boat with its accompaniment of drunken women and "b flats." . . . But in spite of it all we are *in Richmond!*

The Family enter Richmond.

and glad we are,—(knock at the door, and two bouquets with the "compliments of Major Scott, Fourth Massachusetts Cavalry," handed in, for Mrs. Woolsey and Mrs. Woolsey's daughter Carry, with whom he rode on horseback yesterday). We arrived too late for the grand display, but on Wednesday, all day long, Sherman's troops were passing through the city as quietly as possible ; no display of any kind, no review by Halleck ; grim, fierce-looking men some of them, marching along splendidly, but giving no sign. . . . (G. M. W. takes up the letter.) Sherman and Halleck are deadly enemies, since the latter's order to disregard any orders received from Sherman, and a hot interchange of letters, before the troops came up, ended in an announcement by note to Halleck from Sherman that "he had better not show himself in the streets, as Sherman could not answer for the reception he might receive from the soldiers." So they marched sullenly through, leaving the Fourteenth and Seventeenth Corps to follow next day. We were all ready to review them, when, to our horror, at 9.30, as we were finishing breakfast, the announcement came that all the troops had gone through. No one was told of it ; General Curtis,—our wounded Captain of the old Sixteenth, now Brigadier-General of Volunteers, who is here—knew nothing of it, and they began at 5.30 A. M., and went as quietly as possible. Saturday there was still left one corps to pass, and we went up to the State House and watched them, but they broke up, passed through different streets, and took no more notice of our handkerchiefs and the flag, than if we were posts—sullen fellows, espousing Sherman's cause, and determined not to show the slightest interest in the place where Halleck was. So this personal fight deprived us and the army of what might have been a splendid sight. General Curtis is doing everything for us. We have our order for as many ambulances as we want as long as we stay; we never drive with less than four horses and eight outriders; have been all over the city and to Cold Harbor, going there yesterday with four officers and General Curtis and wife, and seeing the field and line of works. To my great pleasure we broke down on this side, and were not obliged to eat our dinner on any battle field, though we did stop where the rebel army must have camped, and somewhere in the neighborhood of *Gaines Mill*, where Joe was wounded....

We came back safely to receive Generals Ord, Turner and someone else, and Captains and Lieutenants thrown in—Mrs. Ord with them. This morning Mother and I have been at home, the girls at a colored church, where, to their great delight, the announcement was made of *Jeff. Davis' capture*. The whole church was overcome with delight, blessing the Lord, crying and kissing Hatty's and Carry's hands. They were charmed to see the northern ladies, and gave them chief places among them, and a bunch of roses each. Numbers of notices were read; people asking information about lost relations, and where to find their own families. To-morrow (Monday), we have been induced by three Major-Generals to go with them to Fort Harrison, and they promise to see that we get off to Petersburg on Tuesday A. M., by General Ord's private boat or special train. What *can* we do against the Union Army? We *have* to stay of course, and shall not get to Washington before Thursday, probably. General Curtis wants me to urge Joe and Eliza to come on soon; he may be sent off from here, and wants them while he is here. They must be sure to, it is all full of interest. Carry is in her glory; goes on horseback with the officers when we are in ambulances, and is delighted with all; Hatty, too. Mother keeps up her interest in all she sees. I shall leave the scraps at Lee's house to-day; we marched by it with General Curtis the other day.

G. had collected for some time past all the striking editorials from the Tribune and Post, on the abuses of the Belle Isle and Libby prisons by the keepers of those shameful pens, which were in daily sight of Lee's own house, and which he could by one condemnatory order have closed. She left the package so collected at his door in Richmond, first ascertaining that he was in the house, and knowing that in the dearth of southern news they would certainly be read.

Jane was at Fairfax Seminary Hospital all this time, and in forwarding the following letter of Mother's she writes to E. at Fishkill, "You will be glad to get this nice letter from Mother. I am so glad she went. All well here. Six hundred and twenty-five men received since this night week, fever, diarrhœa, &c., and many broken down by the 'quick march home' that sounds so pretty in the papers. Come to the 'Great Review.'"

Mother to J. S. W.

RICHMOND! SUNDAY, May 14th, 1865.

My dear Jane: I do not realize the heading of my letter, in spite of the filthy rebel room we are in at the "Spottiswood," and the strange sights and sounds all about us,—and despair of giving you any clear idea of the fact that we are actually in this Rebel capital. . . .

On Wednesday, at 4 P. M., we took the "Adelaide," from which I would warn all who come

after us ! Of all filthy, disgusting conveyances
that is the most so. Crowded with men, women,
children and b. b's. The lowest set of females,
too, that could possibly be congregated together.
We had smooth, pleasant weather, however,
which in some measure compensated, and after
our night of discomfort had a glorious sun-
rising, and at Fortress Monroe we took a joyful
leave of the nasty Adelaide for a nice new boat,
and had a charming sail (or steam) on to Richmond,—stopping awhile at City Point, which,
with the whole of the James River from that on,
was very interesting, with the fortifications,
broken bridges, soldiers at different points
guarding the shores still, and Dutch Gap, etc.
Our own troops now garrison all the rebel
works on the approach to the city. We glided
along to it most peacefully, arriving about 7 P. M ,
an immense crowd waiting the boat's arrival—
civil and military, black and white, Union and
rebel, men, women and children, all mixed in,
and forming a dense mass. It was a sight to
behold ! We got through with difficulty, a military guard taking down all our names as we
passed out of the boat, and we were packed into
the Spottiswood stage and soon found ourselves
in this hotbed of rebels, which name may still
belong with truth to it. We are disgusted to
find as many rebels as Union people here, and
although officers have been forbidden to appear

here in uniform, they swarm in their gray coats,
with their families and friends. We had the
pleasure of dining with a party of them opposite
us at dinner to-day. I have been expecting to
be assailed at every turn by some of my old
Southern friends, but no one I know has yet
crossed my path. . . .

We found rooms kept for us; Robert being
along, he took Charley's. but C. has a cock-loft
by himself now. As we drove up the evening
we arrived, we saw General Curtis to our great
pleasure, who stopped his ambulance in front
till we came up alongside, and told us he would
come immediately to call on us, which he did,
and has been doing ever since. We saw Chaplain Gray too, Charley's friend, and he with all
the staff of the Massachusetts 4th Cavalry have
been at our service all the while. . . .

We have seen the rebel house of Representa-
tives and the Senate; in one of these we waited
for some time, seeing and hearing a number of
rebels taking the oath of allegiance, a poor, forlorn, weather-beaten, hollow-cheeked-looking
set, with sad, disspirited countenances, that made
one feel very sorry for them. We have been to
the cemetery, from which we had a very good
view of Belle Isle,—a wretched, barren point of
land, the very worst spot in the whole country
they could have selected for our poor prisoners.
In the cemetery we saw J. E. B. Stuart's grave,

which has only a headstone, no monument, but
is kept constantly covered with fresh flowers;
so were many rebel graves. We had an ambulance with four horses and four orderlies put at
our service, and wherever we go it is in this
style ! We drove to the cavalry camp of the 4th
Mass., by invitation of Mr. Gray, Major Scott
and Dr. Garvin, who have been our escort all
the while, and their splendid band was called
out on Friday afternoon and gave us charming
music. We make quite a sensation, I assure
you, when we move anywhere with our four
grays and outriders. Yesterday we started off
in this same style, with the addition to our party
of General Curtis and wife, and spent the day
on the battlefields of Gaines' Mill, thrice fought
over, you remember.

It was a most interesting day, the weather
was superb, the trees all in full leaf, and
flowers, seemed in contrast to the lines of
graves, with their wooden stakes marking the
spots, and whole lines, as far as you could see,
of earthworks and rifle pits, with fragments of
garments hanging about them, and still, in many
places, miserable human fragments unburied.
A burial detachment is sent out every few days
to do its sad work. We took a grand lunch of
meats, ice-cream, strawberries and cake, all of
which we collected from confectioneries and
markets, and borrowed a supply of saucers,

spoons, etc. When we had selected a rural spot, not on the battlefield, and spread our cloth, which was the india rubber blanket of one of our aides, we found the officers had also brought from camp a lunch of their own getting up, which, all together, made a large and attractive display of viands. We were sixteen in company and did ample justice to the feast. General Curtis and wife were our guests, Major Scott, Chaplain Gray, Major Garvin, Robert, Charley and ourselves, with our orderlies. Carry rode on horseback with her military escort, feeling grand as possible, and had a real jolly time. Her dress and cap were very handsome, and she rode Major Scott's fine war horse. Altogether the day was a success, and was crowned in the evening by a *line* of distinguished callers, Major General Ord and his wife heading the column, (which we consider a great attention.) General Turner, Captain Gibbs, Captain Baker, Chaplain Trumbull, Captain Franklin, brother of the old General, General Curtis and wife, Major Scott and Chaplain Gray were all our guests here that evening.

I am so glad Hatty and Carry are having such a grand time. We have had every attention these officers could show us, and they are all very busy and pushed hard for time, too. They think it a great treat for themselves to have Northern Union ladies to call on—so they say.

Baker is an English officer of the regular army, and has been in some of our late battles, joining himself with good will to the Union army.

Monday noon.—I wrote this far yesterday and laid it aside to visit the Libby prison and walk round the burnt district, while Robert, H. and C. were at church. I was too tired to finish it last evening, and to-day we have been off on another excursion since 9 o'clock this morning. General Turner sent his own carriage, a very nice low barouche, for my use, in which Georgy, Robert and I went, and in the Headquarters ambulance—which is a very handsome one, cushioned, and seats running across to accommodate eight persons, and which we have had the use of all the time—General Curtis and wife, General Turner and Captain Gibbs accompanied Hatty and Carry. We were very sorry to leave Charley behind with a slight indisposition. We left him a bowl of arrowroot, with a small phial of brandy, and made him promise to keep quiet, which he did, and we found him fast asleep on our return, feeling better, but still out of sorts. This determines us to wait here till to-morrow morning, instead of leaving this afternoon for Petersburg. We drove this morning to Fort Harrison, and all over the battlefields there, getting out and walking all over the forts, and poking our heads into bomb-proofs and rifle pits, and walking into the log tents so recently deserted, first by the rebels, and then by our own soldiers, where their cooking utensils are all left, and their blankets still hanging over poles, and canteens strung on the doors, and old clothing of all sorts strewn about, and everything having the appearance of being left but yesterday.

It is a city of log tents, inside of Fort Harrison, a very extensive one, where the Army of the James were encamped, excellently built and wide avenues between the rows of huts,—their tables, benches, stoves, tin cups and plates all there. We were saying it would be a capital plan to send the poor of Richmond there, either white or black; they could live quite comfortably. To-day has been a more interesting one than Saturday. We saw at the Libby yesterday the quarters of our men and the pit where our officers were buried, without air or light. I wonder any one of them ever lived to tell the story of their sufferings. There are a few rebels there in the upper room still, and we saw them from the street, sitting on the window sills with their legs hanging through the bars outside. Their rebel friends are down there constantly, talking with them, and, until very lately, have been allowed to send them up baskets of provisions, which they managed to draw up by strings furnished them in some way or other. The windows are near enough to the street for their friends to throw up a ball of string, oranges, apples, letters, etc.

This is very different from the rebel treatment of our poor prisoners, who were shot if they showed themselves at a window. We saw the place where the notorious jailer Turner escaped since we have been here, and also the subterranean passage made by Colonel Streight and others, and had some idea of the horrid work it must have been; also, the mine that was prepared by Lee's order in the prison, to blow it up with its inmates in case the city was taken! This same Lee is living here now peacefully in his own residence, and being fed by our military authorities on all the luxuries of the season. We have passed his house repeatedly, but have not yet seen his Satanship. Georgy has plied him well with reading matter from our papers, making any little darky who happens to pass at the moment ring the door-bell and hand them in, having directed them beforehand to Robert Lee, Franklin Street. She sent him a lot of Sunday reading yesterday. I would like much to know the effect it has. Some say he is very much subdued of late, never goes out except early in the morning or late at night, avoids every one, and is *intending* to take the oath of allegiance! I hope he will not be allowed to do so, as it will only be to get to Europe, where his friends will join him. Only think of Jeff. in

his wife's clothes ! It is good to secure him in
any garb, though I am sorry to have womanly
garments so desecrated. I have no doubt he
will manage to slip through the fingers of his
captors, and get off yet out of reach of our
Government. It is to be hoped not, and that
they will make quick work with him.

Judge Campbell is here in this hotel—in the
parlor, sitting near us every evening. General
Curtis pointed him out to us, with the remark,
"There is a man under arrest and who will probably be hung." The house is full of rebel
women, who are here from all parts looking up
their brothers and husbands and sons. It is
annoying to have them swarm into the dining
room at meals, and then to the parlors, occupying all the sofas and chairs. We sometimes
cannot tell whether the new arrivals are rebels
or Union, till we see their gray-coated males
coming in to greet them.

Carry went with Robert yesterday to see Miss
Van Lew, the celebrated Union lady here, and
took her a handsome flag, and some new books
brought from New York for her. She was very
much delighted, and you shall see a letter which
came from her to-day. She sent Carry an elegant bunch of flowers this morning, and wanted
her to promise that by and by, when things are
more settled here, she would come and make her
a visit. She invited Carry and Robert, and any

of us who would accompany them, to tea with her this evening. We are not going to tea, but some of us mean to drive and see her. She lives in a fine old "mansion," with beautiful grounds. We mean also to call on Mrs. Ord and Mrs. Curtis to pay our farewell compliments; and to-morrow morning at 10.40 we take our leave of Richmond, feeling that our visit here has been a brilliant success.

This evening the girls are expecting a bevy of new officers to call on them, and are going in the meantime to General Turner's Headquarters, across the river,—Captain Gibbs coming for them in the General's private carriage. . . .

I don't know how we shall get along at home again without two or more orderlies in full trappings behind us. Wherever we go here on excursions, officers and orderlies are armed, there are so many stragglers and marauders about.

The air is filled with the burning brick and mortar smell through the whole city. The entire block through to the next street in front of us is in ruins, and all the way down the long street not a house is standing; banks, churches, private dwellings and stores without number, all lie in ruins. By moonlight the sight is beautiful. They are putting up slightly-built shanties here and there for the sale of different articles, mostly "beer and cakes," which spoil the picturesqueness.

The city is a beautiful one, with its fine old trees and large gardens, now filled with every variety of roses. We average about four large bouquets a day in our room, from military friends, and our mantelpiece is filled all in a row with roses, syringas, honeysuckles and magnolias. I wish every day you had come with us. I am sure you would enjoy it. Do join Eliza and Joe when they come on. . . .

We shall be in Washington by Wednesday or Thursday sometime. Do not give yourself any trouble about meeting us; we will go and see you as soon as we can, and G. can stay as long as pleases her and you. . . .

Best love to you.　　　　　　Yours,

　　　　　　　　　　　　　　Mother.

Your Grandmother's next letter is given because its anxiety over a slight illness of G's, shows how unusual such a thing was. This was the first "sick leave" in four years. G's campaign had made a hardened veteran of her, though at last the Sanitary Commission came even to *her* rescue.

Mother to A. H. W.

　　　　　　　　　　Petersburg, Va., May 18th.

My dear Abby: The only drawback to our enjoyment of the trip has been Georgy's illness, but I am very happy to speak of this now as

past away. We left Richmond Tuesday morning. She was not very well, I could see plainly,
though she would not allow it, and on reaching
this place, she was in a high fever, and obliged
to give up to the care of a physician. We called
in Dr. Prince, the medical director and surgeon
of the post, who was highly spoken of as a good
man and excellent doctor. The fever raged for
a day and night, so that we were extremely
anxious lest it might run into typhoid, or some
other rapid and fearful disease, but God was
pleased to order otherwise, and she is now so
much relieved that we think of pursuing the journey to-morrow, as it is desirable to get on by
"easy stages" to Washington. We could not
have been better off in every way. . . . An attentive, skilful and gentlemanly physician, and the
Sanitary Commission close at hand to supply us the
wine which we could not get anywhere else; also
excellent black tea. . . . G's bed is literally covered with roses, we have them in such profusion;
our little silk flag (your make) is hung by her
bedside for effect; and on a table near her every
variety of flower the country produces, and this
is a great one, with superb roses of every kind.
Ice, lemonade, ice-cream when wanted, and very
good, too, with whatever else she needs or fan-
cies—looking like an interesting princess. . . .
The 1st Division of the 6th Corps passed through
from Danville to-day. It was splendid ; the

band was drawn up in front of the hotel, play-
ing while they passed, and a crowd of Union
people in the piazzas and windows of the house
looking on. The girls and Charley displayed
our flag, and there was a large collection of
officers in front below us to see them pass along.
Dreadfully burnt and weather-beaten they
looked, too, poor fellows, under their weight of
knapsacks, etc.—they seemed too wearied for
even the thought of going home to cheer them.
There was no cheering or waving at all as they
passed. I do not understand why this is the
case. The feelings of the rebels present everywhere seem to be too much regarded, I think, in
this ; I hope in northern cities it will be different.
These brave fellows should be met with the
applause they deserve, and be made to feel their
welcome from all hearts. . . . We will not stay
long in Washington, just to rest and see Jane,
unless there is something very attractive and
interesting going on. I must say I would wait
there a week to see Jeff. in his wife's petticoats !
This is talked of with great glee amongst
the blacks here ; one or two have asked me,
grinning from ear to ear, if "dey was gwine to
bring Jeff. dis way." Wasn't it a joke ? it finishes
up his reputation amongst his own people. . . .
    I add a P. S. to ask if you will write a line to
Mrs. Turner at Cornwall, or perhaps you and E.
will drive over and see her about a room for

Charley—he seems to want a quiet rest somewhere for a while—an airy, nice room, as he will
sit in it a good deal. . . . We hope to meet Dr.
Bacon at City Point, who will be on hand if
needed.

G. M. W. to A. H. W.

EBBITT HOUSE, WASHINGTON,
SATURDAY, May 21, '65.

We have just arrived; the boat from City
Point touching at Alexandria long enough to
let Mother and Robert off. They were to take
a carriage and drive out two-and-a-half miles to
see Jane, and bring her in to spend Sunday (if
she will come). We came on with Charley to
this House and find it packed. We are all four
put in one room until to-morrow night, when
possibly we may have something better. The
city is full, to see the Review. I hope Joe has
telegraphed for rooms. . . .

I am delighted that they are coming, and very
much disappointed that you are not. We really
thought that you might be induced just to look
at the brave fellows on Tuesday and Wednesday
before everything marched off into the past, forever and ever. . . . I am seeing doctors and taking doses without number in a perfectly docile
way, and you have nothing to say about *me*. . . .
We had Vance of North Carolina a prisoner on
board the boat up, (under guard of officers and

four privates) strutting about,—great fat, chewing fellow.   He called for potatoes at breakfast,
and Mother, sitting next, said, "Here is a very
small, and cold one."   "Thank you," he said,
quite fiercely, "I wish a large and a hot one."
"Small potatoes" might answer his purposes
under the circumstances. . . .

Mother to A. at Fishkill.

WASHINGTON, May 21, 1865.

My dear Abby: Robert will probably have
seen you before this reaches you and told you
all about us. . . . He had telegraphed Joe and
Eliza that he would be at home on Monday, so
that they could come on to the Review. . . .
Georgy is much better, gains every day, but will
gain faster going north, out of this oppressive
air, which seems to have no vitality whatever in
it.   Dr. Smith says it is all malaria everywhere
in this region.   As Robert will tell you, he and
I left the boat on the journey up and drove from
Alexandria to the Fairfax Seminary Hospital.
We found Jane well, and very glad to see us.
It was a very busy time with her, just making
out her orders for special diet, and giving out
the stores.   We only staid an hour, and did not
go into the wards, or to see Mrs. Jerome, only into
Jane's department.   I looked into her poorly
furnished little bedroom, which seemed to me
very bare, and very unsuited to Jane's ideas and

tastes, but which she seems perfectly contented and happy with.

It is a fine building, airy and beautifully situated, very clean, and everything about in perfect order, and Jane the supreme directress. It was strange indeed to see her there, all alone, and hundreds of men waiting their portion at her hands. Things are so arranged that she can sit quietly in her office, (which is a pleasant room, with its seven wardrobes, sure enough, all in a row !) and move the whole machinery of the kitchen and wards, with apparently little labor. This had just been scoured, and a large wood fire was burning, to dry the board floor. The wardrobes ! are fitted up with shelves, and form a row of very nice closets, filling one side of the room ; there is one very large window with a beautiful view, and on the sill a flower box with growing plants ; in the middle of the floor is her business table covered with papers relating to the work of the hospital, her writing implements and piles of diet-lists, etc. Between this table and the huge fire-place is spread her rug, the only piece of floor covering she has anywhere ; across the window, with space from it to admit a chair, stands another table, filled with books and flowers—two vases of beautiful roses, —and I added a splendid magnolia, which I brought her from Petersburg, and managed to keep perfectly fresh in water on the boat.

Jane seemed very well, though she *looks* no stronger than when at home. . . . We left her with the promise from her that she and Dr. Smith would drive up in the afternoon to see G. They did so in spite of the rain, made us a short call, and took Hatty back with them to stay till to-morrow, when Charley is to drive down for her. Jane promises to come up and see the Review on Tuesday, so that we will all *but you*, dear Abby, be here together. . . . Dr. Bacon is staying here in the house, so that we can have his medical advice if needed. . . . General Williams came in last night in his little, modest, quiet way to call, and offered his services in any way to aid us in our getting about ; invited us to a seat in his pew. Will Winthrop was here too, last night. Mrs. John Rockwell, her two sons, and Miss Foote are in the house, and a great crowd of queer-looking people coming to see their husbands and brothers the "Jyggydeers" of the army. Miss Prime and some of her family are here, too ; we have had several little talks with her; she is very pleasant, as usual. Robert will tell you all about our trip on the horrid boat, only a very little better than the Adelaide, and our seeing the vessel with Jeff. Davis and his party on board.

C. C. W. to A. H. W.

The
Great
Review.
The
Army
Dis-
banded.

Dear Abby : Joe and Eliza arrived safely last night at 12 o'clock, and E. was taken into our room, we having fortunately an extra bed, an extraordinary thing in these times. The city is crammed, and no accommodations to be had at any price; hundreds of people have left, finding no sleeping place, and great numbers stay at Baltimore and come up for the day ; among the latter is Charles Rockwell, who with the Tracys came in the train yesterday with Eliza. Charley gave up his third of a room to Joe and took his old quarters with General Williams. The old General has been daily to see us and secured us a window in the avenue for to-day; but as nothing was to be seen from it, we wisely accepted six tickets on a platform which our usual luck threw in our way, in fact forced upon us. Miss Prime's uncle procured in some way twenty seats on the Connecticut State platform, opposite the President's, and insisted on our taking six, which we gladly did. General Sherman's box or covered platform was immediately next, and Admiral Wilkes, who was in it, made several of us come in there. Georgy would not lose the Review and came slowly up, escorted by Joe and Charley, and followed by the family, chiefly Mother, who brought a feather pillow and an air cushion for her to sit on and put at her back,

a box for her feet, and a bag of sandwiches, and
port wine. She stood it remarkably well, and
with three glasses of wine, etc., declared it did
her great good to go. She takes frequent sherry-
cobblers and strong drinks generally, and the
"bar" must think the "sick lady eats and drinks
awful." The Review was sublime! As each
general officer rode up to the President's stage,
which was gorgeously dressed with flags and
hot-house plants, he dismounted and took his
seat in the great circle of great men, till we had
directly opposite us and under our inspection,
President Johnson, Secretary Welles, Mr. Stanton, Generals Grant, Meade, Hancock, Sherman, Butterfield, Merritt, etc., etc. Whenever a
pause occurred the mass rushed to the front of
the staging to get a nearer view of the great
men. Three superb bands relieved each other
and kept up a constant clang of splendid music
just alongside of us. There were no draw-
backs, no accidents. Little General Custer
came near being run away with; his horse took
fright and got beyond his control, tore down
the lines, his hat blew off, and there was a good
deal of excitement, but he finally stopped him
without any damage. One splendid Colonel
there would not have fared as well—a fine looking fellow, sitting like an arrow on his horse, his
sword drawn and a beautiful bouquet in his
hand ; we noticed he made a fine salute, as they

all did, to the President, but with his *left* hand ;
then we saw his right arm was gone to the
shoulder ! What could he have done if his
horse had started, with his sword, his flowers,
and the reins all in one hand ? Have we not
been just in the nick of time everywhere ! To-
morrow we have our same seats for Sherman's
Army ; we could not have had a better time for
Richmond, and our first night here was Sheridan's last. He spent some time in the parlor, so
we had a good look at him ; short and stubby,
but jolly. That night his troops gave him the
most superb serenade you can imagine, right
under our windows ; there must have been three
or four bands united, and all the people of the
city must have turned out, from the cheering.
Early next morning his troops passed, to give a
farewell cheer, and at noon he left for Texas,
the men to follow, I believe.

We have had a number of callers as usual, the
Wilkes, the Knapps, Mr. Huntington Wolcott,
Dr. Smith, Mr. "Conversation Clark," Harry
Hopkins, etc., and Dr. Bacon in the house. We
are glad to have him near in case of need, though
G. really is better. I think the last four years is
the matter with her. It would not be human that
she could endure, without some ill effects, the
constant exposure and trials of that time. We
have only seen Jane for a few moments ; she is
very busy and did not care to come to the procession.

E. and G. were at the Ebbitt House again for the first time since they sailed away with the Sanitary Commission in '62. E. writes:

E. W. H. to A. H. W.

EBBITT HOUSE, WASHINGTON, May 24, '65.

Dear Abby : I wish you could have been here at least for this second day, and have seen Sherman's splendid army. Far from flagging, the interest greatly increased, and there was much more enthusiasm and life to-day than yesterday, both among the men themselves and the lookers-on. Nothing ever was more false than the report that Sherman's braves were all " bummers," and beyond his control, or if so, it would be well for all armies to have " 'alf their complaint." They beat the A. P. all to pieces in their marching, which is an easy swinging gait but in perfect time and uniformity ; and in physique they seemed half a head taller and broad and straight in proportion,—great big, brave, brawny men with faces brown as Indians and a pleased smile on every one. The Army of the Tennessee came first with Logan at its head, though Sherman, of course, preceded him, and both were greeted with roars of delight, as indeed was the case with every general officer, every particularly torn flag, and all the men ! Flowers— many more than yesterday — were showered among them, great wreaths of laurel hung

around many of the horses' necks or over the
flagstaffs, and one of the prettiest parts of all
was to watch Mrs. Sherman, who, with her little
boy, sat next the general all day, cheer and
wave and toss flowers to one after another of
the color-bearers. When she couldn't toss far
enough herself the general himself would throw
them, and they were always caught with great
cheers and tossing of caps by the men. Indeed
Sherman won back our hearts to-day by his perfect delight in watching the ovation to his soldiers
and his zeal in helping it on. Most of the day
he and *Stanton* sat at the two extremes of the
platform, by design we supposed but it could
not have been so, for when it was all over the
last thing we noticed before the grandees separated were the two standing with their arms
around each other ! Perhaps a grand review in
Richmond would have had an equally happy
effect in Halleck's case.

After Logan's army came old Slocum, for
whom we all rose and gave a special cheer—and
who was cheered by everyone,—and the splendid
army of Georgia. The 20th Corps more than
any other impressed us with its immense size.
Each division seemed an army in itself, and after
each came the drollest mule-train loaded with
blankets and camp-kettles and *poultry!* and
darkies of all sizes, just as they came through
Georgia and South Carolina,—"Slocum's bag-

gage," the people shouted, as they laughed and cheered. By this time the crowd of spectators had increased and encroached on the street so much, that the infantry guards were unable to keep them back, and a file of cavalry were detailed to ride in advance of each division or brigade to clear the way, and Joe means to laugh at Slocum for his dodge in making a little force appear like a great one, for the company filed around behind the White House, as in a theater, and reappeared on the scene every few minutes like new troops.

I can't begin to tell you all about it—the newspapers will do that better than I could, but it was a sublime spectacle and one I am very, very sorry you have missed. . . .

I am writing in the parlor with talking all about me, and therefore incoherently. Capt. Joe Rockwell is just telling the girls about his ten months in Libby Prison. . . . Here come General Williams and Mr. Knapp, so I must say good night.

We are very glad you stayed at our home, always *yours*, too, dear, instead of going down to town. Best love to you and the little darlings.

Mother to A. H. W.

Washington, May 27th, Saturday.

My dear Abby : Here we are yet, detained by a cheerless, hopeless, steady pour of rain. . . .

Georgy is at the Fairfax Seminary with Jane,
and cannot get back to us until the weather
changes decidedly for the better ; but such
roads! as this rain made. Their condition reminds me of our McClellan winter here, though
the deep yellow mud is now tramped through
by the " homeward bound," those who have
escaped and survived the hardships and horrors
of the " cruel war" now over. . . . On Thursday we made up a little party to visit Jane, as
she could not come to us—a good-bye call.
Miss Prime and Eliza, with Charley and Joe,
went on horseback, Miss P. riding Charley's
new horse, which is a beauty. Mrs. Clarkson,
with Georgy, Carry and me, in an open carriage,
with Harry Hopkins on the box, all started
together from the door. On reaching the Long
Bridge, we found to our dismay an interminable
line of troops coming this way, the Fourteenth
Army Corps, with all their wagons, etc., and no
chance whatever of getting on in that direction,
—no vehicles are allowed to pass these trains
on the bridge. The equestrians found they
could do so, and rode on. We had the choice of
driving to the boat, with the chance of finding
that too crowded for our carriage, or driving
out over the Aqueduct Bridge, and passing
through Arlington grounds and Freedman's
Village, finally reaching the Seminary road.
All this was very attractive, and we made the

drive, losing very little time and seeing a great
deal that was extremely interesting. On arriving at the Seminary we met the rest of our
party just emerging from one of the wards with
Jane and Dr. Smith, who had been showing
Miss Prime through them, to her great delight.
You know she doats on soldiers and hospitals.
Jane seemed quite well, and did the honors with
a grace that delighted her stranger guests. I
was introduced to the chaplain and wife, Mr.
and Mrs. Jerome, in their own room, and we all
then assembled in Jane's office, where she gave us
some claret and crackers, of her private stores.
We lost our way in coming back ; our driver, a
darkey, unacquainted with the country ; our
horseback party far ahead of us, and cross roads
innumerable everywhere. We drove about over
hill and dale for two hours, and eventually
found ourselves on the Leesburg turnpike!
Where we should have spent the night I know
not, but for an old house on the roadside which
at length showed itself, whose occupant informed us where we were ; and on further inquiry we found we were much nearer to the *Seminary!* than to the Long Bridge which had been
the object of our search. Of course we had
only to drive back there and beg a guide. You
can imagine the surprise and regret of Dr. S.
and Harry Hopkins when we drove up at that
late hour, and told them our experience. . . .

We did not let Jane and G. know anything about it, and Dr. Smith and Harry both ordered horses and saw us safely back. We reached the hotel at a little before 10. . . . Charley is well, but tired out with hanging about here, and I shall be glad to leave. . . . Kisses to the dear children. I dare not look back to this time last year ! or speak of those days of sorrow, but my heart is heavy within me, these *anniversary days*, with unspoken sorrow.

Mother to J. S. W.

WASHINGTON May 28, 1865.
SUNDAY EVENING.

My dear Jane: As we propose leaving Washington to-morrow morning on the 10.30 train, I write you a line of "good bye" to-night, and shall leave it at the desk in case the orderly should call here—and with it some lovely roses which Charley brought in to us this afternoon. I wish you had them now. It is very hard for me to go off and leave you all alone behind us, though you *do seem* happier where you are than at home. I hope, however, when all military hospitals and every vestige of war are done away with, you will be contented to make us happy at home by sharing home with us, and being happy there yourself.

. . . Joe and Eliza went off to Richmond on Friday in spite of the rain. . . . The city has been very quiet the last two or three days—no serenades, no excitements of any sort. To-day Charley and I went to Dr. Gurley's church, while H. and C., attended by General Williams, went to Dr. Hall's. . . . It is very tiresome here now, and disagreeable ; the house is wretchedly kept. If it were not for our colored waiter, young "George Washington Jerome Buonaparte me lord," we should have no attention at all ; he remembered us at Gettysburg, and has devoted himself to us. . . . We shall go through to-morrow, reaching home on Tuesday. . . .

A loving good night to you, my dear child.

MOTHER.

The splendid sweep of the great army passing away for ever, seemed to carry with it out of sight all the stormy four years of our family life. The mad, sad, noble war was over. Those dear to us, who had been in peril, were safe at home once more. All we had longed for, and fought for, was ours. Slavery was dead, and one flag covered the land "*Across a Kindling Continent.*"

" We with uncovered head "
" Salute the sacred dead,"
* * * * * *
" Through whose desert a rescued Nation sets "
" Her heel on treason."

The home circle of which your Grandmother was the center and the charm, was broken and scattered long ago, but it has not been forgotten by those who knew it in the days of war: "Chaplain Hopkins," writing of it after all these years, says:—

"I stopped once on my way to the army at the New York home, and it seemed to me that I got for a little time into a climate and country entirely different from this poor cold world. The house was all aglow with light and warmth; there was an atmosphere of earnest faith, courage, and good cheer, that filled me with a new sense of the sacredness of the cause of our country. Some of the faces in the groups there are dim in my memory, but not your Mother's. She seemed to me very noble and very beautiful the first time I saw her, and later she was good to me after such a fashion, that I put an aureole about her head, and counted her among the saints long before she went to be where the saints are."

A paragraph in a letter from this dear Mother, written six years after the war, expresses her constant love for us, and allows us to close these chapters of our family story with her benediction.

. . . This 9th day of November, 1871, completes my "three score years and ten!" and how has God blessed me all the way along, and in nothing so richly as in my beloved children! What aid, and comfort, and strength, and life have they given me always! and how my heart yearns over each one as my dearest treasure on earth! They have been my staff and support in God's hands, when He was leading me through deep waters, and have kept my head up so that I did not sink. I bless God to-day for *my children.* May He continue to be their God!

www.ingramcontent.com/pod-product-compliance
Lightning Source LLC
Chambersburg PA
CBHW030909270326
41929CB00008B/626